RATIONALITY

Schumacher advances the bold claim that the Christian life establishes not just the plausibility or attractiveness, but the rationality of faith. In this first installment of an ambitious two-part project, she patiently assembles a 'pro-theology philosophy,' i.e., a teleological account of rationality as inherently ordered to ethical ends. The pursuit of knowledge is shown as fully intelligible only when placed within the context of the task of perfecting ourselves as the particular kind of creatures we are. The result is a significant and original contribution that ranges ably over the terrain of ontology, theory of knowledge, virtue epistemology, and virtue ethics.

Jennifer Herdt, Yale Divinity School, USA

Schumacher provides a sophisticated account of how reason and faith should be understood by Christians and philosophers not sympathetic to Christianity. She draws on the work of classical theologians while also paying attention to contemporary thinkers. And she does so to good effect.

Brian Davies, Fordham University, USA

For much of the modern period, theologians and philosophers of religion have struggled with the problem of proving that it is rational to believe in God. Drawing on the thought of Thomas Aquinas, this book lays the foundation for an innovative effort to overturn the longstanding problem of proving faith's rationality, and to establish instead that rationality requires to be explained by appeals to faith. To this end, Schumacher advances the constructive argument that rationality is not only an epistemological question concerning the soundness of human thoughts, which she defines in terms of 'intellectual virtue.' Ultimately, it is an ethical question whether knowledge is used in ways that promote an individual's own flourishing and that of others. That is to say, rationality in its paradigmatic form is a matter of moral virtue, which should nonetheless entail intellectual virtue. This conclusion sets the stage for Schumacher's argument in a companion book, *Theological Philosophy*, which explains how Christian faith provides an exceptionally robust rationale for rationality, so construed, and is intrinsically rational in that sense.

Transcending Boundaries in Philosophy and Theology

Series editors:
Martin Warner, University of Warwick, UK
Kevin Vanhoozer, Trinity Evangelical Divinity School, USA

Transcending Boundaries in Philosophy and Theology is an interdisciplinary series exploring new opportunities in the dialogue between philosophy and theology that go beyond more traditional 'faith and reason' debates and take account of the contemporary reshaping of intellectual boundaries. For much of the modern era, the relation of philosophy and theology has been conceived in terms of antagonism or subordination, but recent intellectual developments hold out considerable potential for a renewed dialogue in which philosophy and theology have common cause for revisioning their respective identities, reconceiving their relationship, and combining their resources. This series explores constructively for the twenty-first century the resources available for engaging with those forms of enquiry, experience and sensibility that theology has historically sought to address. Drawing together new writing and research from leading international scholars in the field, this high profile research series offers an important contribution to contemporary research across the interdisciplinary perspectives relating theology and philosophy.

Also in this series

Resurrection and Moral Imagination
Sarah Bachelard

Ways of Meeting and the Theology of Religions
David Cheetham

Placing Nature on the Borders of Religion, Philosophy and Ethics
Edited by Forrest Clingerman and Mark H. Dixon

Beyond Fideism
Negotiable Religious Identities
Olli-Pekka Vainio

Rationality as Virtue

Towards a Theological Philosophy

LYDIA SCHUMACHER
University of Edinburgh, UK

Routledge
Taylor & Francis Group

LONDON AND NEW YORK

First published 2015 by Ashgate Publishing

2 Park Square, Milton Park, Abingdon, Oxon OX14 4RN
711 Third Avenue, New York, NY 10017, USA

Routledge is an imprint of the Taylor & Francis Group, an informa business

First issued in paperback 2017

British Library Cataloguing in Publication Data
A catalogue record for this book is available from the British Library.

The Library of Congress has cataloged the printed edition as follows:
Schumacher, Lydia.
  Rationality as virtue : towards a theological philosophy / by Lydia Schumacher.
    pages cm. -- (Transcending boundaries in philosophy and theology)
  Includes bibliographical references and index.
  ISBN 978-1-4724-4265-9 (hardcover)
  1. Rationalism. 2. Philosophical theology. 3. Faith and reason. 4. Virtue.
  I. Title.
  BL2747.7.S38 2015
  231'.042--dc23
                                                          2015007098

ISBN 978-1-4724-4265-9 (hbk)
ISBN 978-1-138-05327-4 (pbk)

To my brother,
Elliot

Your fortitude is my inspiration.

There are two ways of looking at our duty in the matter of opinion, ways entirely different, and yet ways about whose difference the theory of knowledge seems hitherto to have shown very little concern. 'We must know the truth; and we must avoid error'—these are our first and great commandments as would-be knowers; but they are not two ways of stating an identical commandment, they are two separable laws ... and by choosing between them we may end by coloring differently our whole intellectual life. We may regard the chase for truth as paramount, and the avoidance of error as secondary; or we may, on the other hand, treat the avoidance of error as more imperative, and let truth take its chance. [W.K.] Clifford ... exhorts us to the latter course. Believe nothing, he tells us, keep your mind in suspense forever, rather than by closing it on insufficient evidence incur the awful risk of believing lies. You, on the other hand, may think that the risk of being in error is a very small matter when compared with the blessings of real knowledge, and be ready to be duped many times in your investigation rather than postpone indefinitely the chance of guessing true. I myself find it impossible to go with Clifford ... Our errors are surely not such awfully solemn things. In a world where we are so certain to incur them in spite of all our caution, a certain lightness of heart seems healthier than this excessive nervousness on their behalf.

—William James, *The Will to Believe* VII

Contents

Acknowledgments

Many institutions and individuals have helped make it possible for me to bring this project to completion. First and foremost, I would like to express my gratitude to the British Academy, which awarded me a postdoctoral fellowship during which I did a good deal of work on this project; and to the University of Oxford Faculty of Theology and Religion and Oriel College, where I took up the three-year fellowship. While writing this book, I also benefited from the support of colleagues at Wycliffe Hall, Oxford, where I became Tutor in Doctrine during the last year of my fellowship. Finally, I am grateful for the time I had to complete this book during my first year in the post of Chancellor's Fellow at the University of Edinburgh School of Divinity.

Over the years I worked on this project, I had many opportunities to present it in different contexts, for example through seminars at the Universities of Cambridge, Oxford, Durham, and Edinburgh, and at the Aquinas Institute, Blackfriars Hall, Oxford. I am very grateful to those who invited me to speak in these and other contexts and for the feedback I received from seminar participants.

In developing this project, I have had the great fortune and pleasure of working with an outstanding editorial team, including Sarah Lloyd at Ashgate and series editors Martin Warner and Kevin Vanhoozer. I am extremely grateful for all that the editors have done to support this work and bring it to the point of publication. In particular, I owe a special debt of gratitude to Martin Warner, who went above and beyond the call of duty, carefully reading multiple drafts and providing detailed comments that helped me significantly improve the final manuscript.

In addition to the above, I would like to extend a special word of thanks to colleagues at Oxford University who encouraged and advised me as I worked on this project, including Sarah Foot, George Pattison (now at Glasgow University), Graham Ward, Stephen Mulhall, David Charles, and Andrew Pinsent. Beyond Oxford, other colleagues have been so good as to provide general feedback on the overall project or specific feedback on certain aspects of it, including Frederick Christian Bauerschmidt, William Desmond, Paul J. Griffiths, Matthew Levering, Rudi te Velde, Denys Turner, Nicholas Lombardo, and Thomas Weinandy. Finally, I would like to thank Pamela Schumacher for her assistance with the index.

Last and most importantly, this book is dedicated to my brother, Elliot, who is without a doubt the most remarkable model of 'rationality' and especially of fortitude of which I have ever known. My brother is not only the reason and inspiration behind my work but also the greatest friend, support, and help I have in doing it. I wish that everyone could have the joy and blessing of knowing and learning from Elliot as I do, and that I could offer him a more adequate token of my love, admiration, and gratitude.

List of Abbreviations

The works of Aristotle are abbreviated as follows:

APo.	*Posterior Analytics*
APr.	*Prior Analytics*
Cat.	*Categories*
DA	*De Anima*
EE	*Eudemian Ethics*
EN	*Nichomachean Ethics*
Int.	*De Interpretatione*
Meta.	*Metaphysics*
Phys.	*Physics*
Pol.	*Politics*
Rhet.	*Rhetoric*
Top.	*Topics*
SE	*De Sophistici Elenchi*

The works of Thomas Aquinas are abbreviated as follows:

Comp. Theol.	*Compendium Theologiae*
De Veritate	*Quaestiones Disputatae de Veritate*
De Ente	*De Ente et Essentia*
ST	*Summa Theologiae*

All references to the *Summa* are derived from the *respondeo* portion of the text unless otherwise noted. In references to Aquinas' *Summa* such as *ST* 1.1.2, *ST* 2.1.1.1, *ST* 2.2.1.1, or *ST* 3.1.1, the initial 1, 2.1, 2.2, or 3 represents the part number of the text, while subsequent numbers respectively indicate the article and question number.

Chapter 1

Introduction to *Rationality as Virtue*

Throughout the modern period, philosophers have debated the question what it means to be rational. In this connection, they have investigated how ordinary beliefs are justified and inquired into the locus of 'objectivity' in human knowledge. According to a fairly widely established consensus, however, many distinctly modern conceptions of human rationality pose a considerable challenge when it comes to defending the rationality of faith.[1]

In response to this threat, theologians and philosophers of religion have tended to employ one of two main strategies for bolstering the contention that faith is rational.[2] The first, defensive, approach involves responding to objections to the faith that have been presented by outsiders on any number of grounds: historical, scientific, intellectual, and even moral.[3] The second approach goes on the offensive for the faith. In other words, it endeavors to give a positive account of Christian belief, which anticipates and implicitly overturns the accusations of objectors.

Although both of the two aforementioned strategies are essential to the overarching apologetic task, the persuasiveness of the defensive arguments turns on the integrity of the positive account of the faith that those arguments defend. Without that preemptive account as a basis, defensive arguments inevitably tend to address objections on the implicit assumption that the objections are legitimate, thus exposing faith to even more and more devastating critiques.

The present work will contribute to the positive dimension of the apologetic project by delineating a definition of human rationality that underlines the rationality of faith, where prevailing definitions evidently call it into doubt. As part of this effort, rationality will be described not merely as an epistemological matter to do with the soundness of human thinking. Ultimately, it will be construed as an ethical question whether knowledge is utilized in a manner that is consistent with the overarching purpose of 'rational animals,' which is to flourish through the exercise of individual abilities and thereby contribute to the flourishing of others. In this regard, the argument outlined here might be described as a moral argument for God's existence, though it is in many respects distinct from and involves a good deal more than most such arguments, which is arguably essential to their sustainability.[4]

In ways on which I will soon elaborate, defining rationality in ethical terms, more specifically, in terms of moral virtue, provides an exceptionally effective basis for establishing the rationality of faith. For Christian faith can be shown to enact or provide a rationale for rationality, defined in these terms, such that faith is already rational—and philosophy already theological. As I will demonstrate below, it takes a full-scale re-configuration of philosophy in terms of what I call 'pro-theology philosophy' to obtain a definition of rationality that is both amenable to faith and intrinsically more plausible than the definitions that tend to undermine faith.

By shedding new light through such arguments on the sense in which faith is intrinsically rational, the project undertaken here aims to lay the foundation not only for defensive apologetic projects but above all for inquiries concerning what it means to live by faith and elucidate the articles of faith—proper to the fields of Christian Ethics and Systematic Theology, respectively—which proceed on the assumption that faith is rational.

Before outlining the more detailed steps of the argument, however, a brief word about sources is in order. In preparing this proposal, I have drawn considerable inspiration from numerous pre-modern thinkers, above all Thomas Aquinas. Because Aquinas for one seems to operate from a theological and philosophical perspective that does not even give rise to the problem of faith's rationality, at least in its modern form, his work represents an especially useful resource for overcoming this problem, which urgently demands resolution today.[5]

Although I follow Aquinas closely on certain matters, the very fact that he operated in a context that is so far removed from our own renders it impossible or at least unprofitable simply to reiterate his thought on, say, the nature of reason or of faith. Thus, the conceptual framework outlined in this context does not entail a reformulation or even interpretation of Aquinas but a constructive effort to resolve the current question of faith's rationality, which appropriates, sometimes quite extensively, and adapts, sometimes quite heavily, principles Aquinas articulated, insofar as these are still relevant in contemporary circumstances.[6]

As hinted above, my treatment of this framework falls into two distinct parts, one of which redefines rationality in ethical terms through the articulation of a 'pro-theology philosophy,' and another, which explains how rationality so construed gestures towards the rationality of Christian faith, such that a pro-theology philosophy turns out to be a theological philosophy.

While the present work undertakes the first part of the project, the second will be the focus of a separate work, entitled *Theological Philosophy*. Because the two distinct works are closely related, I will endeavor in what follows to sketch the overarching line of argument they delineate by summarizing the discussion of each book's chapters. First, however, I will situate this argument in its intellectual context, describing some of the main approaches to asserting faith's rationality that have been advocated in modern times.

The Intellectual Context of Theological Philosophy

Throughout the modern period, two main methods of dealing with the problem of establishing faith's rationality have predominated, namely, rationalism and fideism. The rationalist approach, commonly espoused by proponents of natural theology, turns on several different types of attempt to establish God's existence on grounds accessible to human beings. While cosmological arguments appeal to nature to infer the reality of a cause or creator of the world, for example, teleological arguments invoke the order of the universe and signs of intelligent design to establish God's existence.[7]

In addition to these two types of argument, some, though admittedly fewer, have advocated an ontological argument for God's existence, that is, an argument that derives proof for God from the very definition of God and thus from the mere thought of him, working from 'reason alone' as opposed to invoking the quasi-empirical evidence of creation or the natural order.[8] By contrast to rationalism, fideism tends to trade on the assertion that faith cannot be evidenced or grounded by reason in any way but ought to be adhered to all the same.[9]

In recent years, many scholars have begun to recognize that neither approach to addressing the question of faith's rationality is entirely adequate to the task. While fideism simply evades the question, for example, the natural theological proofs for God's existence mentioned above seem ultimately to beg the question they purport to answer, or to assume what they attempt to prove. They do this by taking God's existence as evident to the senses or self-evident to the mind, when God's reality is clearly not evident in these ways to those who deny or disregard it. As numerous critics have noted, such proofs usually only have the power to persuade those who already believe in God.[10] At very least, this suggests that they do not suffice as a main line of defensive argument for the existence of God.

That is not to say that the proofs have no place in Christian thought, however. They may indeed enrich the faith of believers or even bring unbelievers to faith, particularly when employed as tools for forming a habit of viewing the world from the perspective of belief in God. As I have argued elsewhere, this perspective checks the human tendency to ascribe absolute significance to things other than God and so transforms the thoughts and lives of believers into evidence for the difference belief in God can make when it comes to dealing with ordinary affairs.[11]

Though such a therapeutic or pedagogical interpretation of the theistic proofs is arguably more faithful to the intents of the early Christian and medieval writers who originally developed them, it admittedly diverges rather widely from the modern conception of the arguments, according to which theistic proofs offer direct evidence for God's existence. In fact, it already moves in the general direction of the new approach to asserting faith's rationality that this book contributes to developing.

In presenting a new way of conceiving faith's rationality, however, the present work is not alone. Recently, a number of other scholars have sought to rethink the whole project of proving faith's rationality, in some cases by going so far as to challenge the prevailing standards of rationality that pose problems for faith. For instance, proponents of Reformed Epistemology (RE)—including Nicholas Wolterstorff, William Alston, and especially Alvin Plantinga—ground their religious epistemological agenda on a preliminary reconsideration of the modern 'evidentialist' or 'foundationalist' standard of knowledge. According to this standard, knowledge claims must be backed by empirical evidence, such that cosmological and teleological proofs provide the sole means to proving the existence of God.[12]

In challenging this standard, Plantinga in particular argues that belief in God is 'properly basic', such that God is intuitively and ineluctably known, at least amongst those in whom the Holy Spirit has compensated for the effects of sin upon the will by inspiring faith.[13] By construing belief in God as properly basic, Plantinga effectively reverses the question whether it is rational to believe in God. In diverse and highly sophisticated ways to which this brief description obviously cannot do full justice, therefore, he and other Reformed Epistemologists seek to render it inconceivable not to know that God exists.

Although the work of RE scholars represents an invaluable advance in the field of religious epistemology, it has met nevertheless with various forms of criticism. One of the main objections to the approach of RE thinkers is that it seems suspiciously similar to that of fideism, in that it advocates a sort of 'groundless ground' for belief in God, to wit, a properly basic intuition.[14] Though proponents of RE have sought to exonerate their program of this charge, another has been raised, which points out that the RE agenda, if successful, still only establishes that there is something like a God, not necessarily the Christian God in whom advocates of RE actually believe.[15]

A similar charge could incidentally be laid before the natural theologians who advocate the other forms of proof for the existence of God mentioned above. While cosmological and teleological proofs may validly demonstrate the existence of some kind of God, they provide no basis for confirming that this God is the Christian God or that of any other religious system. Thus, the question remains how conceptually to connect theistic proofs of any kind—whether natural theological or Reformed Epistemological—with belief in, say, the Triune, Incarnate God of Christian faith, as opposed to appending the articles associated with specifically Christian belief at the end of a line of argument for God's existence.

In order to compensate for the lack of doctrinal content inherent in theistic proofs, certain analytic philosophers with Christian persuasions have recently developed a program they call 'analytic theology,' which endeavors to apply the tools and methods of analytic philosophy in elucidating the coherence and rationality of theological doctrines.[16] In principle, this is a commendable project to which this work and its sequel might be seen as contributing, depending on exactly how philosophy is used to illuminate the sense in which Christian doctrines are rational, and, indeed, how the terms 'philosophy,' 'rationality,' and 'doctrine' are even defined.

While it may eventually prove possible and indeed useful to develop an analytic theological account of every major Christian doctrine, and the nature of doctrine overall, it arguably remains the case that such accounts would bring analytic theologians no closer than analytic philosophers of religion to forging a natural and necessary connection between beliefs about the Christian God and the object of attempts to establish the rationality of theistic belief. For it would still be necessary to append arguments highlighting the intelligibility of Christian doctrines to theistic proofs in a seemingly arbitrary way in order to establish that it is the God of Christian belief whose existence is under consideration. That is not a criticism so much as an observation about the possible limits of analytic theology, and the need for a larger framework in which the connection between theistic proof and specifically Christian beliefs is integral, as it is in a theological philosophy.

In addition to the accounts already mentioned, a number of other promising approaches to resolving the question of faith's rationality have been presented in recent years. One account, which is highly congenial to my own, is that of Denys Turner in his *Faith, Reason, and the Existence of God.* In this book, Turner contends that reason itself needs to be re-defined in terms that are more compatible with faith before the question of the rationality of faith can be resolved.

As Turner himself states, however, his essay only 'clear[s] away a little of the clutter of misconception, philosophical and theological, which has for several centuries stood in the way of a more theologically positive understanding of reason.'[17] In doing this, however, he effectively calls for a more comprehensive effort to re-define reason in a manner that is amenable to faith, and to address the question of the rationality of faith on that basis, thus anticipating the project I undertake here.

According to another line of argument that has been advanced in recent years—by figures as diverse as the philosopher of religion, Paul Moser, and the Christian ethicist, Stanley Hauerwas—the proof for the rationality of faith in God ultimately derives from the Christian life, or from the life of the Church.[18] While I certainly arrive at a similar conclusion in the last analysis—indeed in the last substantial chapter of this book's sequel—my own argument over the course of two books should serve to indicate that a good deal of preliminary philosophical and theological work needs to be conducted before this compelling conclusion can really hold up to scrutiny or even carry much meaning—whether for Christians or non-Christians—thus providing a fully intellectually satisfactory alternative to, say, natural theology.

This preliminary work would involve re-construing ordinary rationality in terms of a certain style of life—that is, a virtuous life—and showing subsequently that this life is paradigmatically instanced in or enabled by life in the Church. Such a line of reasoning alone seems plausibly to support the claim that the Christian life is the proof of faith's rationality. Yet it is just this line of thinking that is lacking in the work of the aforementioned thinkers and particularly that of Hauerwas, who seems to deny the very need for it.

By developing precisely this line of thinking, in contrast, theological philosophy aims to provide a basis for the claim that the Christian life is the proof for faith's rationality. At the same time, it lays the foundation for the efforts of theological ethicists to articulate what the Christian life involves and the reasons for living it, without which the Christian life and Christian ethics might easily be perceived as arbitrary, irrational, or irrelevant to all but Christian believers.

Although I have acknowledged above the creativity and promise of a variety of accounts of faith's rationality, I have suggested nonetheless that much remains to be desired when it comes to affording resources conclusively to overturn the question whether it is reasonable to believe in the God of Christian faith.[19] Of course, a single work like this one could scarcely overcome completely the skepticism about faith's rationality that has grown in recent years. Success in that regard would depend not only on the plausibility and persuasiveness of the work's argument but also on the will of skeptics to receive it. Nevertheless, the present discussion begins to forge a conceptual pathway past the problem of faith's rationality and on to a plane of systematic and moral theological inquiry that presupposes it. In its way of doing this, as outlined below, therefore, it provides conceptual resources to those willing to employ them to make slow but steady progress towards the victory of faith over doubt.

The Precursor: Pro-Theology Philosophy

The effort the present work undertakes to outline a pro-theology philosophy begins in Chapter 2 ('The Ontology of Participation') with a discussion of the sub-discipline of philosophy which deals with the most fundamental area of philosophical inquiry, namely, ontology, which describes 'what there is' and the way in which it exists. In particular, the chapter outlines an ontology of 'participation' such as can be found in various forms in the work of Thomas Aquinas and other pre-modern thinkers. As I understand it, 'participation' refers to a being's engagement in the activities or form of existence proper to its specific nature or essence, which is acquired at its inception. This essence makes the being one type of thing as opposed to another and provides it with a potential to actualize through ongoing participation in a certain mode of existence, or life.

Since the human essence is that of a rational animal—or embodied intellectual being—I further describe in this chapter the faculties of perception, imagination and intellect that allow human beings to actualize their cognitive nature. Subsequent to this discussion, I detail the three main areas in which human beings may have an aptitude or 'intellectual virtue' for exercising rationality. These areas include wisdom, which might be understood in terms of the study of theology and philosophy; science, which simply concerns the ordered study of any object of inquiry whatever; and skilled or craft knowledge, which includes all practical, productive, and creative arts.[20]

After treating the faculties that enable human beings to acquire knowledge, I turn in Chapter 3 ('The Ontology of Knowledge') to articulate an ontology of knowledge, or an account of the elements or cognitive functions that factor into and facilitate the cognitive process. These include concepts, statements, and definitions, and inductive and deductive modes of reasoning. In this context, I also consider the relationship between language and knowledge, which allows me to account for the way and extent to which thought is inevitably shaped by and carried out within particular traditions or spatio-temporal contexts.

In the course of this discussion, I review the various aspects of the Aristotelian system of formal logic, which Aquinas implemented as a tool for the expression of his own thought.[21] In doing so, however, it might be argued that I overlook the fact that traditional logic stemming from Aristotle's works has largely been replaced in contemporary philosophy by modern symbolic logic, especially the predicate calculus.[22] The main difference between the two systems is this: while modern symbolic logic operates in an entirely hypothetical mode, 'traditional logic makes the assumption that no term is empty.'[23] That is to say, it presumes that there are real instances of all the terms assessed. The advantage of the predicate calculus, many would assert, is that it allows deductions to be carried out independently of the meaning or content of the propositions involved, thus enabling distinctions to be articulated far more precisely than would be otherwise possible.

In an effort to affirm the fundamentality of modern symbolic logic, certain logicians have endeavored to show that the results of the theory of syllogism may be obtained in predicate calculus, provided certain existential assumptions are made.[24] By these means, they have tried to show that traditional logic is reducible to predicate calculus.[25] Rather than proving that there is a fundamental discrepancy between the two systems, however, this effort simply establishes that traditional logic is a sub-set of predicate calculus, insofar as it makes assumptions about reality, where predicate calculus is also concerned with empty and thus all conceivable terms.[26]

Although predicate calculus may for this very reason successfully enable professional philosophers to explore hypothetical questions, its corresponding tendency to sever ties with reality renders it rather less suitable for the purposes of the present work. One of those purposes is to elucidate the sense in which logic serves as a training ground or facilitator for ordinary cognitive efforts that promote 'reason's self-government, with respect to one's own practical choices and those of others.'[27] In other words, the aim of this work is to explain logic in a way that illustrates that it ultimately 'points beyond itself to a valuable ethical end.'[28]

Aristotelian logic is highly compatible with this purpose, precisely because it deals primarily with actual realities that are the concern of ordinary knowing agents. By clarifying some difficult aspects of Aristotle's logic, consequently, this chapter sets the stage for Chapter 4's effort to illustrate the vital role logic plays in the successful execution of the cognitive process. As I will show in later chapters, particularly Chapter 7, this process through which reason properly governs its own operations in turn predisposes the mind effectively to govern the self and its relation to others and thus to tailor logic to larger ethical ends.

On the grounds that human knowledge like all things is subject to development, Chapter 4 ('The Conditions for Knowledge') demonstrates how the ideas whereby humans realize their potential also undergo growth and change. As I will elaborate, the dialectical process of intellectual development, facilitated by the elements of logic, takes place in three stages, which I will treat in terms of expectant, fulfilled, and informed faith.

One of the main reasons why I appeal to the concept of faith, generically not religiously defined, to explain the process of development in knowledge is that it testifies to the fact that unknowing, the sub-conscious or tacit knowledge, fuels the knowing process.[29] On another level, the concept of faith bespeaks the goal-orientation of knowledge, or the fact that we do not start out knowing whatever we want to know but set objectives to know which we must strive gradually to fulfill over time in the belief that we will eventually do so.

In this connection, the first phase of expectant faith is characterized by a lack of knowledge and a desire to know that motivate us to undertake inquiries that are designed to bring about the acquisition of knowledge. That knowledge is achieved in the second phase of fulfilled faith, while the third phase of informed faith involves placing confidence in the knowledge obtained in fulfilled faith in order to make sense of further experiences. In doing this, we not only add clarity and precision to that knowledge but also begin the whole process of moving from expectant to fulfilled to informed faith again, such that the search for truth is interminable, and knowledge never ceases to be a matter of faith.[30]

Because our thinking is always caught in the throes of expectant, fulfilled or informed faith, it is evidently impossible to capture thoughts about things that are true for all persons at all places and at all times, that is, to be objective or rational on one common modern definition of the term. Thus, Chapter 5 ('Rationality') seeks to explain the sense in which human beings engaged in the cognitive process as I describe it may be considered rational. To this end, I follow Aquinas in appealing to the indispensable role the will plays in collaboration with the intellect at every one of the three aforementioned phases of inquiry. The work of this faculty is implied in the previous appeal to the concept of faith, which is suggestive of intellectual as well as volitional components of cognition, that is, both knowledge and the desire to pursue or employ knowledge.

In expectant faith, for example, the will to account for reality alerts us to the fact that there is something important in our experience for which we are unable to account, filling us with the desire and motivation to compensate for the deficiency in our understanding. Moreover, the will signals when we have achieved the understanding we desire, refusing to settle for any solution that fails to satisfy this desire. Finally, the will compels us to apply the understanding we have achieved in order to make sense of further experiences in informed faith. Without the will moving the intellect at all times, in summary, it would be impossible for the intellect to gain and grow in understanding.

In order to uphold the intellect's commitment to the truth, the will seemingly needs a means by which to make contact with the particular realities of experience for which the intellect has to account. Aquinas explains the embodied nature of human knowing by appealing to the 'passions.' Whenever we experience our bodies or an object in the external world, the passions register the object of experience as helpful or inimical with respect to the intellect's purpose of knowing what is true, and thereby help the will determine how to direct the intellect towards or away from that object.

As essential as the passions may be when it comes to helping us testify to the truth, they can also lead us astray from the truth when we fail to evaluate particular objects of knowledge in terms of the larger effort to promote the truth, and instead reduce the pursuit of truth to the promotion of one theory or ideology about which we are particularly passionate. When we become so preoccupied with one perspective, channeling all our passions to promote it, our passions become 'dis-passions.' For they prevent rather than enable the mind to remain receptive to the ongoing discovery of truth. They put us out of touch rather than in touch with reality, often leading us to fabricate, modify, or block out information with the aim of bolstering personal opinions.

When explaining how to counteract the dis-passions, I appeal to Aquinas' famous discussion of the four cardinal virtues of prudence, justice, fortitude, and temperance, arguing that these can be construed not merely as moral but also as intellectual virtues that rectify the intellect, will and passions for their purpose of pursuing the truth. In this regard, I seek to contribute to recent discussions of what is known as 'virtue epistemology,' that is, the growing field of philosophical inquiry in which the success of knowledge is said to turn on various epistemic character qualities such as commitment (i.e. fortitude) or a sense of accountability to the truth (i.e. justice).[31]

In a virtue epistemology inspired by Aquinas, prudence for one can be described as the virtue that compels the intellect to seek contact with reality. On my account, it allows for this possibility because of the justice of the will, which motivates us to testify about reality in a way that does justice to it, inasmuch as it is accessible to our knowledge. As I understand it, the collaborative work of prudence and justice is sustained by the two further 'virtues of the passions,' namely, fortitude and temperance, which can be counted amongst the intellectual virtues insofar as they promote the work of prudence and justice.

While fortitude plays its part in this regard by giving us the passion or strength to overcome challenges to prioritizing truth over personal opinions or agendas, temperance fills us with the passions we need to perform the regular work involved in pursuing truth, thus preventing us from indulging in passions for pursuits that would distract us from this endeavor. To sum up: fortitude and temperance make it possible to follow through on the purposes of prudence and justice by teaching us to have the courage and discipline to do exactly this.

As this confirms, the four intellectual virtues together—and only in that way—enable us truthfully to testify to our experiences. Although they do not allow us to meet the seemingly impossible standard of knowledge according to which our ideas must remain perennially true, they do predispose us to revise beliefs we originally took to be true whenever new experiences require that we do so. As I will show, these revisions are possible—and human beings are rational—because of the work not only of the intellect but also of the will and passions, and the intellectual virtues of prudence, justice, fortitude, and temperance, which form them.

In advancing this argument about the indispensability of the intellect, will, and passions to human rationality, some readers might suspect that I endorse the so-called 'faculty psychology' that contemporary philosophers have found so objectionable, but which is common amongst pre-modern philosophers including Aquinas and, before him, Plato and Aristotle. In the iconic critique of faculty psychology developed in *The Concept of Mind*, Gilbert Ryle contends that the traditional dogma 'that the mind is in some important sense tripartite, that is, that there are just three ultimate classes of mental processes ... namely, thought, feeling, and will,' represents 'such a welter of confusions and false inferences that it is best to give up any attempt to re-fashion it. It should be treated as one of the curios of theory.'[32]

As a quasi-behaviorist, Ryle rejects such a faculty psychology on the grounds that it supposedly 'assumes that there are mental states and processes enjoying one sort of existence and bodily states and processes enjoying another [such that] an occurrence on the one stage is never numerically identical with an occurrence on the other.'[33] According to most versions of this myth of what Ryle calls 'the Ghost in the Machine,'[34] overt actions 'are the results of counterpart hidden operations'[35] in the secret mental life of the knowing agent. For Ryle, in fact, appeals to the intellect, will and emotions are the prime exemplification or ramification of the notion that the mental faculties lead a life of their own, over and above the human acts they affect. Thus, they reinforce the insurmountable mind-body dualism, which Ryle perceives as intrinsic to faculty psychology and as the most problematic feature thereof.

Since the time Ryle first mounted his critique of faculty psychology, numerous philosophers have responded to his arguments in ways that call attention to his fundamental misapprehension of the theory to which he so forcefully objected.[36] For example, David Braine has stressed that the mental states, such as thinking, willing, and feeling, which faculty psychologies postulate, are not real entities in the way Ryle seemingly envisaged them. Rather, they represent logical constructions or explanatory locutions, the purpose of which is simply to elucidate the psychological impetuses behind changes in behavior, without which there could arguably be no changes in behavior.[37]

On the assumption that 'any proper account of the mental involves the physical, and any proper account of the physical involves the mental,'[38] Braine concludes that all statements about human acts are or must be 'hybrid' statements that recognize both cognitive and behavioral components of human action.[39] Far from indicating the existence of three autonomous entities that function on a plane that supersedes that of natural life, his account consequently confirms that language regarding intellect, will and passions of which faculty psychologists tend to avail themselves points up the constraints of language when it comes to giving an account of something as unified and fluid as embodied human action.

In employing this language, my own treatment of faculty psychology in Chapter 5 operates on the assumption that appeals to the intellect, will, and passions serve collectively to explain the occurrence of embodied human acts—whether intellectual or moral. Rather than implying the existence of irreducibly distinct entities that operate over and above the embodied life of the human being on a separate, mental, plane of being, references to these faculties are intended to facilitate understanding of the conditions that give rise to human actions on the only plane of being in question, namely, that of natural life.

As argued in Chapter 2, the pursuit of knowledge by way of the three aforementioned faculties is our means, as human beings, of accomplishing the larger task of becoming what we are. On this basis, I argue, in closing Chapter 5 that our cognitive efforts are best undertaken with a view to the larger moral or personal goal of self-actualization. By situating our intellectual efforts within the context of this greater goal, I submit, we achieve the optimal position from which to utilize our knowledge for rational ends, namely, ones that are consistent with rather than inimical to our maximal moral or personal development as 'rational animals' with skills in the areas of wisdom, science, or art.

On the grounds that moral virtue is the final arbiter or paradigm case of intellectual virtue and thus of human rationality, the remaining chapters of this work explain how the four cardinal moral virtues enable us to become rational in the fullest sense of the term, by cultivating 'an individual orientation towards the highest good,' which is the definition of the moral life, and therefore rationality.

As a preliminary to this discussion, I explore in Chapter 6 ('Deficient Conditions for Pro-Theology Philosophy') certain factors that might prevent us from fully realizing our personal or moral potential. In this connection, I start by explaining that the dis-passions, which sometimes lead us astray in the pursuit of truth, are particularly liable to detract from our efforts when it comes to engaging in the moral task of self-actualization. They acquire the power thus to render us deficient for our human purpose when they lead us to believe that our good or happiness consists in goods that are inferior to that of self-actualization.

In cases where such 'dispassionate' tendencies become entrenched, they create fixed dispositions whereby we cultivate the worst rather than the best possible versions of ourselves, self-destructing rather than self-actualizing. These dispositions are what are called vices. In this chapter, I outline the implications of the seven main vices that are recognized in the pre-modern Christian tradition and the work of Aquinas, drawing on these sources to construct an account of the way that pride, greed, envy, apathy, anger, lust, and gluttony unravel our ability to be and become what we are.

In treating these vices, I call attention to the two extreme forms in which each vice may express itself. For example, I show that pride not only manifests in an excessive form through arrogance or hubris; it can also emerge in a deficient form, namely, false humility. As I further demonstrate, greed may also surface in extremes of excess or deficiency, respectively, that is, in an unbridled lust for pleasure or privilege, or in a sort of 'greed for pain.' Moreover, apathy may appear in the guise of sheer laziness or lack of ambition, or it may assume the form of extreme busyness and preoccupation with pointless activities.

On my argument, drawing attention to the excessive and deficient forms of every vice is absolutely vital to recognizing and thus correcting as opposed to exacerbating the vices individuals actually possess. Once this account of the vices is elaborated, it should become evident that we need to be informed about the fact that self-realization is our highest good, and about that in which self-actualization consists, if we are to avoid confusion on account of the passions regarding what it means for us to live good lives, and thus escape the snare of the vices.

What it means to actualize personal potential, on my understanding, is quite simply to 'bear well' whatever our intellectual aptitudes, resources, and circumstances that are given to us to bear, at any given point in time. Since these may change over time and with experience, it follows that we must always remain open to reconsidering what it means for us to bear our lives well. By bearing ourselves well in the aforementioned respects, we not only realize who we are but also exploit our personal skills for the sake of contributing to the well-being of others, or the common good, in our invariably individualized and finite ways.

On this showing, consequently, there is no dichotomy between the personal goal of striving for our own highest good, which consists in bearing our circumstances to the best of our abilities—thus engaging in self-actualization—and the aim of realizing our potential to promote the common good. The two goals of human and humane being represent two aspects of one phenomenon.[40] In closing on this note, I set the stage for the last major chapter of the book, which will cover how we bear our lives well by cultivating the four cardinal moral virtues of prudence, justice, fortitude, and temperance.

As I explain in Chapter 7 ('Sufficient Conditions for Pro-Theology Philosophy'), the four cardinal virtues operate in the moral context in ways that are recognizable from their work in the intellectual context. For instance, prudence puts us in touch with who we are as individuals, helping us accurately to assess our intellectual and other abilities, without over- or underestimating them, thus predisposing us to make the most of our limited lives, in part through the exercise of intellectual virtues. In general, then, prudence teaches us to 'bear well' whatever we may have to bear in terms of abilities, resources, and circumstances, and thus to strive for the highest good in the way we can from within the confines of our individual lives.

In cooperation with prudence, justice enables us to bear ourselves to the best of our abilities not only because this maximizes our existence and thus our experience of what it means to thrive in the human condition, but also because such self-actualizing efforts double as the actualization of our potential personally to contribute to the good of others, albeit in a limited way. While fortitude further affords the courage we need to fight for the highest or common good in the face of obstacles, temperance disciplines us to carry out the daily responsibilities involved in bearing our lives well, when it is open to us to be distracted from or neglect these responsibilities. In their distinctive ways, consequently, the four cardinal virtues collectively enable us to maintain a personal commitment to the highest good, which ideally entails the exercise of the intellectual virtues as well.

In the final section of this chapter, I address a number of questions, which bear on the larger question regarding the sense in which moral virtue is the final arbiter of human rationality. For instance, I consider the extent to which we can be considered virtuous or rational while still in the process of habituating ourselves in virtue. Additionally, I inquire about the extent to which we can be regarded as rational if we possess only intellectual without moral virtue or moral without intellectual virtue.

Although I affirm that rationality is possible on some level under both circumstances, I conclude by building on the argument of Chapter 5, according to which rationality ideally entails both intellectual and moral virtue, offering reasons to support this contention. Where there is a unity of intellectual and moral virtue—or better, intellectual *for* moral virtue, and moral virtue conversely substantiated by intellectual virtue, in summary, I identify the paradigm case of human rationality.

In Chapter 8, I briefly summarize the argument of the book and extrapolate some additional conclusions from it. In this connection, I show that the process of self-actualization described above doubles as a process of self-discovery, provided it is undertaken in a conscious or deliberate manner. Since all our labor to bear things well strengthens our sense of personal identity and purpose under these conditions, I elaborate, that work in turn facilitates further attempts to engage in self-actualization.

As this brief summary of the book's argument suggests, the effort to re-define rationality undertaken here involves a foray into all the main sub-disciplines of philosophy: ontology, theory of knowledge, and ethics. On the account I have advanced, these sub-disciplines, while distinctive, cannot be treated as altogether unrelated to one another, as they often are in contemporary philosophy, because they collectively describe and prescribe a functional and fulfilling—or rational—human life. While ontology and the theory of knowledge delineate the necessary conditions for that life and thus for pro-theology philosophy in that they respectively describe the way all things become themselves and the cognitive means through which human beings realize their potential, ethics satisfies the sufficient conditions by accounting for the way these necessary conditions are ultimately fulfilled in the lives of moral agents, or human beings.

There are at least two reasons why I call this philosophy whereby rationality is re-construed in terms of a personal commitment to the highest good a 'pro-theology philosophy,' that is, a philosophy that by its very nature gestures towards the rationality of the claims of faith. One reason concerns the fact that the theory of knowledge proper to this philosophy presupposes and explains the vital role that faith plays in human reasoning. Although this faith is not specifically religious, the very fact that faith of any kind is indispensable to ordinary rationality already suggests that religious faith and even Christian faith may have a sort of rational substance that is often overlooked in prevailing conceptions of both reason and faith.

While the account of knowledge developed in this work may afford some initial and potentially fruitful grounds for asserting the rationality of Christian faith, I have suggested that there may be an even more powerful and conclusive approach to doing this, which involves showing how faith explains the possibility of maintaining the individual commitment to the highest good, or moral virtue, that I have described as the final arbiter of human rationality.

In my proposal, in fact, an 'ethical' re-definition of rationality in terms of a personal commitment to the highest good ineluctably calls for a theological explanation as to how this commitment can be upheld. Thus, a pro-theology philosophy, fully enacted, is strictly speaking a theological philosophy. For this reason, I will proceed in the section below to illuminate pro-theology philosophy's relation to theological philosophy by outlining my understanding of this final rendering of philosophy, which will be developed more extensively in a further volume.

Though the ultimate purpose of the present work is to lay the foundation for the elaboration of a theological philosophy, and thereby overturn the question whether faith is rational, I would close my account of pro-theology philosophy by emphasizing its potential uses for philosophers who are not concerned with this particular question. As the discussion thus far will have established, pro-theology philosophy potentially allows for the recovery of a now uncommon way of thinking about philosophy as a 'way of life,'[41] namely, in accord with the highest good, which predominated in many ancient and medieval schools and recurs under various guises in a limited number of more recent schools of philosophical thought.[42]

This way of thinking promises not only to render philosophy more accessible to ordinary people but by the same token to provide them with resources urgently needed in today's world for living good and meaningful lives. That aside, the attempt I will make to show how emphases on logic and the soundness of arguments fit within a larger framework for addressing moral, personal, or one might say existential questions about philosophy as a 'way of life' also holds promise in terms of reconciling analytic and Continental approaches to philosophy, which are often at odds with one another on account of a tendency to perceive these concerns as mutually exclusive. By reconciling those concerns under the auspices of pro-theology philosophy, I not only lay the groundwork for alleviating the problem of the rationality of faith but also potentially for innovations in philosophical methodology.

The Project: *Theological Philosophy*

The first unique chapter of *Theological Philosophy* ('Necessary Conditions for Theological Philosophy') picks up where pro-theology philosophy leaves off, arguing that belief in the God of Christian faith—a God whose nature and work are treated by Christian theology—provides an explanation or rationale for moral virtue or human rationality, and is rational in that sense. Such an explanation is arguably necessary on account of the human tendency to reduce the highest good of 'bearing things well' or self-actualization to lesser goods—like the promotion of a specific cause or institution, the pursuit of knowledge, wealth, fame, pleasure, family, friends, or honor, to name a few—or even to 'goods' that may not be good at all.

To make this reduction is ironically to exchange an ability to utilize our lives and resources in ways that promote our own flourishing and that of others for one of using other persons, objects, and circumstances to the end of reinforcing self-serving interests, and, ultimately, a prideful perspective on the self. It is to undermine rather than support the highest good and therefore compromise rationality. In order to obtain a rationale for refusing to jeopardize our rationality along these lines, therefore, it seems necessary to posit the reality of one ultimate good that cannot be reduced to any finite good: a single highest good that is transcendent, even divine.[43]

Though such an affirmation of divine unity or simplicity, such as can be found in the work of Aquinas, to say nothing of other monotheists, suffices in many respects as a rationale for rationality, there is a level on which an account of the reality of a single transcendent being necessitates an appeal to a Trinity of divine persons, namely, the Father, Son, and Holy Spirit. An analogy derived from human knowing or, better, self-knowing—which presupposes the knower, the object known, which is the self, and the will or desire to know the object known—illustrates why this is so.

Where this analogy is invoked, the Father may be regarded as the first knower who knows the Son in the way one would know oneself. Since the Father's knowledge on this understanding is reflexive—it is self-knowledge—the Son in turn can be said to know the Father. Thus, the Father's knowing of the Son and the Son's knowing of the Father reflect their mutual desire to know one another, that is, God's desire to know himself and make himself known as the highest good that he is, which is encapsulated by the person and work of the Holy Spirit.

From this analogy, it follows that the doctrine of God as Father, Son, and Spirit is essential to accounting for one God who is capable of knowing and communicating himself as God and of willing to do precisely this. Since a God incapable in these respects could scarcely be considered worthy of the name 'God,' the doctrine of the Trinity, which establishes a perfect correspondence between who God is, what he knows, what he says, what he wants, and what he does, satisfies the conditions for the possibility of affirming that God is God: a being who always completely is what he is, which is to be and to know and to utter and to desire and to do all that is good.

Although the doctrine of the Trinity upholds the doctrine of the one God, it remains the case that human beings are incapable of knowing God directly apart from his own efforts to reveal himself, on account of the fundamental incommensurability of transcendent and immanent, simple and complex, infinite and finite, eternal and temporal, beings. By thus affirming that the immediate knowledge of God lies beyond our cognitive reach, I do not mean to suggest that we must abandon the task of thinking about who God is, or to deny that we can articulate a positive or cataphatic theology.

As I will demonstrate in subsequent chapters, the unknowable nature of God simply stipulates that positive theological work be defined in terms of delineating what can be said about God for the sake of confirming that he is God, to wit, a being who by definition transcends human knowledge. Put differently, God's nature requires that claims about him be treated as formal rather than substantial, or indicative of the kind of being that he is, who as yet subsists beyond our ken, as opposed to disclosing him as an object that might be encountered and subjected to direct analysis in this life.

While such an appropriately reserved approach to the theological task allows us positively to articulate a great deal about God's nature, the apophatic or negative theological outlook that nonetheless underlies it prevents us from defeating the whole purpose of theology by describing God as though he were a being that could be rendered intelligible on our terms, that is, an idol.

In order to span the otherwise unbridgeable gap between humanity and God, the Incarnate Son of God revealed the kind of Being God is—indeed, Triune—by expressing his Spirit, which always operates out of a desire to make the Father known as the highest good and accomplish his purposes. In thus revealing the Trinity, the Son provided us with the fully delineated conception of the supremely transcendent or highest good, which we need in order to secure a rationale or motivation for sustaining rationality. By adhering to the doctrines of Trinity and Incarnation, or to belief in the God of the Christian creed, thus engaging in what I call 'Christian creedal reasoning,' consequently we obtain the most robust account conceivable of the conditions that allow for the possibility of maintaining an orientation towards the highest good.[44]

That is not to deny that it is possible to exercise rationality or moral virtue without the relevant rationale for rationality. As native speakers of a language can communicate relatively successfully without knowledge of grammar, so rational human beings may exercise moral virtue or strive for the highest good apart from belief in God. In much the same way that grammatical knowledge is essential to teaching a language or communicating in the most effective and articulate manner, however, a rationale for rationality is arguably constitutive of rationality, when rationality is defined in the fullest sense of the term.

From this, it follows that belief in the God of Christian faith not only allows us fully to account for rationality but also to be rational in the most robust sense. While a capacity to account for rationality by appealing to key articles of Christian faith naturally does not substitute for efforts to be rational, nevertheless the ability to be rational, combined with an explanation of the conditions for the possibility of rationality, guarantees human rationality in its paradigmatic form.

On my account in two subsequent chapters ('Christian Creedal Reasoning,' parts I and II), the Son's revelation of God in the form of a human person does not merely offer us the resources needed to explain and even sustain efforts to promote the highest good. It simultaneously establishes that our efforts to promote the highest good, facilitated by Christian creedal reasoning in light of belief in the Triune, Incarnate God, strictly speaking entail efforts to live by faith in the God of Christian creed. That is to say, they represent efforts to imitate the Son by using the abilities he bestowed on us through his creative work to express our human spirits to the Father's glory, or in light of the knowledge of his absolute significance.

As this suggests, the process of becoming individuals that promote the highest good is one and the same as the process of growth as a Christian believer, at least if it is understood as such.[45] This contention will be bolstered through a further discussion of other doctrines that are the subject of Christian creedal belief, in particular creation, fall, redemption, and church. Towards the end of my discussion of these doctrines, I extrapolate the implications of my arguments thus far for an understanding of the relationship between Christianity and other systems of belief. Far from precluding conversations amongst members of diverse religious and moral traditions, I demonstrate that Christian creedal reasoning holds potential to facilitate them.

In developing the argument of the foregoing chapters, the next one ('Sufficient Conditions for Theological Philosophy') outlines the conditions which, when satisfied, ensure that we operate under the auspices of belief in the simple, Triune, and Incarnate God, such that our ordinary lives become convertible with our lives in God. These conditions are comprised of the three theological virtues of faith, hope, and love. On my account, the process of habituating ourselves in these virtues involves learning to bring the knowledge of God as the sole object of absolute significance to bear in knowing the immediate objects of our knowledge.

By organizing our lives around God along these lines, we are equipped to unlearn our natural tendency to ascribe greater significance to ordinary circumstances than they deserve and to prioritize greater over lesser goods, thus bearing things well at all times. Though we are unable to obtain knowledge of God himself in the process, we do come to understand our experiences rather differently than we might have done otherwise. In much the same way that the grammar of a language helps us conceive the meaning of a sentence, consequently, belief in God provides us with the rules for thinking about reality, which enable us to put the world of our experience into proper perspective, without over or under-estimating the worth of the things we know.[46]

The difference belief in God makes to our understanding of the world in this instance is the sort of indirect knowledge of him that we may presently attain, through the mediation of the things which are directly accessible to our understanding. Provided we cultivate a habit of thinking about these things in terms of the fact that they are 'not God,' we may begin indirectly to experience the God who is 'nowhere' in all the ordinary circumstances of our lives until we may eventually come to sense his presence continuously.

Though the theological virtues of faith and hope are the means through which we actually engage in such Christian creedal reasoning, I call attention in a further chapter ('The Consequences of Theological Philosophy') to the fact that the life of love alone furnishes proof of the orientation towards the highest good that such reasoning fosters. In developing this claim, I show how love creates the optimal conditions for cultivating the four cardinal virtues of prudence, justice, fortitude, and temperance, which are convertible on my account with the personal, inter-personal, instructive, and persuasive powers of Christian love.

On the grounds that rationality construed in terms of moral virtue—or love—constitutes the substance of a life in God, I further argue that a life of love, led on account of the rationale for rationality that faith in the Triune, Incarnate God provides, represents the final arbiter or proof of faith's rationality. By this account, therefore, the rationality of Christian faith and even of particular doctrines like Trinity and Incarnation is established not as the articles or divine object of faith are somehow rendered intelligible on the terms of human reason, let alone any modern standard of reason. Rather, their rationality comes into relief as belief in God, Triune and Incarnate, motivates us to be rational, in the way I have defined rationality in terms of intellectual and ultimately moral virtue, culminating in an authentic life of Christian love.

As I will show in the course of this discussion, efforts to demonstrate love—and thus the theological and cardinal virtues—are bound to involve difficulties and sufferings of various kinds, particularly in a society permeated by the sin tendencies that undermine the virtues. In ways I will explain, the love of God makes it possible to bear these otherwise unbearable sufferings well. In that sense, the proof for the rationality of faith that the life of Christian love affords at once provides a theodicy, that is, a case for the goodness of God in the face of sufferings and evil. After all, it is the love of a fundamentally good and loving

God that makes it possible in the first place to bring the good of bearing things well out of experiences that could not objectively be described as good.

In the concluding chapter ('Towards a Trinitarian Philosophy'), I summarize the argument of the book. Subsequently, I explain how its efforts to overturn the question of faith's rationality open doors for theological inquiries that are based on the assumption that faith is rational, including the inquiries concerning how to live by faith that are proper to the field of theological ethics. More specifically, I demonstrate how theological philosophy lays the foundation for what I call a Trinitarian philosophy, in which the affirmation of the Triune God that this work establishes as constitutive of the final rationale for human rationality is construed as the source and basis for all reality, human knowledge, and human life, which conversely represent modes of participation in the life of the Triune God.

As I have demonstrated, the account of the relationship between philosophy and theology that has been developed in this work and that such a Trinitarian philosophy would presuppose turns on the initial articulation of a pro-theology philosophy that defines rationality in terms of a personal commitment to the highest good, through engagement with all three of philosophy's sub-disciplines, namely, ontology, the theory of knowledge, and ultimately ethics. Since an appeal to belief in God, Triune and Incarnate, is required to explain and even maintain this commitment, or rationality, I have suggested that such a philosophy is strictly speaking a theological philosophy.

Although philosophy and theology are treated as distinct disciplines on this account, the fact that each informs and enables the purposes of the other suggests that a framework for understanding the inter-relationship of the two fields is necessary for the purpose of doing justice to the subject matter proper to each discipline, namely, human and spiritual life respectively. This is the framework I begin to construct in the following chapters, which collectively delineate a pro-theology philosophy.

Endnotes

[1]   Though it is not part of my present project to analyze how this challenge arose, I have shed some light on this question in *Divine Illumination: The History and Future of Augustine's Theory of Knowledge* (Oxford: Wiley-Blackwell, 2011).

[2]   See Paul Griffiths' helpful discussion of the distinction between defensive and offensive apologetics in *An Apology for Apologetics: A Study in the Logic of Interreligious Dialogue* (Eugene: Wipf and Stock, 2007).

³   The most famous early example is Justin Martyr's *Apologies*. Augustine's *City of God* also exhibits some of the characteristics of a defensive apologetic. For a contemporary example of such a response to faith's critics, see David Fergusson, *Faith and Its Critics: A Conversation* (Oxford: Oxford University Press, 2009).

⁴   Immanuel Kant is perhaps the most famous proponent of this form of argument.

⁵   As Peter Geach writes in *Mental Acts: Their Content and Their Objects* (London: Routledge, 1957), 117: 'the usefulness of historical knowledge in philosophy ... is that the prejudices of our own period may lose their grip on us if we imaginatively enter into another period when people's prejudices were different.'

⁶   Thus, the present work 'recovers' Aquinas' thought, not by projecting current concerns back onto his discussions or by nostalgically rehearsing his arguments as if a simple reversion to a past intellectual paradigm could solve contemporary challenges. Rather, it addresses present concerns in part through the use and adaptation of principles Aquinas articulated, which are perennially relevant, or at least true to the nature of reality as we experience it today. This is the general approach to recovering medieval thought that Jean Porter endorses in her book, *Nature as Reason: A Thomistic Theory of the Natural Law* (Grand Rapids: Eerdman's, 2005), 30.

⁷   See William L. Craig, *The Cosmological Argument from Plato to Leibniz* (Eugene: Wipf and Stock, 2001).

⁸   See Graham Oppy, *Ontological Arguments and Belief in God* (Cambridge: Cambridge University Press, 2007). Alvin Plantinga, *The Ontological Argument from St Anselm to Contemporary Philosophers* (Garden City, NY: Doubleday, 1965); see also Plantinga's defense of his own version of the ontological argument in *God, Freedom and Evil* (Grand Rapids: Eerdman's, 1989).

⁹   Blaise Pascal, Soren Kierkegaard, William James, and Ludwig Wittgenstein are often regarded as fideists, though this interpretation of their work may be contested or, at very least, nuanced.

¹⁰   Jennifer Faust, 'Can Religious Arguments Persuade?' *International Journal for Philosophy of Religion* 63:1 (2008), 71–86.

¹¹   Lydia Schumacher, 'The Lost Legacy of Anselm's Argument: Rethinking the Purpose of Proofs for the Existence of God,' *Modern Theology* 27:1 (January 2011), 87–101. See also Victor Preller's re-interpretation of Aquinas' five ways in *Divine Science and the Science of God: A Reformulation of Thomas Aquinas* (Princeton: Princeton University Press, 1967); and a related work by Eugene F. Rogers, *Thomas Aquinas and Karl Barth: Sacred Doctrine and the Knowledge of God* (New Haven: Yale University Press, 1995).

¹²   The most famous statement of the Reformed Epistemological project can be found in Alvin Plantinga, *Warranted Christian Belief* (Oxford: Oxford University Press, 2000). See also William Alston, *Perceiving God: The Epistemology of Religious Experience*

(Ithaca: Cornell University Press, 1993). Nicholas Wolterstorff, *Reason within the Bounds of Religion* (Grand Rapids: Eerdman's, 1988).

[13] See chapters 6 and 8 in Plantinga's *Warranted Christian Belief*, which respectively cover his Aquinas/Calvin and extended Aquinas/Calvin models of warranted Christian belief.

[14] See Richard Swinburne, 'Review of *Warranted Christian Belief*,' by Alvin Plantinga, *Religious Studies* 37 (2001), 203–14.

[15] On this point and other possible objections to Plantinga's religious epistemology, in particular, the charge that it can be employed to defend religions other than Christianity, contrary to Plantinga's intent, see James Beilby, 'Plantinga's Model of Warranted Christian Belief,' in *Alvin Plantinga*, ed. Deane Peter Baker (Cambridge: Cambridge University Press, 2007). See also Deane Peter Baker, *Tayloring Reformed Epistemology* (London: SCM Press, 2007).

[16] See Michael Rae's introductory chapter in, *Analytic Theology: New Essays in the Philosophy of Theology* (Oxford: Oxford University Press, 2009).

[17] Denys Turner, *Faith, Reason and the Existence of God* (Cambridge: Cambridge University Press, 2004).

[18] Paul Moser, *The Evidence for God: Religious Knowledge Re-Examined* (Cambridge: Cambridge University Press, 2009); see also his earlier work, *The Elusive God: Re-Orienting Religious Epistemology* (Cambridge: Cambridge University Press, 2008). Stanley Hauerwas, *With the Grain of the Universe: The Church's Witness and Natural Theology* (Brazos, 2001).

[19] James Beilby makes this point about Plantinga's project in his article, 'Plantinga's Model of Warranted Christian Belief,' 158.

[20] See Mark D. Jordan, *Ordering Wisdom: The Hierarchy of Philosophical Discourses in Aquinas* (Notre Dame: University of Notre Dame Press, 1986).

[21] On Aquinas' presupposition of Aristotelian logic (including grammar, dialectic, and rhetoric), see Mark D. Jordan, *Ordering Wisdom*, 42, 47. See other relevant works by Jordan, including, *The Alleged Aristotelianism of Thomas Aquinas* (Toronto: Pontifical Institute of Medieval Studies, 1992); *Rewritten Theology: Aquinas After His Readers* (Oxford: Wiley-Blackwell, 2005); 'Thomas Aquinas' Disclaimers in the Aristotelian Commentaries,' in *Philosophy and the God of Abraham* (Toronto: Pontifical Institute of Mediaeval Studies, 1991), 99–112.

[22] See E.J. Lemmon, *Beginning Logic* (London: Nelson, 1971), on the propositional and predicate calculi. See especially his section on 'The Syllogism' at pages 169–77. G. Leibniz is generally accredited with being the first to envision logic along modern lines. See the section on 'The Modern Type of Formal Logic', in Heinrich Scholz, *Concise History of Logic*, trans. Kurt F. Leidecker (New York: Philosophical Library, 1961). I am indebted to Martin Warner for bringing these texts and issues to my attention.

²³   E.J. Lemmon, *Beginning Logic*, 175.

²⁴   Ibid.

²⁵   E.J. Lemmon, *Beginning Logic*, 177: 'From these results the relation between the traditional doctrine of the syllogism and the predicate calculus emerges. The square of opposition principles, the laws of conversion, and the 24 valid patterns of syllogism are all derivable as theorems or sequents of the predicate calculus. Admittedly, in some cases, special existential assumptions need to be made. But rather than as a sign of any fundamental discrepancy between the two, this may be viewed as a situation in which predicate calculus helps to make explicit the foundations on which the theory of syllogisms is based. The traditional theory in fact is that fragment of the predicate calculus in which four forms of proposition are selected for special study, it being assumed also that the terms appearing in those forms are not empty. The predicate calculus is the broader study, at least in the respect that it countenances empty terms.'

²⁶   See Peter Alexander's section on 'Criticisms of Syllogistic Theory,' in *An Introduction to Logic: The Criticism of Arguments* (London: Allen & Unwin, 1969), 179–221. His lengthy discussion of modern criticisms of traditional syllogistic theory nevertheless turns on the contention that 'the theory of the syllogism is not wrong in principle but merely incomplete' (179). Also useful in this regard is A.N. Prior's article on 'Logic, Traditional,' in vol. 5, *The Encyclopedia of Philosophy*, ed. Paul Edwards (London and New York: Collier-Macmillan and Macmillan, 1967), 34–45. At page 44, Prior writes that traditional 'themes are not banished from modern logic but are incorporated into a much larger subject. When the Aristotelian forms are thus interpreted however, their laws seem to require modification at some point.' Still, he argues that it is possible to defend the claim that Aristotelian logic is more fundamental than the predicate calculus—as opposed to the other way around, which E.J. Lemmon comes close to endorsing in the discussion I mention above.

²⁷   Martha Nussbaum, *The Therapy of Desire: Theory and Practice in Hellenistic Ethics* (Princeton: Princeton University Press, 2009), 351. For another albeit very brief account according to which traditional logic explains ordinary acts of human reasoning, see S.H. Mellone, *Elements of Modern Logic* (London: University Tutorial Press, 1945), iii and 178ff.

²⁸   Martha Nussbaum, *The Therapy of Desire*, 350.

²⁹   See Michael Polanyi, *The Tacit Dimension* (Chicago: University of Chicago Press, 2009).

³⁰   Josef Pieper, *Belief and Faith* (London: Faber and Faber, 1962): 'to be a creature means to be continually receiving being and essence from the divine source and creation and in this respect therefore never to be finally completed.'

³¹   In the analytic tradition, for example, see the work of John Greco, Ernest Sosa, and Linda Zabzebski. In the Continental tradition, see writings by William Desmond,

such as, 'Doing Justice and the Practice of Philosophy,' in *Social Justice: Its Theory and Practice*, in *Proceedings of the American Catholic Philosophical Association* 79 (2005), 41–59; 'On the Secret Sources of Strengthening: Philosophical Reflections on Courage,' in *Courage*, ed. Barbara Darling-Smith (University of Notre Dame Press, 2002), 11–29. Some scholars have drawn on historical figures like Aristotle in order to develop their virtue epistemologies. For example, see Linda Zagzebski, *Virtues of the Mind* (Cambridge: Cambridge University Press, 1996). However, most have articulated their accounts without much reference to the rich resources offered by pre-modern thinkers, including Aquinas, whose virtue theory arguably entails the most mature synthesis of earlier virtue accounts, including that of Aristotle. In this scholarly context, consequently, the argument of this chapter represents the first major contribution to contemporary discussions of virtue epistemology, which makes use of what might be regarded as the optimal historical resource for developing a contemporary virtue epistemology. See Thomas S. Hibbs, 'Aquinas, Virtue, and Recent Epistemology,' *The Review of Metaphysics* 52:3 (March 1999), 573–94.

[32]   Gilbert Ryle, *The Concept of Mind* (London: Hutchinson's University Library, 1949), 62.

[33]   Gilbert Ryle, *The Concept of Mind*, 63. Alasdair MacIntyre summarizes and responds to Ryle's project in his article entitled, 'The Antecedents of Action,' in *British Analytical Philosophy*, eds Bernard Williams and Alan Montefiore (London: Routledge, 1966), 207: 'the central argument of *The Concept of Mind* is that the criteria for the application of those expressions which we use to describe mental activity are all criteria of success or failure in performance in the realm of overt behavior, and that therefore we neither need nor have reason to postulate a realm of specifically mental acts above and beyond such behavior. Foremost among the reasons which have misled philosophers into supposing that there are such mental acts is the false view that those bodily movements which are to count as human actions must have a special sort of mental cause.'

[34]   Gilbert Ryle, *The Concept of Mind*, 15: 'As a necessary corollary of this general scheme,' Ryle elaborates, 'there is implicitly prescribed a special way of construing our ordinary concepts of mental powers and operations. The verbs, nouns and adjectives, with which in ordinary life we describe the wits, characters and higher-grade performances of the people with whom we have to do, are required to be construed as signifying special episodes of their secret histories.'

[35]   Gilbert Ryle, *The Concept of Mind*, 64.

[36]   In response to Ryle's claims, Alasdair MacIntyre has argued that while we admittedly do not tend to distinguish our volitions, to take one example, and our actions, in common language, but simply treat our acts as fluid motions, his extreme way of making this point risks 'treating ordinary non-philosophical modes of speech as canonical for philosophical analysis.' See Alasdair MacIntyre, 'The Antecedents of

Action,' 208. See also the important critique of Ryle mounted by Hidé Ishiguro in, 'Imagination,' *British Analytical Philosophy*, eds Bernard Williams and Alan Montefiore (London: Routledge, 1966).

[37]   David Braine, *The Human Person: Animal and Spirit* (Notre Dame: University of Notre Dame Press, 1994), 442: 'The having of a thought cannot be logically severed from the change in the structure of behaviour [that is] inseparable from it.'

[38]   David Braine, *The Human Person*, 4.

[39]   Ibid., 35.

[40]   See Jean Porter's excellent article on 'The Common Good in Thomas Aquinas,' in *In Search of the Common Good* (London: T & T Clark, 2005). On Aquinas' virtue ethics, see various works by Alasdair MacIntyre, Herbert McCabe, Josef Pieper, Jean Porter, especially the following: Alasdair MacIntyre, *After Virtue: A Study in Moral Theory* (Notre Dame: University of Notre Dame Press, 2007); Herbert McCabe, *The Good Life: Ethics and the Pursuit of Happiness* (London: Continuum, 2005); Josef Pieper, *The Four Cardinal Virtues: Prudence, Justice, Fortitude, Temperance* (Notre Dame: University of Notre Dame Press, 1966); Jean Porter. *The Recovery of Virtue: The Relevance of Aquinas for Christian Ethics* (Louisville: John Knox Press, 1990).

[41]   On this, see the important work by Pierre Hadot, *Philosophy as a Way of Life* (Oxford: Blackwell, 1995).

[42]   Here I think of philosophical approaches like that of pragmatism, phenomenology, Wittgenstein, and even some branches of German Idealism, although it falls far outside the scope of this inquiry to highlight continuities between these philosophies and pro-theology philosophy.

[43]   David Burrell celebrates 'the distinction' between God and creatures in virtually all of his works. For a brief discussion of this distinction, see his article, 'Creator/ Creatures Relation: "The Distinction" vs. "Onto-theology,"' *Faith and Philosophy* 25 (2008), 177–89. Also see the chapters on 'Distinguishing God from the World' and 'The Christian Distinction Celebrated and Expanded,' in *Faith and Freedom: An Interfaith Perspective* (Oxford: Wiley-Blackwell, 2004). Then refer to *Knowing the Unknowable God* (Notre Dame: University of Notre Dame Press, 1992). Burrell regularly acknowledges his own debt to Robert Sokolowski's account of the 'Christian distinction' in *The God of Faith and Reason* (Washington, DC: The Catholic University of America Press, 1995), as well as to Kathryn Tanner's *God and Creation in Christian Theology: Tyranny or Empowerment?* (Minneapolis: Fortress Press, 2005), and Sara Grant's *Towards an Alternative Theology: Confessions of a Non-Dualist Christian* (Notre Dame: University of Notre Dame Press, 2002).

[44]   On the idea that doctrine facilitates Christian practice, see Ellen Charry, *By the Renewing of Your Minds: The Pastoral Function of Christian Doctrine* (Oxford: Oxford University Press, 1999).

[45]   As Jennifer Herdt has argued in her important work, *Putting on Virtue: The Legacy of the Splendid Vices* (Chicago: University of Chicago Press, 2008), our Christian understanding of virtue—and I might add, vice—needs to be attributed real practical substance, lest it become divorced from the exigencies of ordinary human life.

[46]   On 'theology as grammar,' see Rowan Williams' chapters under the heading 'The Grammar of God,' in *On Christian Theology* (Oxford: Wiley-Blackwell, 2000), 129–80. David Burrell, 'Religious Life and Understanding: Grammar Exercised in Practice,' in *Grammar and Grace: Reformulations of Aquinas and Wittgenstein* (London: SCM, 2010). See also Paul J. Griffiths' highly relevant work titled, *Intellectual Appetite: A Theological Grammar* (Washington, DC: The Catholic University of America Press, 2009).

PART I
Necessary Conditions for Pro-Theology Philosophy

Chapter 2

The Ontology of Participation

In this chapter, my purpose is to outline an ontology of participation. This type of ontology, which was commonly adhered to during the pre-modern period, has garnered a great deal of scholarly interest in recent years.[1] My explanation of the participatory way of thinking about the things that exist and the ways in which they exist will take the form of a threefold taxonomy of things in general, human nature specifically, and the defining feature of human nature, namely, human knowledge.

The first account is the most fundamental and therefore underlies the other two. In point of fact, my description of human nature simply extrapolates the implications of the initial account for beings that are defined by the capacity to reason. Given the length of the material on the ontology of knowledge, I will discuss that topic separately in the third chapter, which will outline the different elements that enter into the knowing process, which will itself be explained in the fourth chapter.

At the outset of the present discussion, it is worth noting that while a participatory ontology can be detected in the works of many ancient and medieval authors, my account is constructive and does not therefore follow the thought of any one thinker to the letter. Though it consequently provides a new synthesis or arrangement of traditional themes, my account for this very reason depends upon and identifies many points of reference in past participatory ontologies, especially the accounts of Aquinas and Aristotle, selecting and adapting their views in accordance with the distinctive purposes of this project and in view of certain more recent developments.[2]

As is well known, Aquinas drew heavily on Aristotelian philosophy in developing his own thought. In fact, he wrote commentaries on Aristotle's major works, evidently in preparation for authoring his magisterial *Summa Theologiae*.[3] Though it might seem relevant for this reason to turn to Aquinas' commentaries on Aristotle's works and the works themselves, to say nothing of Aquinas' other works, to obtain a detailed account of his views on all the matters ontological, which are covered in the *Summa*, it must be stressed that this approach to interpreting Aquinas is only viable in cases where the *Summa* can be shown to presuppose the background provided by one of the commentaries.

This background is not always assumed, however, because Aquinas often transformed, re-framed or even rejected Aristotle's teachings, in the process of bringing them into conversation with many other classical and medieval perspectives and indeed with his own original synthesis of preceding tradition, as presented in the *Summa*, which was designed to bolster Aquinas' distinctly Dominican Christian faith and mission.[4] For this reason, I will take my cues primarily from Aquinas' own works, rather than his commentaries on Aristotle, in the account that follows, turning to the works of Aristotle himself, whenever it seems relevant.

While I will draw on Aquinas more than Aristotle in most sections of this work, the reverse situation will apply especially in Chapter 3, where I take Aristotle's own works, particularly those on logic, as the main source for my treatment of the ontology of knowledge. The reason for this shift in the use of primary source material has to do with the fact that Aquinas' works lack a full-scale treatment of logic. This lack is not the result of a mere oversight. As a scholastic theologian, rather, Aquinas would have taken for granted his readers' familiarity with Aristotle's logical scheme, which students at his time would acquire through an initial period of training in the *trivium*, or grammar, logic/dialectic, and rhetoric.[5] By way of a preliminary to my treatment of this scheme, therefore, I outline in what follows a constructive ontology of participation that draws on both Thomistic and Aristotelian sources.

The Ontology of Things Known

The ontology of participation I wish to develop recognizes three main classes (genera) of natural beings, namely, non-sentient, non-rational beings (vegetation); sentient, non-rational beings (animals); and sentient, rational beings (humans). The beings in all three categories are what they are in virtue of the distinctive ways they accomplish two tasks. The first task is to hold together the component parts of the being in question, ensuring that it remains the same type of being that consistently performs the same sorts of operations.[6]

The second task is to draw into the life of the being a diverse range of things that enable it to perform its proper functions—sunlight and water, in the case of vegetative beings, for instance, and knowable objects, in the case of rational beings. As these examples suggest, beings are what they are by dint of the way they relate or are united to other beings, though it should be noted that the mode of a being's relating to other beings is more fundamental than any of its actual relations to those beings. In fact, the way a being relates to other beings is at once a way of distinguishing the being from the beings to which it relates.

When a being exercises its particular mode of relation by incorporating other beings into itself, it undergoes what can be described as an accidental change, that is, a change in its properties as opposed to its substance. Before an accidental change occurs, there are two separate elements, namely, that from which and that to which the being changes, respectively.[7] These two elements are called contraries. The third element involved in the change is simply the subject or being that undergoes the change from one of the contraries to the other and so endures throughout the change. Accidental changes that alter some aspect of a thing as opposed to its nature or essence can be distinguished from substantial changes, which pertain to the generation and corruption, or coming into being and ceasing-to-be, of beings. In the case of substantial changes, the contraries include a form and the lack thereof. The subject is the matter that underlies both, presumably the male and female contributions to reproduction.

Whenever beings undergo accidental changes, they appropriate what they require in order to perform their operations and at the same time perform those operations. That is, they do what is relevant to their own nutrition, growth, and reproduction and thus ensure the survival of their kind. The interconnection of nutrition and reproduction in this instance bespeaks the reality that beings do not merely operate in accordance with a natural, seemingly selfish urge to preserve their own lives. Rather, they pursue self-preservation for the sake of multiplying and contributing to the thriving of other beings like themselves—and even to their own thriving, insofar as this is impossible apart from cooperation with other beings.[8]

From the discussion above, it follows that the power to unify is what renders a being a 'reality.' In that sense, the ontology in question is in point of fact a *henology* (Greek: *hen*—one).[9] In a henology, realities exist in the way and to the degree they exhibit unity or individual identity and a related capacity to make other things one with themselves. Insofar as the sheer capacity to unify—to be real—is an intrinsic good, to be one is not only to exist or to be but also to be good.[10]

On henological grounds, the three genera of beings can be organized according to a three-tiered hierarchy of being, which illustrates three ascending grades of participation in reality, or three degrees of ability to unify other beings.[11] Non-sentient, non-rational (vegetative) beings rank lowest on this hierarchy because the range of their relations, or unifying capacity, is restricted to beings that act as the initiators of contact. With few exceptions, plants cannot strictly speaking 'feel' this contact, let alone move themselves to make contact with other beings.[12] For these reasons, which pertain to the fact that plants possess nothing more than what Aristotle calls the 'nutritive' and 'reproductive' capacities, they of all creatures are most at the mercy of the environment when it comes to providing for their nutrition and reproduction and thus when it comes to surviving.

The middle place on the hierarchy is occupied by sentient, non-rational beings (non-human animals), because they possess a 'sensitive' capacity in addition to the capacities for nutrition and reproduction. Owing to this capacity, animals are able to sense when they make contact with other beings. They are also able instinctively to infer the consequences of contact with those beings, seeking out entities that promote their survival and avoiding things that threaten it.[13] In this regard, many, though not all, animals are aided by what Aristotle calls the 'locomotive' capacity, that is, the ability to move towards objects of appetite and away from objects of aversion.

Sentient, rational beings (humans) are positioned at the top of the hierarchy in virtue of the rational capacity. This allows for more than the instinctive or conditioned reactions to objects that are proper to non-human animals. It enables humans proactively to draw universally applicable conclusions about objects that are not dependent on the continued presence of those objects or limited by them in any other way. Indeed, the rational ability gives human beings the freedom to think as much as they wish about virtually all things and even to do this in creative and imaginative ways that are not actually true to reality as it stands but may nevertheless shed light on the way things are or could be. In short, it supports a capacity for infinite thought. This capacity to think all things in turn upholds a capacity ultimately to conceive of the general nature of all things, as in the discipline of philosophy.[14]

In addition to enacting the aforementioned capabilities, the intellectual power enables humans to evaluate themselves and their own operations. This is something non-human animals cannot do, because the sensitive faculty, which allows them to perceive realities, does not go so far as to permit them to think about the fact that they perceive realities. Since human beings may reflect upon the desires and abilities they have to explore the world as they engage in exploring it, by contrast, there is a sense in which their work to discover the world doubles as self-discovery, at least if it is understood as such.[15] By unifying what they know, even about themselves, in summary, humans transform the substance of their intellectual objects into their own substance, albeit in a cognitive way, and thus become what they know, in a manner that is analogous to the way all creatures 'are what they eat.'[16]

In virtue of the ultimate unifying power, which they possess, namely, the power to conceptualize anything or even the nature of all things, humans are both competent and responsible to oversee, that is, unify, the beings that are inferior to them in this taxonomy, just as those beings are ordered to govern their own inferiors. A similar principle applies within the classes themselves, where beings are ordered according to their level of ability to unify or govern other beings inside the genus. Within the animal kingdom, for instance, the species that are self-moving participate in the level of reality characteristic of their genus to a higher degree than do those that are only capable of sensation and self-nutrition.

By dint of being governed by superiors, whether within or outside a particular genus, inferior beings participate in the life of their superiors, which do not in turn participate in the life of the inferiors and cannot more generally be united by or reduced to members of inferior classes. As noted previously, the superior classes surpass the inferior ones on account of a power over and above the powers they may share in common with their inferiors. Thus, human beings and dolphins share the nutritive, sensitive, and locomotive powers. But human beings surpass dolphins because of the added rational power.[17] On account of this power, the animal nature of human beings is altogether different from that of beings that lack this power and consequently manifests in a different form of animal physicality.[18]

In addition to the three different levels of participation in reality that represent degrees of capacity on the part of creatures to unify or internalize other beings, there are degrees of participation in the level of reality that is proper to particular beings, regardless of where they fall on the spectrum. Such participation is made possible by the 'triadic' structure inherent in all beings. This structure consists in the essence, existence, and life of beings, which respectively correspond to their unity, truth, and goodness. The essence correlates to the unity of a thing for the two reasons I already mentioned. In the first place, it makes the being one thing as opposed to another, giving the being an identity and a corresponding set of characteristic operations; thereby, or secondarily, it determines the being's way of relating to or unifying other beings.

An essence is what Aristotle describes as a being's formal cause.[19] Formal causality is just one of four types of causality, that is, types of rationale or explanation, to which Aristotle supposes we must appeal in order to explain the state of being of any being at any given time.[20] While a formal cause answers the question why a being possesses a certain identity—why it is what it is—an efficient cause answers the question why the being exists at all, or how it came into being. Thus, the knowledge of this kind of causality—to which modern thinkers have tended to restrict the whole notion of causality[21]—makes it possible to predict its effects.

In addition to formal and efficient causes, there is the final or teleological cause, which accounts for the purpose or goal of a being's existence, which is to act in accordance with and ultimately fully instantiate a formal cause. The highest faculty a being possesses—rational, locomotive, sensitive, or nutritive—derives from its formal cause, which in turn dictates the material shape the being will take and the sort of physical life it will lead, that is, its material cause. Without a formal cause, there would be no material cause or actual entity. After all, matter creates nothing but the potential for formation. That said, forms could not be instantiated apart from matter.[22] Thus, all natural beings are compounds of matter and form.[23]

This conclusion is related to Aquinas' contention that the soul, which can be nutritive, sensitive, or rational, depending on whether the highest form of the being in question is nutritive, sensitive, or rational, is the form of the body. One key upshot of this contention is that the soul or form of a being is not an altogether separate entity from the body, as in dualism, nor is it reduced to the functions of the body, as in materialism, but instead *entails* embodiment and can only be realized through embodied life.[24] Although matter and form may be logically distinguished by this account, the doctrine of the soul as the form of the body denotes that the two entities are not separable in reality. Furthermore, it highlights that the substantial form that all beings of the same species share in common is one in type rather than one in number, as it would be if all human beings possessed a single mind, for instance. This is because the form in question is individualized through its instantiation in matter.[25]

Because beings are composites of form and matter—actual being and the potential to be—they do not fully instantiate their respective essences from their very inception. By contrast to an essentialist ontology according to which essences either exist in their full and final—totalized—form or not at all, the account espoused here presupposes that beings enter the world with the potential to realize a given form or essence, such that they exist more, the more they do so. In short, their existence is a matter of degrees as opposed to an all-or-nothing affair.

An appeal to final causality explains how beings realize their potential or strive for the goal or *telos* of 'becoming themselves,' gradually instantiating their different forms. Indeed, the final cause is closely linked to the formal cause or essence, which not only gives beings the potential to become the realities they are but is at once that which beings strive to become, namely, the final cause that explains what propels beings to fulfill their potential and why they have done so to any degree. By allowing for the fact that beings 'grow into' their forms over time, as in striving towards a *telos* or end, it becomes possible to uphold a more realistic, that is, teleological, version of realism than the essentialist version according to which realities must be fully instantiated at all times, if they are to be said to exist at all.[26]

This brings us to the question how beings gradually become what they are over the course of time, and to the second aspect of the triad, namely, 'existence,' which is the mode in which a being actually becomes itself. Indeed, existence entails participation in the particular mode of being that is determined by a being's essence: the performance of the functions that are proper to the being. Whereas essence corresponds to the unity of a being, existence represents its *truth*. For existing is the means through which a being is true to or actualizes its essence, by uniting within itself the things that enable its characteristic operations.

By affirming that existence is the mode in which the essence of a being is actualized, this account gives credence to the assumption that existence takes priority over essence, although not in the manner affirmed by strict existentialism, which effectively denies the reality of essences.[27] In this connection, the present account recognizes that the very way in which an essence is actualized—the aspects of the essence that are brought to the fore—is heavily determined by the manner in which circumstances call upon a being to manifest that essence—or exist—at different points in time.

That is not to say that the essence of a thing is a mere function of the environment in which it exists.[28] Still, it is to acknowledge that there is no essence without existence.[29] By gesturing towards the fact that there is conversely no existence without an essence to-be-actualized, however, this account also accommodates the affirmation that essence takes priority over existence in its own way, though not in the way of strict essentialism. On this showing, in fact, essence and existence each enable the work of the other, such that neither takes priority absolutely, and both are indispensable to every act of being.

As stated above, the potential a being has already actualized though such acts of being or on-going existence represents the extent to which it has met its final goal or *telos*. This actualized potential constitutes the life of the being. That life is the *good* of the being's existence, that is, the locus of its own thriving as well as the resource it has to offer to the benefit of other beings. Although the shape of a being's life is bound to alter over time, owing to the material or accidental changes that accompany development, I would reiterate that those changes are not fundamental (formal/substantial) shifts in essence or identity but rather represent the actualization thereof, through ongoing existence, which is again the good of life.

While a being may possess more potential to actualize at any point in time, the possibility of further development does not negate the fact that the being achieves the highest level of maturity it can at a particular time, assuming it does so. In fact, it is only by achieving what it is able to achieve at any given moment that a being is predisposed to participate even more fully in its nature at later points in time. In Aquinas' account, the notion of natural law accounts for the way beings tend to maximize their potential to participate in their essences or modes of existence at various times. This law simply holds all beings accountable to achieve the highest degree of goodness or maturity that is possible for them at any time.

Of course, the good in question is bound to differ from species to species.[30] Since species differ in nature or essence, what it means to fulfill the natural law will vary for different beings, especially human beings. As noted previously, humans may exercise rationality and thus fulfill the natural law as it applies to their species in a virtually infinite variety of ways, such that there are as many ways to fulfill the natural law as a human as there are human beings. Though the natural law can only be fulfilled in diverse ways by different beings, which may even fulfill the law in different ways at different points in time, it bears re-stating that the law itself is not variegated or subject to flux but effectively reduces to one law, according to which all things must strive to achieve their own proper or highest good.[31] In the section below, I will discuss the cognitive faculties that enable human beings to do this in their own characteristic and characteristically diverse ways.

The Ontology of the Human Knower

Similar to other beings, human beings are teleological entities and must therefore become what they are through ongoing participation in their proper mode of existence. Since the human essence is that of a 'rational animal,' this mode is cognitive, such that human life involves the acquisition and application of knowledge.[32] In what follows, I will explain the three modes of knowing that cooperate to enact the possibility of knowledge, thus laying the foundation for the discussion of chapters three through five, which elaborate upon the elements involved in the knowing process and indeed describe the process itself, thus filling out an understanding of what it means to actualize human nature through the exercise of human reason.

The aforementioned modes or powers of knowing include sensation, perception, and intellection, which respectively correspond to the three levels of reality previously mentioned, namely, the vegetative, sensitive, and intellectual.[33] The first power of sensation is the means through which objects in the external world are encountered by way of one or more of the five sense organs, namely, the eyes, ears, nose, tongue, or skin. On making contact with an object in sensation, an alteration occurs in the sense organ that corresponds to the sense object, whereby the sense organ takes on the sensible form of the object sensed.[34]

Since like can only be affected by like, the success of this alteration or impression turns on the fact that sensible is impacted by sensible, or sense organs by sense objects, in this instance.[35] The five sense organs are 'like' their objects precisely in virtue of their physicality. Each one of these organs is ordered towards its proper objects, which are the sensible qualities of things.[36] For example, Aristotle notes that the object of sight is color, and the object of hearing, sound.

Of course, some objects may be perceived by more than one sense. For instance, motion may be sensed by both touch and sight. For this reason, phenomena like motion are referred to as 'common objects.' In addition to an organ or organs, there is also a medium proper to each sense, like air or water. By means of the relevant medium, the sensible quality of an external object is transferred to the sense organ of the perceiver when contact with the object is made.[37] Because such an act of sensation is completely tied to the particular object of experience, sensation is the least comprehensive power in terms of the range of objects it is ordered to encompass.

Once a sense impression has been imposed upon an organ of the body, that impression effectively transfers the object sensed 'into' the body, making the object available to the imaginative power of the mind. This perceptive faculty actually registers the objects contacted by the sense organs, making images or 'snapshots' of things seen; 'sound bites' of things heard; and 'sense bites' of things felt, tasted, or smelled.[38] Insofar as these mental images can be recalled when the objects of experience are no longer present, the perceptive faculty is not as bound to its objects as the sensitive power, even though it is tied to them in the sense that it encapsulates them in some way.

By reflecting whatever occurs in the eyes or ears or other sense organs, and thus enacting a change from like to unlike, these images or bites bridge the gap between what is sensible and intelligible.[39] Once formed, such images, also traditionally called 'phenomena' or 'appearances,' are stored in the sense memory or the so-called 'possible intellect.'[40] In human beings, the images formed by the imaginative faculty lay the groundwork for the work of abstracting concepts or ideas, which apply universally to things of a similar kind.

Although abstraction or thinking cannot be conducted without these images or *phantasmata*, it is crucial to note that 'mental images are [not the] objects of the mind in thinking, but ... the objects of the mind are the things imagined, the things which the images are of. It is not, for instance, that we imagine images of cows, but that we imagine cows.'[41] This conclusion must be bolstered against the 'constantly recurring confusion whereby it is supposed that in the imagining of cows there are some extra objects, not cows, but images of cows before the mind's eye.'[42] For 'the role of the imagination in thinking is not to provide non-external objects of reference of a special kind called images ... but to make reference possible.'[43]

On this showing, the concepts achieved through abstraction are not mental representations of the apparent commonalities that particular images stored in the sense memory exhibit, as they are in the interpretation of abstraction theory—and misinterpretation of Aquinas—to which Peter Geach refers as 'abstractionism.'[44] In other words, they are not entities or objects of knowledge, which mediate between the mind and reality, and thereby threaten to sever the mind's direct connection with the world.[45] Rather, concepts represent ways of or capacities for knowing things, whereby particulars of experience that exhibit certain commonalities are comprehended, as the relation of a universal like 'humanity' to a specific human being is perceived.[46]

As Geach affirms, abstraction 'in all cases is a matter of fitting my concept to my experience, of exercising the appropriate concept, not of picking out the feature I am interested in from among others simultaneously given in experience.'[47] On this account, acts of judgment or abstraction simply involve the exercise of a concept, which is nothing but the mental capacity exercised in judgment to illuminate the nature of a particular thing.[48] Thus, concepts are universal, or concerned with unities or commonalities, only insofar as one and the same or a common concept can be applied to render intelligible many different things of a similar kind, that is, things exhibiting commonalities.[49]

That is not to deny that some effort to identify commonalities or 'see unity' amongst related things or qualities is a necessary preliminary to abstractive knowledge, particularly in the inductive mode of reasoning I will discuss in Chapter 3. There would be no basis for deductively exercising a concept to understand particulars apart from such an initial effort. In this cognitive effort as in any other, however, the ultimate object of knowledge is not some abstract representation of the commonalities particular objects may exhibit—a 'third thing' that mediates between the mind and reality.[50] For in drawing an inference about a certain commonality that objects similarly exhibit, I have suggested that the mind does not perceive some reified version of that commonality, but instead determines that one and the same concept can and should be fitted to all those objects when the feature they have in common comes under consideration.[51]

In his own distinctly Thomist defense of this account, John O'Callaghan concludes in accordance with Geach that a 'concept is a nominalized form of talking about our act of conceiving, not a way of referring to an additional class or category of objects or things in addition to our acts.'[52] In other words, 'a concept is the informed activity of the intellect as it grasps'[53] a thing, while 'the intellect is simply the human substance's capacity to engage in just that act.'[54] On these grounds, O'Callaghan concludes that there is no real difference between the intellect and its concepts, no problem of spanning the presumed gap between the knower and the known, for the two are fundamentally one.

Whereas abstractionism assumes that all persons independently form ideas about objects of experience, which mediate between the mind and the world, and are intrinsically inaccessible to others, consequently, Aquinas and his aforementioned readers throw the emphasis back onto the objects of knowledge, about which numerous persons may have the same concept, insofar as they have the same mental capacity to comprehend objects. Although abstract thinking becomes a highly subjective affair when concepts are thus defined in terms of 'a mental capacity, belonging to a particular person,'[55] this definition paradoxically does not render communication about common objects of knowledge impossible. For the Thomistic tendency to prioritize objects of knowledge instead of knowers—ontology rather than epistemology—renders the objects of knowledge commonly accessible to all and thus does away with the problem of knowing other minds.[56]

In light of the discussion above, it remains to elaborate on the mental transition from perception to intellection that occurs in the abstraction of concepts. This involves a change from like to like, inasmuch as the move from mental images to thoughts of images is a move from intelligible to intelligible. Although no substantial change occurs in the transition from perception to intellection, it is nonetheless true that perception—the passive power to be impressed upon by external objects—is not itself adequate to the active labor of abstracting ideas or exercising concepts. That is not to denigrate perception or the sense faculties more generally. As we have seen, these faculties, which produce the raw material or images for abstraction, are indispensable to the intellect's work, even though those faculties are themselves unable to perform that work. Indeed, the mind needs the senses in order to have data to render intelligible, just as much as the senses of the body need the mind, without which it is impossible to render sense data intelligible.

The reason neither the senses nor the intellect can do the work of the other—though neither can do its own work without that of the other—comes down to a difference in the different faculties' means of operation. As explained above, the perceptive faculties rely on the sense organs in order to perform their operations, and these organs are tied to physical objects. By contrast to the imagination, the locus of the mind's operation is not a bodily organ but a capacity, which has 'no physical states or processes internal to it in the way in which we may suppose perception [and] imagination to have physical processes.'[57] Precisely because the mind makes no immediate contact with sense objects but encounters them through the mediation of the imagination, it is able to transcend the particulars of the sensible world by thinking in universal or abstract terms about them, in ways I have already mentioned.[58]

The difference between the imagination and the intellect makes for another fascinating contrast between them. Since perception deals directly with objects, a confrontation with something highly perceptible—such as a very bright light or a loud noise—dulls the relevant faculty of sight or hearing for example until the impact of the perception dissipates. In the case of the intellect, however, the effect is reversed.[59] The mind understands more not less when it understands more things or more difficult things, because it is not tied to particulars and is therefore capable of universal thought.

Despite their differences, I have been trying to show that the senses and intellect operate in mutual interdependence in order to acquire and apply universal knowledge, which is, after all, knowledge of a sense-perceptible world. As I argued earlier, the (rational) soul forms the body in such a way as to render embodied life the sole possible site of the mind's work. Though the mind is invariably embodied and cannot operate without recourse or reference to bodily life, this should not be taken to imply that features of human embodiment like sex and race can in principle prevent persons from exercising their minds with respect to certain issues.

Although such features may inform how individuals address different issues, the rational capacity is by definition a capacity to consider any issue whatever, such that all human beings that possess this capacity can in principle think about all things. This point bears noting in view of the apparently misguided argument advanced by some that intellectual and other tasks ought to be divided on the basis of preconceived gender or social roles, to take just two examples.

While I have tried to make it clear in the above that the material for the formation of concepts arises from experience (*a posteriori*) and is not therefore innate, it would appear nevertheless that the capacity to think in unifying or universalizing terms is itself one that comes to us prior to all experience (*a priori*) and so consequently by nature. In closing this chapter, therefore, I wish to say a word about the different types and levels of ability human beings may have when it comes to thinking along these lines. Aristotle mentions three different types of intellectual ability or 'intellectual virtue,' namely, wisdom, science (knowledge), and arts/skills pertaining to practical 'things done.'[60]

The first two fields of inquiry are primarily speculative, concerned with universals or generalities, although there are practical or applied sciences like politics, ethics, economics, engineering, and medicine. Wisdom accounts for the nature of reality (ontology), the nature of knowledge (epistemology), and the nature of the good life (ethics). In short, wisdom pertains to the work of philosophy. Additionally, wisdom may delineate the transcendent conditions for reality, knowledge, and human life. It may extend to the study of theology.[61]

Whereas wisdom outlines the nature of reality and its transcendent conditions of possibility, science elucidates the nature of particular objects of inquiry.[62] Any object of interest may become the basis for a scientific inquiry, including history, society, language, nature, and so on. According to Aristotle, some subject areas are 'sub-alternate' to others, for example, philosophy to theology, or music to mathematics.[63] Sub-alternate sciences derive their first principles from the conclusions reached by higher sciences, which conversely delineate the reasons for the conclusions reached in the sub-alternate sciences.

The arts or areas of skilled or craft knowledge are practical, and thus concerned with particulars by contrast to universals. Some arts are productive, such as the technical and domestic arts, including cooking, home economics, gardening, farming, and woodworking. Others are artistic in the strict sense of the term, for example, the creative, performing, and visual arts, which include literature, poetry, dance, music, drama, painting, sculpture, and so on.

In addition to the different types of skill for comprehending reality, there are different degrees of ability when it comes to seeking and gaining understanding. For instance, some individuals are able to orientate themselves to one or a number of the aforementioned fields of inquiry very quickly or even immediately. As a result, they can pursue the lines of inquiry proper to those fields much further than others would be able to do. On another level, some individuals possess a penetrating knowledge of a particular subject area, though they may lack awareness of the relation of their area of expertise to other areas.

While those with a broader perspective are generally better equipped to grasp the relations amongst spheres of thought, they may or may not have highly specified understanding of any one of those areas. As this suggests, the perspective of the broad-minded must be counterbalanced by those possessing a more focused outlook, just as those with a narrow focus need the vision of the broad-minded to compensate for their own potential deficiency in comprehensive understanding. The narrow and broad outlooks just described may predispose a person to pursue one or another of the aforementioned fields or types of inquiry.

For example, an individual with broad vision might be particularly well suited to the study of philosophy or politics.

In any event, the nature and degree of a person's intelligence is proportional to the way and extent to which they are able to unify or make sense of reality conceptually. In this connection, ingenuity would seem to be distinguishable from mere talent in an area of inquiry not by an ability to work without appropriating ideas from others, since most great scientists and artists are influenced by the work of others. Rather, geniuses can be set apart from ordinary and even exceptionally gifted minds by the *way* they appropriate the ideas of others, namely, to the end of constructing an intellectual framework of their own invention, where merely talented individuals would simply interpret, alter, or corroborate existing perspectives.[64]

Though the foregoing discussion of the different types and levels of intellectual ability hints that human relations are subject to hierarchical ordering, since some are more capable than others when it comes to navigating certain spheres of understanding, it is not intended to deny the equal value of all human beings, much less to imply that the hierarchy can be established on any grounds other than sheer intellectual ability—such as sex, race, or culture. Regardless of such accidental features, all persons are deserving of the opportunities and support that are equal or proportional to their abilities.

By the same token, they are responsible for utilizing their abilities for appropriate ends, that is, to oversee, aid, or answer to others in ways those abilities render relevant. Since no one is able to achieve their full potential in these respects at any given point in time, however, our value as persons cannot be identified with the type or level of our abilities. Instead, it must be determined in accordance with the extent to which we exercise and indeed maximize those capabilities, however meager or impressive they may be.[65] In that light, those who make the most of modest capacities tap into their dignity as persons more than those with exceptional abilities who neglect to use them, or to use them for good.

Whereas the potential of many persons goes unrealized on account of negligence, that of others may be impeded by a mental or physical disability or some other vulnerable state, such as that of an unborn or newborn child. Under these conditions, individuals have a 'potential for potential,' that is, a potential that cannot be fully actualized—if it can be actualized at all—that makes it difficult for them to protect and sustain their own lives and thrive in very basic ways.[66] In that sense, their existence lays upon those who enjoy unqualified potential a responsibility not only to refrain from neglecting, exploiting, or abusing them but also to administer the special care that is required to compensate for their vulnerabilities.

In turn, those challenged by disabilities might be regarded as responsible to maximize their 'potential for potential' by accepting willingly any appropriate support and aid offered to them, assuming they are not too incapacitated voluntarily to receive it. When they acquire by these or their own means a basis for giving to others in accordance with their own abilities, they become the most remarkable examples of human being, and paradigms of human dignity, precisely because of the weaknesses they overcome in order to exhibit their strengths. As this suggests, equality is achieved amongst human persons, regardless of their state of mental ability or disability, when those who can give, give, and those who can receive, receive, and thus give meaning and purpose to the lives of those who can give, who in turn give inspiration and life to those who receive.

By these means, the distinction between those who give and receive breaks down, thus confirming that what is most important when it comes to exercising our humanity is not so much the type or level of our abilities but whether we make the most of our potential—or potential for potential—whatever it involves. The degree to which we do this, whether by offering or receiving aid, as relevant, determines the extent to which we live up to the name 'human being' and become what we actually are but which we could conceivably neglect to be.

In the next two chapters, I will treat the main tool we have to exercise our humanity, namely, the ability to reason. On the basis of my argument that all ontological realities are subject to development—where the human being is a reality defined by the capacity to know, or rationality—it can be inferred that human knowledge is also subject to development. In other words, the ideas human beings form in order to direct their lives admit of growth and change. In Chapter 4, I will discuss the nature of this knowing process, after investigating the elements of knowledge that enter into the process in the chapter that immediately follows.

Endnotes

[1] See for example Catherine Pickstock, *Truth in Aquinas* (London: Routledge, 2000); and Rudi te Velde, *Participation and Substantiality in Thomas Aquinas* (Leiden: Brill, 1995).

[2] When it comes to offering a general ontology, I draw on Aquinas' account of the natural order at *ST* 1.44–74. Also relevant to this discussion is his important treatise on being and essence, *De ente et essentia*. With regard to the ontology of human nature, I make use of Aquinas' 'treatise on human nature' at *ST* 1.75–102, and where relevant, his disputed questions on truth (*Quaestiones disputatae de veritate*).

³   The major works on which Aquinas commented include Aristotle's *Physics* and *Metaphysics*, which respectively treat the nature of the natural order and the principles that govern reality; the *De anima*, where Aristotle provides his account of the diverse faculties that living beings, including human beings, possess (including the faculties of self-nutrition, reproduction, sensation, and thinking); the *Posterior Analytics*, which concern human knowledge; and the *Nicomachean Ethics*, which describe the life of virtue.

⁴   On the influence of the Dominican mission on Aquinas' work, see Ferdinand Christian Bauerschmidt, *Thomas Aquinas: Faith, Reason and Following Christ* (Oxford: Oxford University Press, 2013). On Aquinas' use of Aristotle, see Mark D. Jordan, *The Alleged Aristotelianism of Thomas Aquinas* (Toronto: Pontifical Institute of Medieval Studies, 1992); *Rewritten Theology: Aquinas After His Readers* (Oxford: Wiley-Blackwell, 2005); and 'Thomas Aquinas' Disclaimers in the Aristotelian Commentaries,' in *Philosophy and the God of Abraham* (Toronto: Pontifical Institute of Mediaeval Studies, 1991), 99–112. As Mark D. Jordan writes in the first of the aforementioned works, Aquinas' commentaries were written as literal expositions of Aristotle's works. While the use of this genre 'need not suggest that the commentator disavows what is taught in the underlying text, it does suggest that additional warrant will be required for attributing what is taught to the commentator ... The literal commentary as such does not assert that the text under explication is true, it asserts that the text merits careful reading' (104). Jordan goes on to argue that Thomas likely wrote the commentaries in part to explore issues he intended to treat in his *Summa*. This would explain why he did not complete some of the commentaries, namely, because there would have been no need to complete them after finishing the necessary preliminary studies for the *Summa* (106). As such, Jordan contends, the commentaries 'can give us only scattered indications of Thomas' philosophical doctrine, indications to be followed into other works of his corpus,' (110) especially for the present purposes, the *Summa*. For this reason, Jordan submits, we can only identify where Aquinas' thought coincides with Aristotle's retrospectively, that is, in light of the knowledge of other texts like the *Summa* that represent Aquinas' own points of view. As Jordan affirms, 'this exegetical practice derives from the presupposition that Thomas' philosophical teaching may break through its Aristotelian precedents at many decisive points' (111). While a reading of the *Summa* can lead us to the passages in the commentaries that actually represent Aquinas' thought, in other words, the commentaries themselves are not necessarily indicative of Aquinas' own views.

⁵   See Mark D. Jordan, *Ordering Wisdom: The Hierarchy of Philosophical Discourses in Aquinas* (Notre Dame: University of Notre Dame Press, 1986), 42, 47.

⁶   Herbert McCabe calls attention to both the differences and similarities between living beings and machines in his article, 'Animals and Us,' in *The Good Life* (London:

Continuum, 2005), 95–114. Although machines represent imitations of animals in virtue of the fact that their parts are assembled to facilitate the performance of coherent operations, McCabe contends, they differ from animals in that their parts can be disassembled and used for different purposes, which is not for the most part true of natural animals. While animals can reproduce and heal themselves, moreover, machines must be produced and repaired by rational beings. However they may appear to 'live,' consequently, they are not alive in the true sense that they are capable of sustaining their own lives. For this reason, the human ability to construct machines should not be confused with an ability to master natural life. This confusion is especially important to avoid because the presumption of an ability to manipulate a life may significantly affect the way human beings decide which machines to make and what to do with them, leading them in many cases to make and employ machines in ways that actually harm or undermine natural life.

[7]   Aristotle, *On Generation and Corruption; Phys.* I.7.

[8]   On altruism, see Stephen J. Pope, *The Evolution of Altruism and the Ordering of Love* (Washington, DC: Georgetown University Press, 1995). See also *Evolution, Games and God: The Principle of Cooperation*, eds Sarah Coakley and Martin A. Novak (Cambridge, MA: Harvard University Press, 2011), especially the entry by Jean Porter on 'Nature, Normative Grammars, and Moral Judgments.' See also Justin L. Barrett, *Cognitive Science, Religion and Theology: From Human Minds to Divine Minds* (West Conshohocken: Templeton Press, 2011), 86: 'from an evolutionary perspective, the core argument is that individuals with moral inclinations (even if they do not always act in accordance with them) will outcompete the wholly immoral for survival and reproduction. It is not an adaptive strategy to be completely selfish, cheating, stealing, fighting, and murdering. Such behavior would discourage others from cooperating or trusting such an individual and lead to their having less access to the resources and other benefits of large group living.'

[9]   Leo Sweeny, *Divine Infinity in Greek and Medieval Thought* (New York: Peter Lang, 1992). Josef Pieper, *Living the Truth* (San Franciscan: Ignatius Press, 1989), 82: 'The higher the form of existence, the more developed becomes the relatedness with reality, also the more profound and comprehensive becomes the sphere of this relatedness, namely the world.'

[10]   *De Veritate* 21.

[11]   *ST* 1.18.3.

[12]   *ST* 1.78.1–2.

[13]   On this topic, see Martha C. Nussbaum, *Upheavals of Thought: The Intelligence of the Emotions* (Cambridge: Cambridge University Press, 2001), ch. 2; and *The Fragility of Goodness* (Cambridge: Cambridge University Press, 2001), ch. 9. See also Alasdair MacIntyre, *Dependent Rational Animals* (London: Duckworth, 1999).

[14]   *ST* 1.80.1.

[15]   *ST* 1.87.

[16]   *ST* 1.87.1; *ST* 1.119.1. Joseph Owens, 'Aquinas on Cognition as Existence,' *Proceedings of the American Catholic Philosophical Association* 48 (1974), 74–85.

[17]   *ST* 1.76.4: the intellectual soul virtually contains the sensitive and nutritive souls; cf. Martha Nussbaum, 'Humans and Other Animals,' in *Upheavals of Thought*.

[18]   On this, see Herbert McCabe, 'Change, Language, Reasons, and Action,' in *On Aquinas*, 44–5.

[19]   *De Ente* 1.

[20]   *Phys.* II.3, *Meta.* I.3: on the four causes. R.J. Hankinson, *Cause and Explanation in Ancient Greek Thought* (Oxford: Clarendon Press, 2001).

[21]   See Simon Oliver, *Philosophy, God and Motion* (London: Routledge, 2005).

[22]   Etienne Gilson, *The Arts of the Beautiful* (Dalkey, 2000), 93. In fact, 'Thomas Aquinas was so sure that the existence of a matter without any form is impossible that he even denied God the power to create it as such ... The reason for this is simple: being is only what it is because of its form. In losing its form it would cease to be anything; it would lose the very possibility of existing.'

[23]   This is the upshot of Aristotle's doctrine of hylomorphism as described in *DA* II.1 (Greek: *hylo*—matter; *morphe*—form).

[24]   *ST* 1.76.1: the affirmation that the soul is the form of the body also implies that the rational soul is what causes the body to act in the ways peculiar to human beings (which pertain to nourishment, sensation, local movement, and understanding). See David Braine's refutation of both dualism and materialism on Aristotelian and Thomist grounds in, *The Human Person: Animal and Spirit* (Notre Dame: University of Notre Dame Press, 1994).

[25]   See Anthony Kenny, *Aquinas on Mind* (London: Routledge, 1993), 27: 'three men share a common substantial form of humanity, but they are not one single form of humanity because matter individuates them, and individuating substances, it also individuates their substantial form.' See also p. 119: 'the essence of a human being is what makes him a human being, which includes having a body, but the essence does not include having this body or a body composed of this matter.'

[26]   Jean Porter offers a compelling account of teleological realism with a view to the challenges of modern science, in *Nature as Reason: A Thomistic Theory of the Natural Law* (Grand Rapids: Eerdman's, 2005), ch. 2.

[27]   The renowned medievalist Etienne Gilson has advanced this argument in various works, for example *The Christian Philosophy of St Thomas Aquinas* (Notre Dame: University of Notre Dame Press, 1994).

[28]   Though beings 'evolve' into their essences, Herbert McCabe stresses in *The Good Life* (108), that species themselves need not be regarded as evolving, in the way

they evidently did prior to the dawn of human history. On his account, the end of the pre-historical era and the arrival of the linguistic animal replaces evolution with 'history and tradition, which is just the inheritance (not biological but social) of acquired characteristics. The linguistic animal can adapt itself within its own lifetime and by language transmit the new art or technology or wisdom to the next generation. This is very much quicker and more efficient than natural selection.'

[29]   See Aquinas' *De Ente*; and David Burrell, 'Mulla Sadra on Substantial Motion: A Clarification and a Comparison with Thomas Aquinas,' *Journal of Shi'a Islamic Studies* 2:4 (2009), 369–86.

[30]   *ST* 2.1.94.2. Jean Porter, *Nature as Reason*, 53–82.

[31]   *ST* 2.1.94.4–5. Jean Porter, *Nature as Reason*, 28: as Porter writes in this context, the natural law is often regarded as a 'system for deriving a comprehensive set of specific moral rules or at least a framework for assessing existing rules, confirming them and placing them in systematic relation to one another.' In her work, Porter contests this common interpretation of natural law, particularly as articulated by John Finnis and proponents of the 'new natural law.' In challenging this interpretation of the natural law as involving 'substantial' rules for proper functioning, or rules that dictate precisely how it is appropriate for human beings to act in certain situations, she presents an interpretation of the law as 'formal,' or as a law that provides guidelines regarding the type of activities that are appropriate for human beings, but which can normally be carried out in a wide variety of ways, depending on individual circumstances.

[32]   Jean Porter, *Nature as Reason*, 82–125. In this passage, Jean Porter outlines and defends a 'teleological' conception of human beings, to say nothing of other beings, which takes questions arising from modern science into consideration.

[33]   *ST* 1.85.

[34]   *DA* II.5.

[35]   Any given act of sensation is essentially triadic in structure, insofar as it involves an external sense, object sensed, and medium. Similarly, perception entails an internal sense, the image that sense produces, and the sense impression from which it is produced.

[36]   *DA* II.6.

[37]   *DA* II.7.

[38]   *ST* 1.78.4. See also Herbert McCabe, 'Interior Senses I,' 'Interior Senses II,' in *On Aquinas*, 115–42

[39]   In this connection, Herbert McCabe writes that the brain is the organ of the interior senses, or perception, and thus oversees the exterior senses, among other voluntary and involuntary physical functions ('Interior Senses II,' in *On Aquinas*, 132ff.). That is to say, it is the organ of the nervous system, which coordinates perceptions of objects grasped by the five senses in order to capture images or the meaning of those objects. As McCabe writes, 'a vital difference between experience and the signifying [of it] is

that experience is what happens to me because of the material apparatus of my nervous system, but significance is the way I use the material things which are words or other symbols. Significance is in my use of the symbols. It is a matter of my creative activity; experience by comparison is passive' (*On Aquinas*, 49). On the grounds that thoughts represent meanings in a language, as opposed to the nervous system, and that meaning transcends and makes sense of natural phenomena, McCabe concludes that the organ of thought cannot be physical and cannot therefore be the brain.

[40]   When construed along the lines outlined above, the relationship between the powers of sensation and perception is similar to the relationship between matter and form. While the work of these faculties is distinguishable, it is not separable. For the faculties seem to need one another in order accomplish their joint task of grasping empirical realities. Insofar as this is true, perception is not a purely physiological process that entails physical contact with external stimuli, nor a merely cognitive event that lacks physiological changes. Rather, the physiological changes that occur in sensation constitute and enable the mental imaging that is executed in perception, such that perception turns on the coincidence of both phenomena.

[41]   David Braine, *The Human Person: Animal and Spirit* (Notre Dame: University of Notre Dame Press, 1994), 421.

[42]   Ibid.

[43]   Ibid., 433.

[44]   Peter Geach, *Mental Acts: Their Concepts and Objects* (London: Routledge, 1957), 18: abstractionism is 'a name for the doctrine that a concept is acquired by a process of singling out in attention some one feature given in direct experience—abstracting it—and ignoring the other features simultaneously given—abstracting from them. The abstractionist would wish to maintain that all acts of judgment are to be accounted for as exercises of concepts got by abstraction.' In the appendix to his work (130–31), Geach discusses the case of Aquinas. While conceding that Aquinas is 'very often regarded as an abstractionist,' he argues concerning Aquinas that it can nevertheless 'be decisively shown that in his mature work, the *Summa Theologica*, his views are opposed to what I have called abstractionism ... [for] he says that when we frame a judgment expressed in words, our use of concepts is to be compared not to seeing something but rather to forming a visual image of something we are not now seeing or even never have seen.'

[45]   Anthony Kenny, *Aquinas on Mind*, 35. In Aquinas' theory, as this suggests, 'there are no intermediaries like sense data which come between the perceiver and the perceived. In sensation, the sense faculty does not come into contact with a likeness of the sense object. Instead it becomes like the sense object by taking on the sense object's form. But it takes on the form not physically but intentionally.' Like any other philosopher, 'Aquinas had to deal with problems of error in sense perception, but the way in which this problem presents itself to him is a question of describing and accounting for the

malfunctioning of a faculty. It is not a question of building a bridge between a correctly functioning faculty or a correctly functioning cognitive apparatus and an extra-mental reality. But that is what through Scotus and often in Descartes the epistemological problem more and more explicitly became' (114).

46   Peter Geach, *Mental Acts*, 7: 'concepts, as we shall see, are capacities exercised in acts of judgment.' See also Herbert McCabe, *On Aquinas*, 41.

47   Peter Geach, *Mental Acts*, 77.

48   Peter Geach, *Mental Acts*, 40; cf. 45, 98: 'having a concept never means being able to recognize some feature we have found in direct experience; the mind *makes* concepts, and this concept formation and the subsequent use of the concepts formed never is a mere recognition or finding; but this does not in the least prevent us from applying concepts in our sense experience and knowing sometimes that we apply them rightly.'

49   As Geach writes in *Mental Acts*, 78–9: 'a concept is a capacity for certain exercises of the mind; and as regards capacities generally, if a man formerly capable of certain performances in one domain comes to perform similarly in another domain, it is quite arbitrary whether we say that his former capacity now extends to a new domain of exercise or that he has acquired a new capacity closely related to his old one. I shall say indifferently "analogical concepts" and "analogous exercises of concepts."'

50   According to John O'Callaghan, the fact that a mental process or effort is in question here leads many to assume that the process 'implies the existence of a product distinct from it.' As he further writes, however, the 'nominalization of verbs into substances is a way of talking about our activities, not a way of recognizing another realm of things in addition to our activities.' On this score, O'Callaghan quotes Wittgenstein, who wrote that 'one of the greatest sources of philosophical bewilderment [is that] a substantive makes us look for a thing that corresponds to it.' See John O'Callaghan, 'Concepts, Beings, and Things in Contemporary Philosophy and Thomas Aquinas,' *The Review of Metaphysics* 63:1 (September 1999), 77. In this article, O'Callaghan more generally refutes the idea that Aquinas advocates a representational theory of knowledge in which thoughts constitute 'third things' that mediate between the mind and reality, such that the mind does not directly know reality. In this connection, see also his rebuttal of the representationalist interpretation of Aquinas, as developed by Robert Pasnau in *Theories of Cognition in the Later Middle Ages* (Cambridge: Cambridge University Press, 1999), in his article, 'Aquinas, Cognitive Theory, and Analogy: A Propos of Robert Pasnau's *Theories of Cognition in the Later Middle Ages*,' *American Catholic Philosophical Quarterly* 76:3 (2002), 451–82.

51   On this understanding, John O'Callaghan writes, in 'Concepts, Beings, and Things in Contemporary Philosophy and Thomas Aquinas' (76), that the difference between the mind and its object concerns a distinction between 'modes of existence, not modes of location,' such that there is no real difference between the object as it is

known by the mind and as it subsists external to the mind, but only a logical difference concerning the manner of an object's existence in itself and in the mind, in the first case, in reality, and in the second, cognitively.

52   John O'Callaghan, 'Concepts, Beings, and Things in Contemporary Philosophy and Thomas Aquinas,' 79.

53   Ibid., 78.

54   Ibid.

55   Peter Geach, *Mental Acts*, 14.

56   Ibid., 3: an account like the one outlined above affirms the possibility of private references to experiences but denies 'the possibility of giving them [experiences] a private sense,' or mode of presentation, known only to the seemingly solipsistic knower. As Martin Warner helpfully brought to my attention, the understanding of 'sense' (*Sinn*), which Geach presupposes in this context is derived from Frege, who characterized 'sense' in terms of the 'mode of presentation' of a thing. See 'On Sense and Reference' in *Translations from the Philosophical Writings of Gottlob Frege*, ed. and trans. Peter Geach and Max Black (Oxford: Basil Blackwell, 1952), 57.

57   David Braine, *The Human Person*, 447. See also Braine's defense in chapter 12 (pp. 447–79) of the claim that the intellect possesses no bodily organ. In this connection, Braine refutes both the materialist view which identifies the mind with the brain and the dualistic outlook, the mistake of which does not consist 'in saying that the thinker is a spirit but in supposing this spirit to be some inner thing analogous to the body capable within its own physical soul-stuff and inner-soul world of an inner non physical speaking and hearing' (458).

58   For an excellent discussion of the way the human mind transcends the body, which does not fall prey to dualism or materialism, see chapters 14–15 of David Braine's *The Human Person*.

59   *DA* III.4, 429a29-b5.

60   See Gregory M. Reichberg, 'The Intellectual Virtues,' in *The Ethics of Aquinas*, ed. Stephen J. Pope (Washington, DC: Georgetown University Press, 2002), 131–50.

61   Aristotle discusses the 'intellectual virtues' including wisdom, science, and art in *EN* book VI.

62   George E. Karamanolis, *Plato and Aristotle in Agreement* (Oxford: Oxford University Press, 2006). In ancient schools of thought, Karamanolis contends, Plato and Aristotle were not regarded as mutually exclusive thinkers as they often are today, with the former focusing on higher, metaphysical questions and the latter primarily treating questions concerning empirical realities or the natural realm. Though distinct, the work of the two thinkers was believed to be complementary.

63   *APo* I.13, 78b34–79a16.

64   Etienne Gilson, *The Arts of the Beautiful*, 48–50.

65   *ST* 1.79.3. In this passage, Aquinas suggests that the intellect is a power and not the essence of the soul. By this he seems to mean that the human capacity to know is not fully actualized, such that human beings are able to obtain ideas that are true once and for all. Rather, it represents a potential to know objects with increasing clarity and precision, which must be gradually realized.

66   Jean Porter, *Nature as Reason*, 114–15. According to Porter, the value of a teleological realism, which accounts for human deficiencies or disabilities in terms of the 'thwarted expression of formal principles,' is that it can explain incomplete, immature, or defective states of being with reference to complete, mature, or ideal forms and thereby affirm disabled beings as instances or expressions of a given essence or nature.

Chapter 3

The Ontology of Knowledge

On the basis of the ontology developed in the last chapter, I turn now to treat the ontology of knowledge—what knowledge is and involves—discussing what might be described as the 'integral parts' of knowledge, which factor into and facilitate the knowing process. These parts include the elements of logic—categorical propositions and syllogisms—language, inductive reasoning, deductive reasoning, and logical fallacies. For reasons I detailed in my references to this chapter in the introduction, my discussion in this context takes the traditional system of logic articulated by Aristotle as distinct from modern symbolic logic as its point of departure. In particular, I devote attention to Aristotle's six logical works, which are often collectively referred to as the '*organon*' or 'tool' for human reasoning. These works are normally listed in the order in which they build upon one another, which may not be their chronological order: *Categories, On Interpretation, Prior Analytics, Posterior Analytics, Topics*, and *Sophistical Refutations*.

As a preliminary to my discussion of the integral parts of knowledge, I offer in what follows a brief account of these works and the instruction they provide in grammar, logic/dialectic, and rhetoric, or the *trivium* of subjects, the study of which affords the tools for inquiry that facilitate learning in any subject area whatever. In the first place, the *Categories* treat the fundamentals of grammar, to wit, the parts of speech, including nouns, verbs, adjectives, and adverbs. This text therefore enumerates the basic components of statements and consequently thoughts about any issue.

Presupposing the grammar of the *Categories*, *On Interpretation* deals with different ways of forming statements or propositions about objects. According to this text, every sentence must include a subject—that about which something is said—and a predicate—or whatever is said of the subject. Such a statement may be affirmative or negative; universal (applying to all) or particular (applying only to some). As I will soon demonstrate, any ordinary statement can be translated, with a little reorganization, into a universal/ particular and/or affirmative/negative 'categorical proposition' that takes the form 'S is (not) P.' These propositions are foundational to Aristotle's system of logic.

The two aforementioned works lay the groundwork for the *Prior* and *Posterior Analytics*. The *Prior Analytics* contain Aristotle's signature system of formal deductive logic, or the categorical syllogistic. The teachings of this text have been distilled over the years to the fundamentals that are now generally found in many standard introductions to traditional logic—fundamentals I will incorporate into my discussion of the ontology of knowledge in the present chapter. As Aristotle acknowledges, deductive reasoning transpires any time existing understanding is used to comprehend new objects of experience.

Oftentimes, reasoning along these lines takes place unconsciously, for example when the conclusion that 'the college is not open today' is automatically reached on the grounds that 'today is a holiday' and 'the college is closed on holidays.' Aristotle's system of formal logic effectively 'freezes' the mental connections that are made in such cases, first by translating the assumptions at stake into categorical propositions in the form of 'S is P,' and then by inserting those propositions into a 'categorical syllogism.'[1] While contemporary readers have become accustomed to using the term 'syllogism' only to refer to arguments in categorical form, it is worth noting that Aristotle sometimes employs it to speak more broadly of any argument in any form.

Whether syllogisms are categorically structured like the example below or instances of ordinary thought like the one mentioned above, they necessarily contain three and only three terms, namely, the two terms that are connected in the syllogism and the term that connects them.[2] The connection between the terms is established by three and only three premises, as below:

S is M   The college is closed on holidays
P is M   Today is a holiday
S is P   The college is closed today

In his *Prior Analytics*, Aristotle elaborates on a wide variety of types of syllogism including those that will be outlined later in this chapter, explaining why some are valid and some are invalid in that they contain illogical or unjustified mental leaps. Furthermore, he shows how some syllogisms can be rearranged and so rendered valid. In treating the various patterns of reasoning, *Prior Analytics* sets the stage for a discussion of the actual process of reasoning. That process is the subject of Aristotle's *Posterior Analytics*, which is the only logical work by Aristotle upon which Aquinas composed a complete commentary.

Posterior Analytics explains how discoveries are made and definitions formulated through inductive reasoning. These discoveries and definitions in turn provide a basis for drawing conclusions through deductive acts of reasoning, which are again the primary concern of *Prior Analytics*. In covering the inter-relationship of inductive and deductive reasoning, *Posterior Analytics* not only presumes familiarity with *Prior Analytics* but also provides a broader framework for the whole *organon*.

Though *Posterior Analytics* enjoys a sort of priority amongst the works of the *organon*, *Topics* is also a significant work in that it treats the dialectical process through which inductive or deductive conclusions are reached. As something of an appendix to *Topics*, *Sophistical Refutations* covers various fallacies in reasoning, which I will discuss both at the end of this chapter and under the heading of 'Intellectual Vices' in Chapter 5.

A further work, namely, Aristotle's *Rhetoric*, which is not strictly speaking part of the *organon*, is relevant to the present discussion in that it instructs readers how persuasively to articulate arguments in front of diverse audiences. Since the ability to articulate thoughts intelligently and convincingly is the ultimate test whether a capacity to think soundly has been cultivated at all, rhetoric arguably represents the final consummation of all previous study in grammar, logic, and dialectic.

The Elements of Logic

In light of this overview of the ontology of knowledge, I will proceed to offer a more detailed account of the integral parts of knowledge, starting with the elements of logic, namely, categorical propositions and syllogisms. In order to treat categorical propositions, it is first necessary to discuss the four different and increasingly complex ways of identifying unity in things, or making propositional statements, which traditional logic seems to presuppose.

The first manner of appreciating unity involves what has been called the 'simple and absolute consideration' or 'simple apprehension' of a thing. This amounts to grasping that a thing exists, conceptualizing or naming it as 'one thing,' say, a man, without necessarily articulating fully what a man or specifically 'this man' is or is like. The next two ways of perceiving unity can be described as 'complex apprehensions.' In such apprehensions, the relatively empty concept of a thing, simply apprehended, is filled out as it is qualified in different ways.

One way of qualifying a thing involves saying what it is, that is, offering a definition of it. A definition is a statement that indicates the property or properties that make a being the one thing that it is.[3] Ordinarily, the subject of a defining statement indicates the *definiendum*, or thing being defined, while the predicate offers the *definiens*, that is, the definition itself. Through these two components, the definition displays the essence of a thing, which often entails both form and matter.[4] In the case of human beings, for instance, the relevant form is that of rationality, while the matter is that of an animal, such that human beings are defined as 'rational animals.'

The second way of qualifying an object through a complex apprehension involves saying something about what it is like, that is, listing attributes other than those that are essential to its definition. As I will explain further below, these attributes may be essential (but not defining) or accidental and wholly contingent. Statements of the sort under consideration conceptually unite two entities and/or properties, such as 'human beings' and 'bi-pedal creatures,' affirming, for example, that, 'human beings are bi-pedal creatures.' While such statements may take the form of an affirmation as in the previous example, they may also be construed as denials, as in the case of the proposition that 'human beings are not winged creatures.'[5]

Such affirmations and denials are parasitic on definitions in the sense that their truth is contingent upon the way in which the terms that are affirmed or denied of one another are defined. For example, the claim that 'human beings are capable of language' obtains truth on account of the fact that human beings are defined as 'rational animals,' and rationality entails a capacity for linguistic communication, that is, 'grammaticality.' Whether complex apprehensions assume the form of definitions, affirmations, or denials, they are the universals or principles of knowledge, which serve as the rules whereby judgments are formed about entities including but by no means limited to rational animals.

As I will shortly demonstrate, complex apprehensions are the by-product of inductive lines of reasoning. Taken together, three such apprehensions allow for the development of a deductive argument, which presupposes three premises. In such an argument, I have noted, existing knowledge is employed to render new objects of knowledge intelligible. Thus, the conclusion of a deductive argument represents the fourth way in which intellectual unity may be achieved.

Before moving on to discuss the inductive and deductive modes of reasoning in greater detail, I wish in the remainder of this section to elaborate further on how complex apprehensions may be articulated in the categorical form that enables the analysis of human thoughts. Obviously, thoughts are frequently articulated through statements, which are not necessarily expressed in the form of a categorical proposition, in which the subject and predicate are always connected by a verb that indicates a state of being. In colloquial language, for instance, we might say that 'Mary runs' instead of speaking in the categorical form according to which 'Mary is a runner' (X is Y).

In his *Categories*, Aristotle distinguishes between 10 different types of category that may supply the subject or predicate term in categorical propositions representing complex apprehensions. The first of these categories is what Aristotle calls a substance, which is generally designated by a noun, that is, a person, place or thing. The rest of the categories can be predicated or 'said of' a noun.[6] These categories include 'quantity' (e.g. two-footed, five-pound); 'quality' ('capable of learning to speak'); relation (larger, shorter); location (at school); time; position (sitting, lying down); action (seeing, doing); being acted upon (being hurt, being helped); and possession (a state resulting from being acted upon, e.g. 'hurt').

The categories correspond to the basic parts of speech that are impressed upon students of grammar. Hence, quantity, quality, relation, and possession are adjectives, describing nouns. Location, time, and position are adverbs, modifying verbs or adjectives. Action and passion (being acted upon) are verbs, indicating movement or state of being. According to Aristotle, all of the categories are 'beings' of one kind or another. Clearly, however, being in this instance is defined in many ways, some primary, and some secondary.[7] A being as defined in the primary sense is an ontologically basic entity, in which other things may inhere, but which does not inhere in other things; such a being is designated by a noun. Beings that fall into the other categories owe their existence to substances and are consequently called beings in the secondary sense.

Assuming the grammar of the *Categories*, Aristotle discusses the types of subject-predicate proposition that can be formed with the various parts of speech in *On Interpretation*. In this treatment of syntax, he distinguishes between two ways of attributing properties to a subject. Some properties are 'essential,' which means that they belong to a subject because of what it is. For example, being 'grammatical' is essential to human nature, because language is part of rationality, and human beings are rational by nature. Other properties are 'accidental' in that they do not belong to a thing because of what it is, but just so happen to qualify it on a temporary basis. At this moment, for example, I am seated in a chair, but it is not essential to who I am that I be seated in a chair.

As this illustration confirms, accidental properties can be otherwise in beings belonging to the same class. According to the law of non-contradiction, fundamental to Aristotle's logic, which states that contradictory terms cannot both be true and false at the same time (i.e. A is B; A is not B), however, such properties cannot be otherwise in one and the same being at same time.[8] In other words, I cannot be seated and standing simultaneously. Incidentally, the law of non-contradiction is closely related to the other two of the three main laws of thought, namely, the law of identity, according to which any thing is the same as itself;[9] and the law of the excluded middle, which states that either a proposition or its negation is true.[10]

In categorical propositions, I have mentioned, the subject and predicate, or the 'terms' of the proposition, are always linked by a form of the verb 'to be' as opposed to an action verb, such that 'Mary runs' becomes 'Mary is a runner.' The 'being' verb ensures that the two terms or categories that are united in the proposition are clearly identifiable. As I have already stated, categorical propositions may be affirmative or negative in quality and universal or particular in quantity.[11] Thus there are four different forms of categorical proposition. The first form (A) is the 'universal affirmative,' e.g. all A is B: 'all men are mortal.' The second (E) is the universal negative, e.g. no A is B: 'no cats are dogs.' The third (I) is the particular affirmative, e.g. some A is B: 'some humans are women.' The fourth is the particular negative, e.g. some A is not B: 'some men are not tall.' The abbreviations A-E-I-O are taken from the Latin words for 'affirm' and 'deny,' respectively: *AffIrmo, nEgO.*

When all members of a class are referred to in any one of these propositions, the term for that class is regarded as 'distributed.' In A propositions, consequently, the subject but not the predicate is distributed. In E, the subject and the predicate are distributed; in I, neither is distributed, and in O, only the predicate is distributed. Here, it is also worth noting that all A-E-I-O propositions are 'immediate.' In other words, they draw a connection between two terms, rather than connecting two terms through the mediation of a third term. This is the kind of connection that is drawn in the categorical syllogisms that will be discussed later in the chapter.

From immediate propositions, it is possible to infer some further propositions, which differ in form but retain effectively the same meaning as the original propositions on which they are based. When in possession of an A proposition which is known to be true, for example, we can come immediately to conclusions about the truth or falsehood of E, I, or O propositions containing the same terms in the same order. An immediate proposition that is drawn out from another immediate proposition is called an 'immediate inference.' On the basis of the law of non-contradiction, it is acceptable to make the following immediate inferences:

If A is true: E is false; I is true; O is false
If E is true: A is false; I is false; O is true
If I is true: E is false; A and O are undetermined

If O is true: A is false; E and I are undetermined
If A is false: O is true; E and I are undetermined
If E is false: I is true; A and O are undetermined
If I is false: A is false; E is true; O is true
If O is false: A is true; E is false; I is true

In addition to these immediate inferences, others may be drawn out through some additional efforts, which are described in terms of 'conversion,' 'obversion,' and 'contraposition.'[12] With the foregoing discussion of the four general types of statement in view, it is now possible to consider the specific type of statement known as a definition. As I mentioned above, a 'definition is a phrase signifying a thing's essence.'[13] Although Aristotle devotes a good deal of attention to categorical propositions in *On Interpretation* and *Prior Analytics*, he reserves his more extensive account of how to formulate definitions for the *Posterior Analytics*.[14]

Whereas affirmations and denials may take the form of A, E, I, or O propositions, definitions must always take the form of a universal affirmative (A) proposition, which indicates those features that set all individuals within a specific class of beings apart from other species. In order to signify the essence of a thing, Aristotle states, it is imperative to specify the 'genus and differentia' of the entity—or species—in question.[15] The genus is the larger class to which a number of different species belong, that is, a collection of species that possess some very general shared characteristic. For example, human beings (*homo sapiens*) belong to the genus 'homo' along with other hominids.[16]

In the effort to define a particular species that falls under a specific genus, we must first isolate the further attribute or attributes that all members of the species share in common, but which they do not share with other species in the genus.[17] These distinguishing properties are the 'differentia' that must be added to the genus to construct a definition of the species in question. The most basic difference—the one that causes or entails the other differential properties, which do not do not conversely entail this most basic difference—is the one that should be listed first in the definition.[18] The same rule applies when it comes to determining which differential property, if any, to list next.

Without exception, the differentia of a definition must designate essential rather than accidental properties. As suggested above, they must represent the most 'essential' essential properties the thing under consideration possesses, that is, the essential properties that allow for the very possibility of exhibiting all the other essential and accidental properties the thing could exhibit.[19] Since linguistic ability is implied in the rational ability, consequently the definition of a human being refers to rationality as opposed to grammaticality.

Although non-differential essential properties to say nothing of accidental properties cannot be included amongst the differentia of a definition, it is worth noting that the differentia may be derived from any one of the categories, depending on what is being defined. While a father is what he is largely on account of his *relations* to other people, for instance, a geographical region is defined in terms of its *location*.

One reason why it is crucial to list differentia in the order in which they unfold or follow from one another is that giving greater or lesser weight to a property than it deserves by enumerating differentia out of order can skew understanding of the object being defined.[20] By the same token, mentioning too many or too few differentia than is appropriate can render the definition of a thing too narrow or too broad, such that instances that should or should not fall under the definition are excluded from it or included in it, respectively.[21]

According to Aristotle, the reason many make such mistakes often comes down to a lack of wide-ranging experience, or at least a broad or open mind.[22] Those that have only experienced an object one way, or are only open to experiencing it one way, for example, will naturally assume it always presents itself in the way they have seen it or wish to see it and discredit other cases accordingly. For example, human beings who regard humanity as quintessentially instanced in a certain skin tone, sex, or socio-cultural or religious background will tend to discount the humanity of those that differ from their ideal in race, sex, or religion and objectify them in different ways.

By contrast, broad-minded or experienced persons refrain from making judgments based on such prejudices and unify under the definition of, say, humanity, all classes of human being, regardless of race, sex, or religion, excluding only those classes of being that cannot be counted amongst rational animals. In the effort to identify a place for everything, and everything in its proper place, they isolate the differentia that, taken together, apply *entirely and only* to members of the class in question, so that none of the members of the class are excluded from and nothing irrelevant is included in the definition.

Such a definition that unifies all that is relevant and precludes all that is irrelevant to its subject matter can be described as *true*, provided that truth is a form of unity.[23] As Aquinas writes, truth 'consists in a certain mean, by way of conformity with things themselves, in so far as the intellect expresses them as being what they are, or as not being what they are not: and it is in this that the nature of truth consists. There will be excess if something false is affirmed, as though something were, which in reality it is not: and there will be deficiency if something is falsely denied, and declared not to be, whereas in reality it is.'[24] To summarize, true definitions state no more and no less than is correct concerning the objects of definition.

As I have mentioned, the truth of affirmations and denials regarding any two of the four categories of genus, species, (essential) property, or accident is parasitic on the truth of definitions. In other words, such statements make sense or hold true in light of the definitions of the associated or dissociated categories. Where the operative definition of either category is faulty in some respect, persons will be predisposed to project it on to their perception of the associations or dissociations amongst things and will misconstrue reality accordingly. Insofar as definitions observe the law of non-contradiction, however, registering their objects in a manner that is consistent with the actual nature of those objects, the intellectual resources are secured rightly to associate beings—in the primary or secondary sense—and thus to comprehend experiences accurately.

Language and Knowledge

Although it is crucial to our knowledge to delineate real definitions, which display the essence of a thing by indicating its genus and differentia, it is virtually impossible to do this apart from an ability to articulate thoughts about the nature of things through language. The question of the relationship between knowledge and language is what I take to be at stake in Aristotle's distinction between real and nominal definitions.[25]

Whereas real definitions are necessarily true, in the sense that they hold true on account of the essence of the thing defined, nominal definitions are only accidentally true, because they do not indicate what things are but rather tell how words are used to refer to things.[26] Since this usage is generally fixed rather arbitrarily or by convention, a given object may be called by different names in different contexts, and a name used to signify one thing in one situation may just as easily be employed to signify another thing under other circumstances.[27]

Because names do not signify things on account of *what* they are, nominal definitions cannot tell us *why* things are the way they are. As Aristotle repeatedly insists, we only obtain 'knowledge-why' when we possess 'knowledge-what.' Short of that knowledge, we can only know *that* something is the case. Thus, knowledge-*that* is all we can acquire through nominal definitions, or language. Within a given context, there is normally some kind of analogy or 'family resemblance'[28] amongst the different uses of a word within that context. In other words, there is at once a similarity as well as a difference between the varying uses of the word in a particular setting.

To take Aristotle's well-known example, a diet, exercise regime, and urine are all healthy in the sense that they promote the functioning of the body. However, they do this in very different ways. In this example, as in other cases of analogous word usage, one focal meaning—which here involves the promotion of the life of the body—not only upholds the similarity in the meaning of diverse words but also allows for the different ways in which that meaning is extrapolated with reference to various matters, such as diet, exercise, and urine. On this account, in fact, the full range of a word's accepted usage to designate things in the world, such as diet, exercise, and urine, can be identified with its meaning.

Because any given word may be used in many ways that are analogous rather than univocal or uniform in meaning, the focal meaning that unites all the existing uses of the word can always be extrapolated in unprecedented ways in new and unforeseen circumstances.[29] Thus, the range of a word's usage—its meaning—remains potentially subject to change, whether by expansion or restriction, even within one context. This claim reinforces my earlier contention that names or words have little or no necessary connection with the things they signify. That is to say, words have no intrinsic meaning but are assigned meaning in relation to a role they are determined to play in a larger system of communication or 'language-game.'[30]

In order to grasp what names mean, consequently, it is necessary to attend to the objects to which words are used to refer. Although referents disclose a great deal about the meaning of words, it is worth noting that they also go a long way towards revealing the prevailing concerns and priorities of individuals operating in a given context. In this connection, they betray the close connection between language and the culture or common practices of the community, school of thought, or group that speaks the language.[31] For the ways of going about things—the things that are done and never done—in different social sectors not only impact ordinary choices about which words to use and how to use them but also conversely enlist language in the subtle induction of its speakers into specific forms of life.

Where a particular phenomenon is of special significance to speakers of the local language, for instance, there may be numerous words to specify the nature of that phenomenon. On the other hand, there may be only a few words or even no words to denote realities that seem insignificant or are unfamiliar to players of the relevant language-game. Aristotle himself arrived at this realization in his attempt to offer a relatively exhaustive taxonomy of human vices and virtues. In a departure from what was apparently a common philosophical assumption at his time, Aristotle rejected the idea that vices and virtues come in opposing pairs—such as wrath and temperance—and argued instead that virtues represent the mean or balance between two extreme forms of vice, one of excess and one of deficiency.

In his subsequent attempt to identify the two extreme forms of every vice, Aristotle discovered one of the main reasons why so many thinkers at his time simply opposed every virtue to a single vice. The reason was that members of society at the time—at least those with power and influence—tended to be prone to one of the extremes to the point of ignorance of the other extreme. Owing to the stigma attached to cowardice in Hellenistic society, for example, members of this society—at least male members—were not generally 'over-willing to reconcile with enemies.' For this reason, this vice was never given a name and recognized as a vice until Aristotle identified it as the deficient extreme of temperance, as it pertains to anger, which is opposed to the excessive extreme of wrath.

As this example demonstrates, the range of vocabulary—and not merely the manner in which vocabulary words are used—is part of the way language subtly compels us to attend to some realities or ignore others, indoctrinating us in common opinions about the way things are or should be, and indeed, a whole way of being—in the aforementioned example, a form of life that precludes a cowardly willingness to give in to opponents or oppressors. In light of the ways that language bears on thought, it seems plausible to conclude that the things that give themselves to us through experience can never be encountered in an unmediated way but are always perceived through the mediation of some linguistic—and broader cultural—framework.[32]

Most individuals will be accustomed to operating within any number of such frameworks for communication, which correspond to different forms of life, proper to involvement in various different communities: cultural, political, vocational, familial, or even religious. As participants in any such community, we have access to a common language, which we must employ to express ourselves, and as a result of which our thoughts about the matters that concern us, unlike our sense perceptions, are intrinsically public.[33]

That is not to say that we cannot 'use the common public language in which our thoughts are formulated to think silently to ourselves. For a fact, it is entirely open to us to keep our thoughts to ourselves or to lie about them to others. There is no mandate to make our thoughts public.'[34] Even so, our thoughts are not essentially private and can theoretically be made public, using the tools of language, to which all have access that share or could come to share in a given form of life.[35]

Of course, learning to use language for the sake of engaging in public communication can take a good deal of time and effort.[36] Although all participants in a community in principle have access to any knowledge exchanged within that community by means of language, such access is obviously contingent upon facility in the use of the relevant language. Since names are accidental to the things they signify, and there is no necessary connection between a word and what it represents, however, there is nothing about a name itself that gives away the full range of its acceptable usage and thus its meaning in a given context.

In order to understand what words mean, consequently, we must acclimatize ourselves to the scope of their acceptable usage by observing and imitating how those that already know the language use words. Through the trial and error of ongoing practice, and with the help of correction from others, we may eventually learn to discern the difference between appropriate and inappropriate uses of words; we may become skilled at employing language within the given conventions and so acquire the means of thinking, to say nothing of articulating thoughts.[37]

Although these thoughts, made possible by the acquisition of language, enable us to grasp that things are the case, it is important to reiterate that they do not yet elevate us to the knowledge what things are, and why they are the way they are. They give us nominal, not real, definitions, that is, the ability to use words—not necessarily to know what we are talking about. Because real definitions can only be articulated through language, however, there is always a risk of confusing the acquisition of language or nominal definitions with the acquisition of knowledge-what and knowledge-why.

One problematic consequence of this confusion is that it leads to operating on the assumption that the truth of things has already been captured, which in turn closes the mind to the possibility that things could be other than they are currently understood to be—that there is more to learn. While we must acknowledge that human reasoning always transpires in some context or another, therefore, we should not by the same token presume that it is impossible or unnecessary to think outside the conceptual constraints associated with a given linguistic context in order to pursue real definitions.

Though the acquisition of such a definition may not fundamentally alter opinions held previously, it helps us come to a more principled understanding of our preconceived notions and thus to know what we are talking about when we talk about anything whatever. As I will demonstrate in the final section of the next chapter on 'Informed vs Uninformed Faith,' this understanding not only enables us to communicate meaningfully with those that speak of the same realities in different terms, or who speak of different realities altogether.[38] Where relevant, it also enables us to correct and improve our ideas and thus uphold the law of non-contradiction on an ongoing basis.

Inductive Reasoning

These preliminary considerations aside, we may now embark upon a discussion of inductive and subsequently deductive reasoning. As a rule, inductive reasoning involves accumulating seemingly related empirical facts and drawing a general conclusion about the nature of their similarity.[39] That is not to say that the images of objects on the basis of which such conclusions are drawn represent a 'third thing' that mediates between the mind and reality: it is not to suggest that there is any object of human knowledge other than the actual object of knowledge itself.

As I argued in Chapter 2, conclusions or concepts are not so much objects of thought as means to making sense of objects. In other words, they are not things but ways of thinking about things. In discussing the process through which universal concepts are inferred from multiple encounters with related objects, consequently, I do not treat a process through which the objects of inquiry become mentally reified but rather describe the activity through which a capacity for knowing things of a similar sort is acquired.

In the case of inductive conceptualization, perceptual experience represents what Aristotle calls the 'pre-existing' knowledge, which gives us the potential to know that we actualize when we come to a universal conclusion about that which our various experiences have in common, or through which all those experiences can be rendered intelligible.[40] Inductive reasoning may be conducted in either one of two ways. For reasons I will soon explain, the second way exclusively counts as an instance of inductive argument in the full sense of the term. The first way of inducing a concept may be symbolically displayed along the lines of this example:

S1 is P
S2 is P
S3 is P
Therefore, all S is (probably) P

In this example, the conclusion that all S are likely to be P is drawn on the grounds of successive or concurrent experiences of numerous instances of S and

P, which corroborate one another to the point of warranting that conclusion. As Aristotle writes, each encounter with S as P creates in us a memory, and when enough memories of a similar sort converge, they eventually form a single experience, which enables us to make a pronouncement about some universal state of affairs. Although the instances of S may have very little in common besides P, and they may exhibit P in varying ways and degrees, the argument outlined above nonetheless confirms that they have P in common.

While the symbolic depiction above may mask the fact, it is worth noting that it can take considerable time and experience to reach an inductive conclusion such as the one stated above. For it may take time to encounter S2 as P after an initial experience of S1 as P, and it is not always under our direct control to determine when and whether a further encounter ever occurs.

Though the inductive approach described above is useful in terms of telling us *that* the terms under consideration exhibit some commonality, it does not disclose *why* they have P in common. Strictly speaking, then, it does not afford an argument or reason for the conclusion that all S are probably P, consisting in a third term that connects the terms S and P. Without such a term, which gives the reason for the relation between S and P, the inductive line of reasoning outlined above can be easily overthrown by a single counter-example to the general rule that S are P. That is why it is necessary to proceed to the discussion of inductive arguments.

The term that connects S and P in a proper inductive argument is what Aristotle describes as the 'middle term' (M). While what he calls the major term (P) always appears in the first or major premise, the minor terms (S) are presented in both the major and the second or minor premises of inductive arguments. Such an argument, which evidently makes use in its premises of the conclusions of simpler inductive claims, may be symbolically depicted as below:

S1, S2, S3, S4 is P
S1, S2, S3, S4 is M
Therefore, all P is (probably) M

Whereas the first approach to inductive reasoning only confirms that S have P in common, this argument shows *why* they have P in common. The reason why the S have P in common is that they also have M in common. On the Euclidian principle, fundamental to Aristotle's logic, according to which things equal to the same thing are equal to one another, the conclusion 'P is M' is inferred on the grounds that all the S are both P and M. Thus, M is the reason for its own connection not only with the S but also with P. It provides the reason for the connections between all the terms under consideration, because it tells us something about what the S and P are or are like. As soon as we realize that the S belong not only to P but also to M, in fact, we have the conclusion that all P probably belong to M.

Although it can prove difficult to lay down hard and fast rules for establishing the soundness, that is, truth and validity, of inductive arguments, there are a number of criteria that can be taken into consideration in this regard.[41] The first criterion for a sound inductive argument concerns the number of experiences upon which the argument is based. The more experiences that can be accumulated of the same or a similar kind, the stronger the case in question will be. In spite of this, there is no fixed method for determining how many experiences warrant a conclusion in a given instance, for this depends upon many factors, above all the nature of the object under consideration.[42] While it may be possible to draw a conclusion after a few encounters, or even just one, in the case of very concrete objects, many experiences are generally required in order to draw conclusions about matters that are more abstract in nature, concerning which there is more room for disagreement.

The second criterion for a sound inductive argument has to do with the number of respects in which different experiences exhibit similarities. In general, an inductive conclusion is more probable the more commonalities exist amongst the experiences in question. That stated, numerous similarities only add to the force of an inductive argument when those similarities are relevant to the argument. In this connection, a single highly relevant factor outweighs many factors of lesser significance.[43] Thus, inductive reasoning always comes down to a judgment call. The final criterion concerns the conclusion itself, which should be modest relative to the premises and should not therefore claim more than is warranted by the supporting evidence, nor suppress evidence that undermines a preferred conclusion.

Ultimately, conclusions reached by inductive to say nothing of deductive reasoning are stored in what has been called the intellectual memory or passive intellect.[44] In virtue of these conclusions or concepts, the intellectual memory also contains all the images from which they are derived. What it does not possess and only the sense memory can possess are the additional images that have never been conceptualized inductively, because they were not understood, noticed, or regarded as significant at an initial encounter.

As the next chapter will explain in greater detail, these images can prove very useful when it comes to increasing our understanding in certain situations. At present, however, our concern is to investigate in general terms how ideas stored in the intellectual memory may be further applied to clarify the significance of sense images, whether these are acquired through new experiences or summoned up from the depths of the sense memory where they formerly lay in neglect. This brings us to deductive reasoning.

Deductive Reasoning

Whereas complex apprehensions—whether definitions or statements about non-essential properties—are the goal of inductive reasoning, deductive reasoning employs these concepts as means to the end of comprehending new experiences. Stated otherwise, deduction employs concepts as rules or criteria to determine what things are, as opposed to *whether* they exist along the lines of skepticism.[45]

While induction searches for a middle term that unites particulars under one universal, consequently, deduction seeks the middle term that brings some universal to bear on a particular object of experience. As Aristotle summarizes, 'a deduction is a discourse in which, certain things being stated, something other than what is stated follows of necessity from their being so.'[46] In deduction, then, the potential for knowledge is actualized that is latent in the complex apprehensions achieved in induction. An example of a deductive categorical syllogism can once again be outlined as follows:

> All M are P
> All S are M
> Therefore, all S are P

As the predicate of the conclusion, P is the major term in this syllogism, such that the first premise of the argument is the major premise. The subject of the conclusion, namely, S, is the minor term, and the second premise is the minor premise. M is the middle term that is included in both premises and with which both extreme terms have something in common. As such, M is absent from the conclusion, which connects the extremes. As in induction, so in deduction, the mind grasps its conclusion in the very moment it grasps the middle term that connects the extremes, S and P.

Already I have mentioned that categorical syllogisms like the one outlined above help us determine whether the arguments we make are valid. The question of an argument's validity has to do with whether its conclusion is adequately supported by the foregoing premises—whether it is a well-founded claim or an unfounded logical leap. Insofar as validity comes down to internal consistency, it pertains to the 'form' of the argument.

As truth can only be a property of the premises or categorical propositions that make up categorical syllogisms, arguments comprised of three as opposed to merely two terms can alone exhibit form and thus possess or lack validity. In fact, an argument may be valid regardless of the truth of its premises. Thus, Aristotle acknowledges that true premises can be framed within an invalid argument, while a valid argument may contain false premises.[47]

Where a syllogism contains both true premises and a valid form, it is described as sound. Since each syllogism contains three categorical propositions, and there are four forms of proposition (A, E, I, O), it follows that there is a total of 64 possible categorical syllogisms. A syllogism like the one above, in which all three propositions take the form of a universal affirmative (A), is commonly described as an 'AAA' syllogism. An abbreviation like 'AAA' depicts what is known as the 'mood' of the syllogism.[48] In addition to its mood, each syllogism is characterized by a figure, which is determined by the location of the middle term in the syllogism. In the first figure, the middle term is placed thus:

M—P
S—M
S—P

In the second figure, thus:

P—M
S—M
S—P

In the third figure, thus:

M—P
M—S
S—P

And in the fourth, as follows:

P—M
M—S
S—P

By multiplying the 64 possible moods by the four possible figures, we obtain a total of 256 possible forms of categorical syllogism. As it turns out, however, only 15 of these syllogisms are valid in the sense that the conclusion is the logical corollary of the premises.[49] Those which are valid in the first figure include: AAA, EAE, AII, EIO; in the second, AEE, EAE, AOO, EIO; in the third figure, AII, IAI, EIO, OAO; and in the fourth, AEE, IAI, EIO. The rest of the possible syllogisms are eliminated in the process of applying two formal rules for deductive reasoning. These rules state that: 1. The middle term must be distributed in at least one premise; and 2. If either term is distributed in the conclusion, it must be distributed in the premises.[50]

Where these rules are observed, the major term is sure to belong to the middle, which may or may not encompass more than the major; and the minor will belong the middle, such that the minor falls under the major, in virtue of falling under the middle, under which the major also falls.[51] As a result, the premises provide adequate grounds for drawing the connection proper to the conclusion, which cannot be validly drawn where the aforementioned rules are not observed.[52]

In addition to these rules, there are a few more 'formal' guidelines for deducing a conclusion that follows logically from the preceding premises. According to these, deductive arguments cannot: 1. Contain two negative premises, since no conclusion can be drawn on those grounds; 2. Draw an affirmative conclusion where one of the premises is negative, since a negative and a positive do not make a positive; and 3. Draw a particular conclusion from two universal premises.

In this context, there is insufficient space to provide a case-by-case explanation as to how the rules delineated above render all but 15 of the 256 possible syllogisms invalid, though Aristotle himself goes into some detail on this score in his *Prior Analytics*. Suffice it to say that in all but the 15 instances mentioned above, syllogisms involve some sort of unwarranted logical leap: they infer more or less than is justified on the basis of the information given in the premises.

In addition to ordinary deductive arguments, traditional logic also generally treats what are known as conditional or hypothetical (if/then) and disjunctive (either/or) syllogisms, which allow us to envisage possibilities that could arise and consequently plan for the future. These types of syllogism were actually developed more by the Stoics than by Aristotle. In that sense, the Stoics anticipated the eventual development of modern logic, in which pure hypotheticals are the main subject of logical inquiry.[53] 'Hypothetical syllogisms are divided into "pure" in which premises and conclusion are all of the form "if p then q," and mixed, in which only one premise is hypothetical and the other premise and the conclusion are categorical.'[54]

In the case of mixed hypothetical and disjunctive syllogisms, there exist two valid moods. These are known as *modus ponens* ('the mode of affirming') and *modus tollens* ('the mode of denying'), which take the following forms, respectively:

modus ponens

Hypothetical	**Disjunctive**
If P then Q (major premise)	Either P or Q
P (minor premise)	Not P (or: not Q)
Therefore Q	Q (or: P)

modus tollens

Hypothetical	**Disjunctive**
If P then Q	Either P or Q
Not Q	P (or: Q)
Therefore not P	Not Q (or: not P)

In the first case, the consequent (Q) is affirmed as a result of affirming the antecedent (P); in the second, the consequent is denied, such that the antecedent must also be denied. 'The fallacies of affirming the consequent and denying the antecedent (i.e. of doing these things to start with in the minor premise) consist of reversing these procedures, that is, in arguing "if p then q, and q, therefore p," and "if p, then q, but not p, therefore not q."'[55]

Many traditional logicians have reacted against hypothetical and disjunctive forms of reasoning by trying to show that they can be reduced to categorical syllogisms. As I noted in the summary of this chapter in the introduction, modern logic does just the opposite, demonstrating that categorical syllogisms can and really should be construed hypothetically. This controversy notwithstanding, it is arguable that hypothetical and disjunctive syllogisms are useful even to the traditional logician who is primarily concerned with actualities, insofar as anticipating and preparing for future possibilities is part of what it means to lead a responsible human life in the actual present order.

Perfect vs Imperfect Syllogisms

In discussing the 15 valid syllogisms, Aristotle distinguishes between syllogisms that are 'perfect' and others that are 'imperfect.'[56] By his account, a deduction is perfect if it 'needs no external term in order to show the necessary result.'[57] In other words, a syllogism is perfect if the validity of the syllogism is immediately apparent, in virtue of its structure, as in the case of first-figure syllogisms (AAA, EAE, AII, EIO). While the validity of imperfect or second, third, and fourth-figure syllogisms is not immediately obvious in this way, the conclusion produced by such syllogisms nevertheless follows from the foregoing premises.

In his *Prior Analytics*, Aristotle demonstrates that any imperfect syllogism can be reconfigured such that the logical connection between its premises and conclusion, or validity, is immediately evident, like that of a perfect or first-figure syllogism.[58] The process of transforming a second, third or fourth-figure syllogism into a syllogism of the first figure is known as reduction. When syllogisms are left unreduced, Aristotle observes, it takes a longer chain of reasoning and thus more time to see the point being made. In short, the argument in question is less concise and efficient, less simple, unified, satisfying, and ultimately useful as an explanation for real states of affairs.[59]

The effort to reduce a syllogism to the first figure relies heavily on the immediate inferences I mentioned above, through which one or more of the propositions comprising the syllogism is recast in a new form, which conveys the same basic meaning. Indeed, the insertion of immediate inferences can transform the structure of the syllogism in a way that makes its validity obvious in an immediate way.[60] Although it would take more space than I have here to show how every imperfect syllogism can be rendered perfect, I will offer one example of what reduction involves, invoking a *Cesare* or first mood, second-figure syllogism. Such a syllogism posits that:

> No A is B
> Every C is B
> No C is A

On closer examination, it is not immediately apparent that the conclusion of this syllogism follows from the given premises. Since the first premise entails a universal negation, however, it can be transformed by conversion into the proposition, 'No B is A.' When this proposition is substituted for the original premise within the syllogism, the syllogism can be re-construed along the lines of a *Celarent*, first-figure syllogism:

> No B is A
> *Every C is B*
> No C is A

As this example illustrates, supplementing a *Cesare* syllogism with a premise that represents the converse of one of its original premises reconfigures the syllogism in a way that makes it possible to grasp instantly that its conclusion does indeed follow from the premises. Once a syllogism has been reduced to one the four first-figure syllogisms, Aristotle shows that the syllogisms that can only be reduced in the first instance to one of the particular-mood syllogisms may be further reduced to one of the two universal-mood syllogisms.[61] Through a series of steps, for instance, an EIO can be reduced to an EAE.[62]

Furthermore, an AII-1 can be reduced to an AAA-1 by means of a *reductio ad absurdum* or proof *per impossibile*.[63] Such proofs involve showing that something is the case because it is impossible for it not to be the case. The problem generally associated with these proofs is that they may involve a false dilemma, in which only two alternatives are presented when in fact there may be others. Given the possibility of other options, it will be assumed for the sake of the argument of this and the next chapter that a proof *per impossibile* cannot necessarily be relied upon in argumentation, notwithstanding the appeal of its ability to produce universal and affirmative conclusions.[64]

These conclusions are superior to particular and negative ones, respectively, insofar as it is more useful to know what is always as opposed to occasionally the case, and to know what is rather than what is not the case.[65] On these grounds, we can conclude that second through fourth-figure syllogisms should be reduced as far as possible, and wherever possible, to an AAA syllogism.

Deduction vs Demonstration

In addition to his concern for the validity—perfect and imperfect—of arguments, Aristotle was preoccupied with the truth content of deductive arguments, and especially the question whether any given argument gives a reason for the conclusion it draws concerning the object under consideration, which appeals to the nature or essential features of the object itself. In order to distinguish between arguments, which lack and offer such a reason, respectively, Aristotle separates mere deductions from full-blown demonstrations, insisting that a 'demonstration is a sort of deduction, but not every deduction is a demonstration.'[66]

While a syllogism of any figure can in theory take the form of a deduction or a demonstration, a demonstration is distinct from and superior to a deduction insofar as its major premise—or first principle—meets the following criteria, namely that it is immediate, true, logically prior, primitive, better known, and the cause or explanation of the conclusion that is ultimately drawn from it.[67]

Of the aforementioned criteria, the first stipulates that the first principle must be an immediate or 'un-middled' inference.[68] As noted above, an inference is immediate if there is no middle or third term that explains the unity amongst the two terms that are connected through the inference.

The second criterion posits that the first principle of the syllogism must be true; it must reflect the facts of human experience. The third criterion holds that the major premise must be logically prior to all that follows from it. In other words, it must not be derivable from the conclusion itself, which would involve circular reasoning. That is not to deny that, 'no principle can be first as such; [for] to treat a principle as a first principle is always to choose to do so for some particular purpose within some particular context.'[69] Thus, it is entirely feasible for a principle that follows from certain conclusions in one context to be logically prior to other conclusions in another context.

The fourth criterion states that the first principle must not merely be logically prior to the conclusion that is drawn out from it; it must be the most immediately prior or primitive premise available in reference to the conclusion. In other words, there cannot be a conceptual gap between the principle and what it proves, particularly if a principle is available that leaves no such gap and bears directly on the particular, the nature of which is being demonstrated. Such a gap leaves room for doubt about the legitimacy or strength of the grounds offered for the conclusion.

The fifth criterion maintains that the first principle must be better known than the conclusion derived from it. There are two senses in which one thing can be better known than another, namely, in itself or by us. While particular objects of experience are better known by us, for example, the universals or concepts we infer on the basis of them are better known in themselves, inasmuch as they render particulars comprehensible. For the purposes of demonstration, Aristotle mandates that the first principles of our knowledge be better known in themselves.[70]

The last criterion follows from the fifth, stating that the first principle must be the cause of or rationale behind the conclusion. Though a given principle may provide such a reason in certain contexts, with reference to certain matters, it is of no use if it cannot supply a rationale for the conclusion under consideration. While I may explain why I took my umbrella to work today by appealing to the morning weather forecast, which predicted rain, for example, I cannot offer the relevant explanation by affirming that I enjoy my job, because enjoying my job does not count in most circumstances as a reason for taking my umbrella to work. To summarize, the principles we select to found our conclusions must be directly related to those conclusions as reasons for them.

In Aristotle's account, we can be sure we have isolated the appropriate explanation or reason for our conclusion when the major and middle terms are co-extensive, that is, when the universals are 'commensurate.'[71] By describing a universal as commensurate, we assert that the extension of the middle term is not wider than or 'positioned outside'[72] that of the major term. In other words, the middle term is an essential as opposed to accidental property of the major term, possibly even part of the real definition of it, in which case the middle term describes entirely and only the major term and other instances like it.

By appealing to the essence of a thing in offering the rationale for what we conclude about it, we offer what can genuinely be described as a demonstration, insofar as we prove that one thing is true of another by appealing to the very nature of the object being demonstrated or described.[73] Such an appeal to *what* the object under consideration is enables us to say not only *that* it exists in a certain way but also *why* it is what it is.[74] Incidentally, the explanation why a thing is what it is may invoke any one of the four causes or types of explanation: formal, efficient, final, or material.

As noted previously, an argument that invokes what something is in order to explain why it exists or exists in a certain way produces a conclusion that is necessarily true in the sense that it follows from an understanding of what the thing in question is.[75] In this context, the term 'necessary'[76] is contrasted with terms like 'accidental' or 'incidental,' which refer to those features of a thing's existence which are not essential to its being and are therefore subject to change. In cases of accidental truth, where relationships of belonging hold for a reason other than one to do with the nature of the thing that belongs to a class, we can only know *that* the relationship exists, not why or what it entails.[77] This is as far as mere deduction can take us.

The following example, provided by Aristotle, should help to clarify the difference between deduction and demonstration:

> Thunder is the extinguishing of fire in the clouds.
> The extinguishing of fire produces a noise in the clouds.
> Therefore, thunder is a kind of noise in the clouds.

The first line of this syllogism invokes an essential feature, in fact what Aristotle takes to be the real definition of thunder.[78] The definition of thunder, namely, 'an extinguishing of fire in the clouds,' thus becomes the middle term of the syllogism, which in turn affords the reason for the conclusion that thunder is a kind of noise in the clouds, explaining the cause of the noise. Such an explanation is important for various reasons, but especially when it comes to ruling out implausible explanations for noise in the clouds, such as the wrath of the Greek god of the sky, Zeus.

While there is obviously considerable value in deductions that do not rise to the standard of demonstrations—a value that will become clearer in the discussion of the next chapter—that value is enhanced and consummated when deductions are in fact elevated to the level of demonstrations, thus satisfying the six conditions of immediacy, truth, logical priority, primitiveness, familiarity, and causality or explanatory value.[79]

In some cases, however, a simple three-premise syllogism does not suffice to supply a demonstration that meets all the aforementioned criteria. While the middle term of the syllogism may create a loose and thus vaguely plausible connection between, say, A and B, the mind's grasp of that connection resembles the vision of a distant object, in which it is impossible to make out all that the connection between A and B involves. In other words, the connection in this instance is undifferentiated, such that it is necessary to identify further points of mediation between the two terms until the connection between them is as clearly delineated as possible.[80]

The process of elaborating the further middle terms that allow the relationship at stake in the syllogism to be fully analyzed is known as the 'thickening' or 'increasing' of the middle term of a demonstration. In summary, thickening the middle term means detailing every single step or middle term that it takes, in the order it must be taken, to move logically from A to B, until the connection between every term is immediately or directly related to the one that follows from it, and from which it follows.[81] The initial syllogism might look something like this:

> All A is C
> All C is B
> All A is B

Once fully thickened, however, the syllogism will actually consist of a chain of syllogisms ('sorites'), in which the conclusion of the first syllogism serves as the major premise of the next one, as follows:

> All A is E
> All E is D
> All D is C
> All C is B
> All A is B

Though the middle term cannot be thickened infinitely, since A and B set upper and lower limits on the inquiry, it is both possible and necessary to continue thickening until every middle term that is introduced to intervene between A and B involves a connection that is as tight as it possibly could be, and all the stipulations for logical priority, primitiveness, familiarity, and so on are fully satisfied.[82]

While demonstrations can be offered and the middle term thickened in any figure whatever, I would conclude by re-iterating the value of reducing demonstrations to the universal and affirmative syllogism of the first figure, namely AAA.[83] Precisely because this syllogism, and this syllogism alone, consists entirely of statements that are universal and affirmative, it can offer information that applies to all instances of the type of being demonstrated.

Although demonstrations in other moods may do this as well, I will show in the next chapter that the understanding an AAA syllogism affords is unique in that it simultaneously enhances our understanding of the essential or even differential properties of the definition by which we demonstrate. Other demonstrations obviously cannot do this, because they are particular and/or negative in mood and cannot consequently produce conclusions that apply to all instances of a thing, and thus, to its definition. Through the use of an AAA syllogism exclusively, consequently, two of the most important cognitive tasks can be accomplished at once, namely, demonstration and definition.[84] The section on informed faith in chapter four will explain how this is so.

Logical Fallacies

Before closing this chapter, I wish to say a word about logical fallacies, which I will describe in chapter five as 'intellectual vices.' In the sections on inductive and deductive reasoning above, I mentioned a number of rules that must be observed in order for arguments of either kind to obtain both validity and truth. Albeit in different ways, truth and validity pertain to the unity of our thoughts. While answering to the truth, for instance, ensures that claims are united to or bear on reality, striving for validity secures the unity of or correlation between evidence offered and the claims made on the grounds of that evidence.

When the criteria for validity are disregarded, one of the formal logical fallacies I mention below will inevitably be committed. Such a fallacy turns on affirming more or less than is warranted on the basis of the evidence presented in the premises of an argument. In that sense, formal fallacies arise from an internal inconsistency in the structure of an argument. Whereas formal fallacies pertain to the form of arguments, informal fallacies have to do with the matter or truth content of the propositions that constitute them. In the case of these fallacies, then, the question is whether an argument fulfills the content-related criteria mentioned above.

Formal Inductive Fallacies

There are two ways to break the formal rules for inductive syllogisms, namely by: 1. failing to distribute the minor terms in both premises (but not the conclusion); or 2. failing to distribute the middle term in the conclusion (but not the premises).

Formal Deductive Fallacies

A number of formal fallacies correspond to the rules for validity pertaining to deductive syllogisms. The rule to 'distribute the middle term in at least one premise,' for example, correlates to the fallacy of the undistributed middle. The rule to 'distribute in the premises any term that is distributed in the conclusion' corresponds to the fallacies of the illicit major and the illicit minor (in which the major and minor terms, respectively, are not distributed). The rule to 'avoid four terms' corresponds to the fallacy of four terms. This fallacy is often committed when one word or turn of phrase is used in two different senses within the course of a single argument. The rule to 'avoid two negative premises' is broken by the fallacy of exclusive premises. The rule to 'draw a negative conclusion where either premise is negative' is broken by the fallacy of 'drawing an affirmative conclusion from a negative premise.' Finally, the rule 'not to draw a particular conclusion from two universal premises' corresponds to the existential fallacy.

In addition to formal fallacies, there are a number of informal fallacies related to the truth content of the propositions produced in induction or the arguments presented in deduction. I will treat these in turn.[85]

Informal Inductive Fallacies

In the section on induction, I set down a few criteria for induction. These criteria hold us accountable to draw general conclusions that are based on an adequate number of examples, which exhibit the number or the types of commonalities necessary to warrant the conclusion, and which are ultimately modest relative to the available evidence. In what follows, I name some fallacies of 'defective induction' that can be committed when these criteria are overlooked.[86]

- Hasty Generalization: jumping to conclusions without enough evidentiary support. Conversely, it is possible to procrastinate on drawing a conclusion when evidence demands a verdict.
- False Cause: naming a definition as the cause of certain circumstances when it is not in fact their cause.
- Argument from Ignorance: concluding something must be true because it cannot be proven false.
- Cherry Picking: picking and choosing evidence in order to support a particular conclusion, ignoring or suppressing evidence that might undermine that conclusion.
- Oversimplification: assuming that one definition is the explanation for many instances, which in fact have different causes.

Informal Deductive Fallacies

Most informal deductive fallacies are the by-product of a failure to meet the six stipulations for demonstration I set out above, and if necessary, to thicken the middle term. Indeed, the failure to fulfill these stipulations is bound to result in one of the deductive informal fallacies of presumption, which assume something that the deductive argument should itself prove. These fallacies include the following:

- Accident: applying a general definition to a particular that the definition does not define.
- Complex Question: posing a question that presupposes the truth of some assumption upon which the question itself rests.
- Begging the Question: stating or assuming the conclusion of an argument in one of the premises.
- Circular Reasoning: proving A on the basis of B when B itself derives support from A.
- Missing the Point: refuting a thesis other than the one a conversation partner is advancing.
- Argument from Fallacy: assuming that an invalid line of reasoning cannot have a true conclusion.
- Appeal to Probability: insisting that something must happen if it can happen.
- Argument from Repetition: presuming that an issue does not need to be explored because it has already been the topic of extensive conversation.
- Argument from Lack of Consensus: positing that an issue cannot be addressed or even resolved if there are many conflicting opinions about it.

- Shifting the Burden of Proof: presupposing the truth of personal assumptions, thus shifting the burden of proof on to those who adhere to different assumptions, which may not require proof.

While all of the aforementioned fallacies presuppose the existence of an actual argument, the following 'fallacies of relevance' do not. Rather, these fallacies represent ways individuals may try to hide the fact that they do not actually possess a cogent argument. Such fallacies are also known as 'red herring' fallacies, which employ a distraction or irrelevancy to mislead or confuse interlocutors.

- Appeal to Validity: citing the validity, and/or clarity, rigor, and precision of an argument as grounds for accepting it as true.
- Appeal to the People: assuming that something is true because many people affirm its truth. It is also possible to invoke the principle of solidarity, that is, to endeavor to convince others of an argument on the grounds that they owe their support, respect, or gratitude to those who already affirm that argument.
- Appeal to Emotion: playing on emotions of fear, envy, pity, and so on, in order to persuade others.
- *Ad hominem*: attacking a person, rather than their views.
- The Straw Man: misrepresenting an opponent and criticizing them on the basis of that misrepresentation.
- Appeal to Force: using threats to persuade others.

Finally, there are fallacies that arise from ambiguities in language:

- Equivocation: confusing two or more meanings of the same word or phrase (as in the formal deductive fallacy of four terms).
- Amphiboly: combining words in a loose, awkward or mistaken way, which may create ambiguity in meaning.
- Accent: giving a term or phrase a different meaning in the conclusion of an argument than it had in one of the premises.
- Composition: assuming that the attributes of parts also apply to the whole of which they are a part.
- Division: assuming that the attributes of a whole also apply to its constituent parts.

To summarize, all of the aforementioned fallacies unite things that are not united or distinguish things that are not distinguished. Some do this in a formal sense, asserting more than is warranted by the evidence laid out in the argument—or less, as in the case of fallacies from repetition, lack of consensus, or shifting the burden of proof, to name a few examples; others are fallacious in an informal or material sense: they claim that things that contradict or are not united to one another are in fact united, or true.

Conclusion

Over the course of this chapter and the last, I have argued that all beings, including human beings, are subject to development; and that human beings are defined by rationality, such that their development or the actualization of their potential is accomplished through the acquisition of knowledge. From all this, it follows that human knowledge is also subject to development. The next chapter will explain the process through which human understanding develops, indicating where relevant how the elements of knowledge treated in this chapter factor in to and facilitate this process. Chapter 5 will then return to the larger question as to how our cognitive processes fit into the greater process of becoming what we are already, if not yet in full, namely, individual human beings.

Endnotes

[1]   Peter Geach explains how any English sentence can be transformed into a logical syllogism in his chapter on 'Logical Schemata' in *Reason and Argument* (Oxford: Blackwell, 1976), 46–51.

[2]   *APr.* I.25.

[3]   *Meta.* VII.12, 1037b9–1037b28.

[4]   *De Ente* 16.

[5]   *Int.* 6ff.: on affirmations and denials.

[6]   *Cat.* 4.

[7]   *Meta.* IV.2, 1003a33–1003b18.

[8]   *Meta.* IV.4, 1005b34–1006a11.

[9]   *Meta.* VII.17, 1041a6–1041a32.

[10]   *Meta.* IV.7, 1011b23–1012a17.

[11]   *APr.* I.116–17, 'a proposition, then, is a statement affirming or denying something of something; and this is either universal or particular or indefinite.'

[12]   In conversion, the subject and the predicate terms change places. The four standard categorical propositions can be converted in this way:

A	All S is P—I: some P is S (this is an example of 'conversion by limitation' in which the quantifier 'some' instead of 'all' is applied, since the statement that 'all S is P' does not necessarily warrant the conclusion that 'all P is S')
E	No S is P—E: no P is S
I	Some S is P: some P is S
O	Conversion is not possible

Obversion is a type of immediate inference in which the quality of a proposition is changed and the predicate term is replaced with its complement, that is, a negated version of the original term, e.g. mammal vs non-mammal. The obverted propositions are as follows:

A	All S is P—E: no S is non-P
E	No S is P—A: all S is non-P
I	Some S is P—O: some S is not non-P
O	Some S is not P—I: some S is non-P

In the last type of immediate inference, contraposition, the subject term is replaced by the complement of the predicate term, and the predicate is replaced by the complement of the subject term, as follows:

A	All S is P: all non-P is non-S
E	No S is P—O: some non-P is not non-S (by limitation)
I	Contraposition is not possible
O	Some S is not-P: some non-P is not non-S

---

[13]   *Top.* I.5, 101b30–31.

[14]   On this score, see David Charles' excellent work, *Aristotle on Meaning and Essence* (Oxford: Oxford University Press, 2002).

[15]   *Top.* VI.4, 141b15–142a13.

[16]   Irving M. Copi and Carl Cohen, *Introduction to Logic*, 14th edn (Upper Saddle River: Pearson, 2011), 94. See Paolo Crivelli's account of the *Prior Analytics* in *The Oxford Handbook of Aristotle* (Oxford: Oxford University Press, 2012), 113–49.

[17]   *APo.* I.13, 97b.

[18]   *APo.* I.13, 96a-b.

[19]   *Apo.* I.4, 73a-b: what belongs to a thing because of its nature is essential, and what does not belong in this way is accidental.

[20]   *APo.* II.13, 96b-97b.

[21] There is a legend that rather comically illustrates the point stated above. At one time, Plato's successors at the Academy in Athens apparently settled on a definition of man as a 'featherless biped.' On learning of this conclusion, their critic, Diogenes, plucked a chicken and tossed it over the wall of the Academy, giving Plato's followers a 'featherless biped,' which was by no means human. In this amusing way, Diogenes proved that the definition of 'man' Plato's followers had formulated was too broad. See Irving M. Copi and Carl Cohen, *Introduction to Logic*, 97.

[22] *APo.* I.31, 88a12, 'some of our problems are referred to want of perception.'

[23] *ST* 1.85.6: falsehood is in the intellect only as regards composition and division.

[24] *ST* 2.1.64.3: *Consistit in quodam medio, per conformitatem ad ipsam rem, secundum quod dicit esse quod est, vel non esse quod non est; in quo ratio veri consistit. Excessus autem est secundum affirmationem falsam, per quam dicitur esse quod non est, defectus autem accipitur secundum negationem falsam, per quam dicitur non esse quod est.*

[25] See Peter Geach, *Reason and Argument* (Oxford: Blackwell, 1976), 42. Here, Geach writes that 'one sort of nominal definition accepts established usage, and is concerned to sort out and characterize as accurately as possible the actual uses of a word; this is the sort of definition you find in a good dictionary, though dictionaries will also contain a certain number of what would count as real definitions. Another sort of nominal definition does not merely accept whatever happens to be current usage, but constitutes a proposal for tightening up the use of a term; under the proposal, the term would mostly be applied as it now is, but with stricter criteria; or again, the proponent of the definition may suggest that we abandon some current uses and retain only one preferred use. Finally, an old word may be arbitrarily given a quite new meaning.'

[26] *Int.* 2, 16a19, 27–8, 'a name is a spoken sound significant by convention ... I say "by convention" because no name is a name naturally but only when it has become a symbol.' See chapter 4 on 'The Signification of Names,' in David Charles, *Aristotle on Meaning and Essence*, 78–109.

[27] Contrary to a longstanding opinion, consequently, words are not signs or images of the things they name. As David Braine argues in *The Human Person: Animal and Spirit* (Notre Dame: The University of Notre Dame Press, 1994), 399, speaking involves 'neither images of external objects nor representations of states of affairs, nor abstracted images.' On this score, see also the important work by John O'Callaghan, *Thomist Realism and the Linguistic Turn: Towards a More Perfect Form of Existence* (Notre Dame: University of Notre Dame Press, 2003), which refutes the common interpretation of Aristotle and Aquinas according to which the two conceived of language as signifying actual realities. In an earlier article on 'Concepts, Beings, and Things in Contemporary Philosophy and Thomas Aquinas,' *The Review of Metaphysics* 63:1 (September 1999), 70, O'Callaghan points out that this conception of language results from the view that

a mental representation or 'third thing stands within the mind of the language user and the world he would speak of. Because of the interposition of this mental representation, words are thought to be directly related to or directly to signify things in the world ... [71] Moreover because words signify concepts without mediation ... it is by knowing concepts as primary objects of knowledge ... that the language user knows what extra-mental objects are talked about.' See also his related article on 'The Problem of Language and Mental Representation in Aristotle and St Thomas,' *The Review of Metaphysics* 50:3 (March 1997), 499–545.

[28]   This phrase was coined by Ludwig Wittgenstein. See David Burrell, *Analogy and Philosophical Language* (New Haven: Yale University Press, 1973).

[29]   David Burrell, *Aquinas: God and Action* (London: University of Scranton Press, 2008), 64. According to Burrell, scholars have generally overlooked the quasi-Wittgensteinian character of Aquinas' account of analogy; in the attempt to acquire linguistic precision, they have often construed analogy in terms of an analogy of proportion, which is a form of univocity.

[30]   'Language game' is another phrase that was coined by Ludwig Wittgenstein.

[31]   David Burrell, *Analogy and Philosophical Language*; John P. O'Callaghan, *Thomist Realism and the Linguistic Turn*; Alasdair MacIntyre, *Whose Justice? Which Rationality?* (London: Duckworth, 1999).

[32]   G.E.L. Owen, '*Tithenai ta phainomena*,' in *Logic, Science, and Dialectic* (London: Duckworth, 1986), 239–51, especially at 240: 'an appeal to *legomenon* may be an appeal either to common belief about matters of fact or to established forms of language or to a philosophical thesis claiming the factual virtues of the first and the analytic certainty of the second.' Experience includes 'not only the supposed evidence of the senses but the common assumptions and specifically the common use of language which form men's picture of the physical world' (242).

[33]   Herbert McCabe persuasively argues that this is one upshot of Aquinas' contention that matter is the 'principle of individuation.' See *The Good Life* (London: Continuum, 2005), 35ff. See also Herbert McCabe, *The Good Life*, 84: 'A concept is a skill in using a word which has its meaning from its part in the structure of the language. If words have their meaning in the language which does not belong to anybody but to everybody, then ... the capacity to deploy meanings is not a capacity for any individual bodily process as a sensation is.' See also Herbert McCabe, *On Aquinas* (London: Burns and Oates, 2008), 50: while 'what we see is more or less determined by how the world is around us, what we say is not so determined.'

[34]   Herbert McCabe, *The Good Life*, 84.

[35]   Ibid., 37.

[36]   On this showing, the problem of demonstrating that it is possible to know other minds—and indeed, to get outside our own—that arises for some modern theorists of

knowledge is clearly circumnavigated. By contrast to some such theorists, who hold that we possess thoughts, which we are unable to express short of learning to articulate ourselves through language, the present account turns on the assumption that our ability to conceive and communicate meaningful thoughts is proportional to the extent to which we have learned fluidly to communicate verbally, and vice versa. In other words, we grow in understanding as we find ways to articulate our ideas, and we articulate our ideas more effectively as we grow in understanding. In sum, we know what we can name, and we name only what we know. Fergus Kerr, *Theology After Wittgenstein* (London: SPCK, 1997). See also David Braine, *The Human Person*, 357: 'the capacity of children to speak and think advances simultaneously.'

³⁷   See chapter 4 on 'The Signification of Names,' in David Charles' *Aristotle on Meaning and Essence*.

³⁸   Robert Sokolowski, *Presence and Absence* (Bloomington: Indiana University Press, 1978), 6. Though what 'we learn in our inherited language will urge us to notice certain aspects in an object ... it does not predestine us to see only these; words compel only those persons who cannot resist an urge. It is always possible to break through the pressure of language and notice aspects that others may not see, aspects that have not yet been institutionalized in the language.'

³⁹   *APo.* I.19, 100a4–9: 'so from perception there comes memory, as we call it, and from memory (when it occurs often in connection with the same thing, experience); for memories that are many in number form a single experience. And from experience, or from the whole universal that has come to rest in the soul (the one apart from the many, whatever is one and the same in all those things), there comes a principle of skill and of understanding—of skill if it deals with how things come about, of understanding if it deals with what is the case.'

⁴⁰   *APo.* I.1.

⁴¹   Irving M. Copi and Carl Cohen, *Introduction to Logic*, 452.

⁴²   *APo.* II.19.

⁴³   Irving M. Copi and Carl Cohen, *Introduction to Logic*, 454.

⁴⁴   *ST* 79.6. The intellect retains universals; sense memory retains individuals.

⁴⁵   On this, see Ludwig Wittgenstein's *On Certainty* (Oxford: Blackwell, 1969).

⁴⁶   *APr.* I.1, 24b19–20; *Top.* I, 100a6–7.

⁴⁷   There are a number of possible permutations of truth and validity. There can be a(n): valid argument with all true propositions; valid argument with all false propositions; invalid argument with only true propositions; invalid argument with true premises and a false conclusion; valid argument with false premises and a true conclusion; invalid argument with false premises and a true conclusion; invalid argument, with all false propositions.

⁴⁸   Irving M. Copi and Carl Cohen, *Introduction to Logic*, 207.

⁴⁹   Although this is strictly speaking true, Martin Warner has helpfully pointed out to me that the number of valid syllogisms can be elevated to 24, with six in each figure, provided we make an extra existential assumption, albeit not always the same one, in each of the additional nine cases. See Lemmon's discussion of the syllogism in *Beginning Logic* (London: Nelson, 1971), 175–7.

⁵⁰   Irving M. Copi and Carl Cohen, *Introduction to Logic*, 229.

⁵¹   *APr.* I.4, 25b35–6: 'I call that term middle which both is itself in another and contains another in itself.'

⁵²   Though I have noted that there are no such rules strictly speaking, since inductive arguments ultimately come down to a judgment call, the rules outlined above can be inverted to produce the following two rules for validity in inductive syllogisms: 1. The minor terms must be distributed in both premises but not the conclusion; and 2. The middle term must be distributed in the conclusion but not the premises.

⁵³   See E.J. Lemmon, *Beginning Logic*, on the propositional calculus.

⁵⁴   A.N. Prior, 'Logic, Traditional,' in vol. 5, *The Encyclopedia of Philosophy*, ed. Paul Edwards (London and New York: Collier-Macmillan and Macmillan, 1967), 42.

⁵⁵   Ibid., 42.

⁵⁶   *APr.* I.1, 24b23–6.

⁵⁷   *APr.* I.1, 24b23–24.

⁵⁸   *Apr.* I.7, 29a30–1, 'all the imperfect deductions are made perfect by means of the first figure.'

⁵⁹   *Apo.* I.25, 86a34–36: 'let that demonstration be better which depends on fewer postulates or suppositions or propositions. For knowing will come about more quickly in this way, and that is preferable.'

⁶⁰   Patrick Byrne, *Analysis and Science in Aristotle* (Albany: State University of New York Press, 1997).

⁶¹   Traditional logicians have devised some mnemonic devices to help students remember which reductions are possible and how to execute them. They have assigned a Latin name to each of the 15 valid syllogisms. Each name contains three vowels that represent the mood of the major premise, minor premise, and conclusion (e.g. AAA). The valid moods in the first figure are called *bArbArA, cElArEnt, dArII, fErIO* (AAA, EAE, AII, EIO, respectively). The names of the second-figure syllogisms are, *cEsArE, cAmEstrEs, fEstInO, bArOcO* (EAE, AEE, EIO, AOO, respectively). The titles assigned to the third-figure syllogisms include *dIsAmIs, dAtIsI, bOcArdO, fErIsOn* (IAI, AII, OAO, EIO, respectively); and the fourth: *cAmEnEs, dImArIs, frEsIsOn* (AEE, IAI, EIO, respectively). These mnemonic devices prove helpful when it comes to reducing syllogisms to the first figure, because the first letter of the name that denotes a syllogism of the second, third or fourth figure corresponds to the first letter of the name of the syllogism in the first figure to which that syllogism can be reduced. Thus, the following reductions can be performed:

AOO-2—reduces to—AAA-1 (*reductio ad absurdum*)
AEE-2—reduces to—EAE-1
EAE-2—reduces to—EAE-1
EIO-2—reduces to—EIO-1
AII-3—reduces to—AII-1
IAI-3—reduces to—AII-1
EIO-3—reduces to—EIO-1
OAO-3—reduces to—AAA-1 (*reductio ad absurdum*)
AEE-4—reduces to—EAE-1
IAI-4—reduces to—AII-1
EIO-4—reduces to—EIO-1

From the above, it is clear that all the second, third, and fourth-figure syllogisms can be reduced to either a universal/negative (EAE) or universal/affirmative (AAA) syllogism in the first figure or to a particular/negative (EIO) or particular/affirmative (AII) syllogism in the first figure. For more on this score, see Patrick Byrne, *Analysis and Science in Aristotle* (50), where the author discusses the Aristotelian claim that imperfect deductions are made perfect by means of the first figure.

[62] *APr.* I.7.

[63] *APr.* I.23; cf. *APo.* I.26.

[64] *Apo.* I.26. This is a somewhat contentious claim, as there has been some debate as to whether *reductio ad absurdum* arguments represent a sound basis for drawing conclusions. In *Reason and Argument* (28), Peter Geach argues forcibly that they do. There, he asks his readers to suppose that someone asserts 'premises P and Q and now adds a third premise R just as a supposition. If from the premises P, Q and R all together, the falsehood of R logically follows, then the reasoner's assertion of P and Q warrants him in going on to assert that R is false, and in offering this as a provided conclusion to anyone who agrees in accepting P and Q. For if R could be asserted along with P and Q, the set of asserted premises P, Q, R would logically lead to the assertion both of R and R's falsehood, and this is absurd. This powerful argumentative move is called *reductio ad absurdum*.'

[65] *APo.* I.24–25.

[66] *APr.* I.4, 25b30–1; cf. *Apo.* I.13. With regard to the same science, there are some deductions that state the fact and others the reason why; in cases where the middle term is positioned outside the genus of the other terms, there is no real explanation of the reason why the conclusion holds true.

[67] *APo.* I.2.

[68] *APo.* 72a8–10: 'a principle of a demonstration is an immediate proposition, and an immediate proposition is one to which there is no other prior.'

⁶⁹   Alasdair MacIntyre, *The Tasks of Philosophy* (Cambridge: Cambridge University Press, 2006), 145.

⁷⁰   *APo.* I.2, 72a29–33: 'a thing always belongs better to that thing because of which it belongs, hence if we know and are convinced because of the primitives, we both know and are convinced of them better, since it is because of them that we know and are convinced of what is posterior.'

⁷¹   *APo.* I.4.

⁷²   *APo.* I.13, 78b13.

⁷³   *APo.* I.6.

⁷⁴   *APo.* II.2, 90a32–34: 'what it is and why it is are the same ... to know what it is the same as to know why it is and that either *simpliciter* and not one of the things that belong to it or one of the things that belong to it, e.g. that it has two right angles.'

⁷⁵   *APo.* I.9, II.8.

⁷⁶   *APo.* I.4.

⁷⁷   *APo.* I.6.

⁷⁸   *DA* I.1, 402b25–403a2: 'in all demonstration, a definition of the essence is required as a starting-point, so that definitions which do not enable us to discover the derived properties, or which fail to facilitate even a conjecture about them, must obviously, one and all, be dialectical and futile.'

⁷⁹   *APo.* I.2, esp. 71b29–33.

⁸⁰   Patrick Byrne, *Analysis and Science in Aristotle*, 121.

⁸¹   *APr.* I.28: on filling in the middle term.

⁸²   *APo.* I.22.

⁸³   *APo.* I.24–5.

⁸⁴   *APo.* I.14.

⁸⁵   For details, see Aristotle's *Sophistical Refutations*.

⁸⁶   Irving M. Copi and Carl Cohen, *Introduction to Logic*, 155.

Chapter 4

The Conditions for Knowledge

The purpose of this chapter is to explain the process through which knowledge is acquired. One underlying assumption of the chapter is that formal logic, as outlined in the previous chapter, renders this process perspicuous and accounts for its success.[1] That is not to say that the study of formal logic is a necessary condition for the success of inquiry. Many individuals possess a natural ability to distinguish between sound and unsound arguments. Since many others require training in order to think critically, however, the study of logic is arguably helpful and in many cases necessary for this purpose.[2]

On the account I develop here, the knowing process is characterized by three phases. Although Aristotle and Aquinas described these as phases of inquiry, judgment, and directing reason, I will treat them in terms of expectant, fulfilled, and informed faith, where faith is defined in a generic rather than a religious sense, which simply denotes the element of personal investment involved in achieving understanding in the face of unknowns.[3] Taken together, the three stages of faith represent the conditions for the possibility of acquiring and applying knowledge.

The reason I describe the three-stage cognitive process in terms of faith is twofold. First and foremost, the concept of faith underlines the goal-orientated nature of knowledge, or the fact that we do not start out knowing whatever we wish to know, but must instead work to acquire the knowledge we desire over time. As the initial phase in this pursuit, expectant faith is characterized by a lack of the knowledge of the desired object of knowledge as well as the desire to know it. This preliminary type of faith therefore gives us an objective to know as opposed to an object of knowledge. That objective leads us to believe that the object exists and consequently gives us the motivation we need to follow through on inquiries that are ordered towards attaining the knowledge we desire.

In the second phase of fulfilled faith, we achieve that knowledge. That is to say, our desire for knowledge is satisfied. In the third phase of informed faith, we employ or place faith in the knowledge we have obtained in order to make sense of further experiences. Whenever we do this, the whole process of moving from expectant to fulfilled to informed faith begins again. As soon as we reach the end of an inquiry, therefore, we come to the point of departure for another one.

In that sense, the search for truth is interminable, and knowledge never ceases to be a matter of faith.

The second main reason I describe the knowing process in terms of faith is that the concept of faith implies both a lack of direct vision of faith's object and the anticipation of such vision. Put differently, the concept of faith underscores the essential role that tacit or subconscious awareness plays in obtaining and maintaining explicit or conscious knowledge.[4] In expectant faith, for example, the mind entertains a concept, which is empty or unseen. Though that concept is substantiated in fulfilled faith, I will demonstrate later in this chapter that attaining such a concept comes at the cost of direct attention to all the particulars on the basis of which the concept is ultimately formed. When the concept is consciously contemplated, consequently, the particulars are only known on a pre-suppositional level.

In informed faith, the opposite is true. Here, a concept cannot be consciously or directly considered, insofar as it is employed to understand objects of experience. At every stage in the process, therefore, acts of knowing entail the interplay of sightlessness and vision, that is, the anticipation or presupposition of direct knowledge and the enjoyment of direct knowledge itself. As will soon become clear, it is precisely this tension between the two forms of knowing—tacit and explicit, unconscious and conscious—that promotes the advance of knowledge.

The First Condition: Expectant Faith

At the outset of this section on expectant faith, it is relevant to consider how such a faith or desire to know arises. This kind of analysis is important, because the intellect tends to take in objects or features of objects that its existing ideas predispose it to grasp, as opposed to registering all the objects or features of objects that may present themselves objectively.[5] As Aquinas puts it, the mind receives images of things according to the mode of the intellect, rather than the mode of the thing.[6] Because the mind does not generally feel compelled to investigate realities that its existing definitions cannot explain, it is not constantly subject to the desire for knowledge or expectant faith. When the mind registers seemingly insignificant realities at all, Aquinas' account implies, it simply stashes them away in the sense memory for possible future reference.

While such 'selective seeing' might seem at first glance like a hindrance to human knowledge of reality, it is actually a considerable help when it comes to conforming our mode as knowers to the mode of reality itself. For the screening function pre-existing ideas perform gives us a point of departure or frame of reference for making progress in the acquisition of knowledge, without which we might be so over-stimulated by the available data as to succumb to intellectual paralysis.

Within this frame of reference, an expectant faith generally only arises when a new piece of information, a new perspective, or new approach comes to our attention, which our pre-existing ideas predispose us to desire to explain but can not actually explain. The ironic upshot of this conclusion is that the experiences that initially enable us to formulate ideas eventually force us to dismantle and reconsider those ideas, for the sake of comprehending an anomaly that seems important in light of them. The larger the anomaly or perceived gap in our understanding, the more urgent and dedicated our expectant faith is likely to be, to say nothing of the eventual growth in understanding that results from following the lead of this faith. In that sense, really remarkable discoveries result when our most fundamental assumptions are thrown into doubt; they are not the product of minor intellectual upsets.

There are a number of ways in which an anomaly may call our preconceived notions into question. Sometimes, an anomaly simply raises awareness of a reality that was never previously known to exist, giving rise to the question, 'what is X?' Similarly, an anomalous experience may call attention to an object that seemingly should but does not fit under one of our existing definitions, indicating that there may be a problem with the definition itself. In other cases, X may be discovered to be something other than it was always believed to be, such that we are forced to consider whether X is something else. In still further cases, an anomaly might motivate us to inquire if X exists at all.[7]

In all of the aforementioned cases, our primary task is to reconstruct an existing definition or construct a new one that explains the anomaly in question. In the event that the perceived problem concerns a complex apprehension about the essential but non-differential properties of a thing, reckoning with that problem may involve more work than can be undertaken in a single inquiry, that is, the work of adjusting the definitions of all the terms referred to in the apprehension until an affirmation or denial is obtained that once again reflects the available evidence. Though this process may require the alteration of more than just one definition, it always at base involves a search for definitions.

This search must be conducted through a series of steps. Though the overall goal of defining or re-defining entails the delineation of an object's genus *and* differentia, expectant faith only enables the initial step of identifying the genus or general category under which an anomaly falls and thus the production of a preliminary or basic definition of it. As I will soon demonstrate, it falls to

informed faith to elaborate differentia. In order to formulate a preliminary
definition, it is necessary to engage in acts of inductive reasoning, through which
images of particular objects are added to or subtracted from the mix of minor
terms that fell under the definition—now challenged by the anomaly—until
an inductive syllogism can be constructed that contains a middle term, which
locates the anomaly under a genus.

While the new genus obviously cannot be specified short of its actual
discovery, the old definition and the anomaly fill us with foresight or expectant
faith as to the nature of the middle term that will eventually reconcile the two
terms. These extreme terms therefore prepare us to recognize the new middle
term when we come across it.[8] In the moment this term is identified, I noted
in Chapter 3, the conclusion is obtained that points up the generic nature of
the anomaly. Once the genus of an anomaly has thus been specified through
inductive reasoning, a trial must be performed in which the conclusion of the
inductive syllogism serves as the first line in a deductive syllogism.

Supposing the trial proves that the newly identified genus does not fully
explain the anomaly, the process of inductive reasoning must be re-instigated
and continued until the middle term is located that most effectively accounts for
the anomaly and the other images or 'appearances' that were formerly explained
by the old definition. As this suggests, the process of confirming the genus of an
anomaly is twofold, in that it involves phases of both inductive and deductive
reasoning. In the first phase, inductive lines of thinking, which I will describe in
more detail below, facilitate hypothesizing about possible genera.

In the second, a newly identified genus is tested as an explanation of the
anomaly in order to determine if it satisfactorily explains that anomaly. Thus,
deductive reasoning clearly plays a part in facilitating the work of expectant
faith, even though the exercise of this faith is mainly a matter of inductive
reasoning, which alone allows for the eventual explanation of anomalies. That
again is not to say that it is necessary to know logic in order to achieve cognitive
success. Still, it is to suggest that those who grasp the truth do so by following
the rules of logic intuitively; that those rules therefore account for the success
of those who come to understand the truth; and that the knowledge of the rules
may for this very reason increase the chances of both succeeding and avoiding
logical failures in reasoning.

The alternation between inductive and deductive reasoning that ultimately
enacts cognitive success can be described in terms of a dialectic through which
two previously irreconcilable elements, namely, the anomaly and the original
definition, are synthesized or reconciled. So construed, the dialectic is not its
own distinctive mode of reasoning but employs both inductive and deductive

reasoning to achieve understanding. The fact that both forms of reasoning play a role in facilitating the dialectic bolsters the contention that logic—far from an arcane or irrelevant discipline—is crucial to enabling the dynamic process through which our thoughts are rendered consistent with new experiences.

In this connection, it bears noting that the dialectic facilitates the search for truth not only at the personal level, or within the confines of an individual's own thinking, but also at the collective or collaborative level. In other words, the dialectical process I describe in this chapter can explain how individuals as well as communities achieve and grow in understanding both within distinct periods of time and over the course of history.

At the start of such a dialectical search for understanding, the mind instinctively turns to the cognitive resources that are closest to hand, namely, the definitions in the intellectual memory that most regularly play a guiding role in our knowing. In this connection, it tends to turn intuitively to the definitions that seem most immediately united to the problem under consideration, or which seem most conducive to explaining the anomaly, marshaling them forward in the order of their apparent relevance to addressing the problem in view.[9]

Although one of these definitions may instantly offer an account of the anomaly, it is usually necessary to undertake further efforts to tap into a definition's latent explanatory powers. These efforts often involve drawing immediate inferences from pre-existing definitions, possibly through conversion, obversion, or contraposition, whereby the meaning of existing definitions is recast, consciously or unwittingly, in new argumentative forms.[10] On drawing an immediate inference, the powers of deduction must be employed to determine if it explains the anomalous experience—that is, to identify whether it highlights a middle term that connects the definition and the anomaly.[11] Where no such term emerges, it remains to proceed to the next most promising inference and try again.

As this suggests, the search for the anomaly's definition resembles puzzle solving. Such puzzling as it were is not subject to rules, since there are no rules for explaining a matter that has yet to be explained. For this reason, the exact procedure for explaining an anomaly cannot be determined in advance. That is not to say that efforts to account for an anomaly are bound by no rules whatsoever, however. For there is a finite number of possible middle terms that are capable of drawing any given anomaly under a definition, and we are or should be seeking the one that is best: the one that possesses the greatest degree of explanatory power with respect to the anomaly and so creates the highest level of unity between the extremes of anomaly and definition and is in that sense supremely true.

Though there is considerable room for improvisation in cognition, consequently, as a result of which it is impossible to predict exactly how the knowing process will unfold, human reasoning is far from random or devoid of logic. The logic it presupposes is simply not that of the intellect but of the will's desire to pursue whatever is best—most unifying and therefore true—in every single instance. As I will elaborate in the next chapter, this desire compels us systematically to turn down deficient solutions to the problem of accounting for an anomaly and continue the quest to understand it until the best possible explanation is found.

As I have mentioned, the explanation in question should identify the genus of an anomaly. In ideal circumstances, this explanation would not only define the class of the anomaly but would also do the same for all the images or phenomena or appearances that previously fell under the definition the anomaly disrupted, thus 'saving the appearances,' even if reconfiguring our understanding of their status or role in our conceptual apparatus for interpreting reality.[12] At times, of course, it is not possible to save the appearances. In other words, we must forfeit a definition that explains matters accounted for by our old definition in order to settle on a definition that explains our anomaly. Provided the explanation of the anomaly seems vital to our whole framework for thinking, it may be worth incurring this loss, at least initially. An effort to save the appearances may always be exerted through further inquiries, if this seems an important undertaking.

Though the reconfiguration of existing definitions may successfully explain an anomaly in certain cases, there is always the chance that it will fail to do so. In such cases, it is imperative to move on and actually reconstruct or construct altogether new definitions. To do this, we must turn to the next most unifying level in our knowledge, that is, the sense memory. There, as in the intellectual memory, we begin by collecting facts that seem relevant to our inquiry. Here, however, the facts are not preconceived definitions, but images that seem to resemble the anomalous image in ways that might help us induce a definition of it—images that have previously served as the basis for constructing definitions or that have possibly never been scrutinized at all.

In order to conduct our search at this stage, it may prove necessary to break down an old definition, add new images from the sense memory into the mix of images on which the definition is founded, perhaps eliminating some of the old images that now seem insignificant, inferring the genus of our anomaly on the basis of the images that remain. On doing so, we attain the position to test our findings by deduction. If we find by these means that the genus provides a middle term under which the anomaly falls, then our work is finished. Otherwise, another attempt must be made to locate the middle term, which resorts to the first and least unifying level of our knowledge, namely, sense perception.

In this case, the world outside our minds must be consulted as we search therein for data that seem relevant to explaining our anomaly. Here, as ever, an order of priority is intuitively observed, such that reason automatically makes first recourse to material that seems most useful or 'united' to our purposes, most promising, obvious, or urgently in need of our attention. In this connection, we naturally start by revisiting earlier areas of inquiry where we suspect we may find useful information, the explanatory powers of which we did not fully explore previously. The next obvious course of action is to delve into completely new areas of inquiry, starting with the ones that seem most fruitful for our purposes.

Each time enough images are gathered that resemble our anomaly, the inductive process must be initiated whereby we formulate or reformulate a hypothesis about the possible genus of our anomaly, which is in turn tested in deduction. In the event that test fails, another attempt must be made to find the appropriate middle term—indeed as many attempts as prove necessary for this purpose. Though these failed attempts take time, it is important to recognize that they are far from a waste of time. For whenever possibly relevant facts are enumerated, a deductive line of reasoning is completed, the conclusion of which is represented by an A, E, I, or O statement.

At first glance, this information may not seem useful for explaining the anomaly. Insofar as the aforementioned deductive lines of reasoning can be reduced to first-figure EAE (universal/negative) or AII (universal/particular) demonstrative syllogisms, however, the conclusions they produce may ultimately afford information about that which the anomaly is *not* or what it is in part but not in full. While the accumulation of knowledge of what the anomaly is not helps us eliminate possible genera, gathering knowledge of aspects of our anomaly gradually attunes us to its generic nature until we eventually identify what that is.

Since we know very little on both counts early on in the inquiry, our hypotheses as to the nature of the anomaly are bound to be rather imprecise and imperfect at this time. Moreover, our sense of how to go about identifying the anomaly's genus will usually be rather vague. For this reason, our progress towards understanding is initially rather slow. As we eliminate possibilities or enhance our sense of the feasibility of others, however, we not only gain a better idea of the nature of the object of knowledge we seek but also acquire a fuller understanding of where and how to look for it.

Though the expectant faith that guides us at the start of our search is in one sense stronger than the faith that marks this stage because it rests on less evidence, the expectant faith that governs the more advanced phase in our investigation is stronger than the faith we have at the beginning, insofar as we now know how to work more efficiently towards our goal and are closer than ever to achieving it. Before long, the cumulative effect of our efforts is bound to set in, such that we may begin to make out the shape of the desired object of our knowledge, that is, the genus of the anomaly.

In the very last step of the inquiry, the new genus is tested as an explanation of the anomaly in an AAA-1 syllogism. This syllogism represents all our efforts to turn the 'negatives' of our knowledge of what the anomaly is not or is not in full into a positive understanding of its generic nature. Through this *via negativa*, the things we already know—which are not what we want to know—are used to speculate about the nature of the object we want to know and so ultimately to come to know it. In sum, the unknowing that characterizes faith is employed to achieve understanding.

Of course, this understanding may become outmoded and require revision as a result of further experiences. Since the law of non-contradiction, so fundamental to Aristotelian logic, only stipulates that one and the same thesis cannot hold both true and false at the same time, however, the possibility of achieving fuller understanding of truth over the course of time does not undermine the truth of earlier claims, assuming they unified all relevant information and were therefore as true as they could have been when they were made.

Actually, it is by testifying to the truth insofar as it can be known at a given time that we achieve the optimal position from which to see when and how our ideas require further revision. In that sense, the truths that turn out to be partial or inferior play an essential truth-bearing function and are not therefore strictly speaking false. In an order where truth takes time to realize—where it is impossible to know what is true for all people, at all places, at all times—in summary, our commitment to the truth consists in doing our best at any given time to testify to the truth while remaining willing to acknowledge when our ideas need to change.[13]

Within the present order, it sometimes proves difficult to identify the middle term that subsumes an anomalous particular under a genus. Although all promising lines of inquiry may be pursued over a long period of time, the sought-for solution may still evade us. The disappointment this outcome tends to engender is considerable, precisely because the work invested in the inquiry to this point renders us more prepared than ever to recognize its solution, and thus more aware of all that is at stake in finding it. Because of this discouragement, our expectant faith may hit a sudden plateau. We may be tempted to think our work was for nothing and to write the inquiry off as a lost cause.

On reaching this point of frustration or even boredom with a problem, it is necessary to give up the will to deal with it, though perhaps not permanently. In seemingly failed inquiries such as I have described, it may be the case that more information, which is not yet available, is needed in order to complete the project at hand. Alternatively, information already available may not be recognizable as relevant for our purposes because we need to grow in other areas of understanding, which would enable us to perceive this relevance. Such obstructions to an inquiry often arise when the definition we are trying to construct rests on other definitions we have not yet constructed, or upon existing definitions that require revision before the definition we are currently seeking can be articulated. In cases like these, the resources needed to deal directly with the problem under consideration simply are not accessible to us, such that we gain nothing but added frustration from trying to address it.

At this point, consequently, it behooves us to step away from the problem with faith that its solution will eventually be found, transferring our attentions to other, though possibly not unrelated, investigations. In this regard, our mental energies must be invested in whatever line of inquiry seems most urgent, most interesting or most important at the time. However unrelated to our initial concern it may appear to be, such an inquiry may have some as yet unrealized bearing on explaining the anomaly.

Since that anomaly can scarcely be forgotten, even if focused efforts to explain it have been temporarily suspended, we tend instinctively to go about further researches differently than we might have done otherwise. We proceed in ways that contribute indirectly to the accumulation of facts relevant to resolving the original problem. In the process, we revise and construct the definitions that are at the background of our initial concern to explain a particular anomaly, and so perhaps without realizing it, gradually achieve a perspective from which to reconsider the nature of the anomaly itself.

Whenever a new discovery seems obviously relevant to this end, consequently, it seems appropriate to pause and add the new information into the mix of resources we previously possessed to reckon with the anomaly to see if it makes a difference to our understanding. Although the new data may enable us to make further progress towards achieving understanding, it may nevertheless not generate a full understanding of the anomaly. When we thus confront again the limits of our knowledge, we must set aside the inquiry once more, returning to other lines of inquiry that seem significant for our knowledge until we make another discovery that is relevant to explaining the anomaly.

In this connection, our focus must be shifted off and back on to the anomaly as many times as it takes to gather all the information relevant to explaining it. Furthermore, our attention must be transferred to as many other areas of study as prove necessary, for as long as seems necessary, eventually to be in a position to provide the relevant explanation. In the case of problems involving a comparatively small number of variables, the moment of discovery may immediately follow an initial period of rest from investigative efforts. Other larger or more fundamental questions may take generations to achieve resolution precisely because there are oftentimes many background issues that need to be resolved before such questions can be addressed.

While it is impossible for this reason to exercise direct control over when or how the solution to a problem is obtained, a sort of indirect control can be exerted over the timing of our discoveries as we undertake the tasks that seem most urgently to demand our attention in the immediate context. At this stage, then, expectant faith is evidenced as we simply do our best to pursue the lines of inquiry that present themselves to us, in the order of priority in which they present themselves, trusting that we will eventually see the fruit of our labor.

The Second Condition: Fulfilled Faith

Paradoxically, insight into the nature of an anomaly tends to arrive when it is least expected; for example, when the inquiry concerning it has been abandoned, when mental energies are focused on another investigation, or in the midst of a simple respite from work. In such unanticipated moments, expectant faith is fulfilled; the 'mode' of the knower expands conceptually to encompass the 'mode of the thing' under consideration.[14] An aspect of reality is grasped that was waiting to be discovered but towards which we had to make our own way through various researches.

When insight into an anomaly's genus is gained in this way, an intellectual gap is spanned between the images of particular things that were entertained prior to the moment of discovery, and the knowledge of their synthesis, which consists in the knowledge of a middle term that categorizes the anomaly under a genus. Though these particulars, including the anomaly, are the basis for the synthesis, nevertheless the synthesis represents more than the mere sum of its parts. For it highlights the meaning of the parts, which cannot be perceived, even immediately prior to the moment of discovery, when all the particulars relevant to the synthesis have been registered but as yet not the synthesis itself.

Whereas expectant faith is placed in this synthesis—which still cannot be perceived—so long as the search for particulars continues, the focus on the synthesis or whole that characterizes fulfilled faith obstructs the explicit consideration of the particulars that constitute it. Thus, it is impossible to attend to the particulars without losing sight of the whole, at least momentarily, in the wake of fulfilled faith. For the two modes of attention, namely, to the parts or to the whole, are mutually exclusive.

As hinted above, therefore, the unplanned moment of discovery that transfigures the particulars in terms of their meaning or synthesis—the parts in terms of the whole—brings about an irreversible paradigm shift in our knowledge. That is not to say that the old and new paradigms are incommensurable, even if they are characterized by radically different points of view.[15] Although an old outlook may be rejected on obtaining a new one, it is precisely the old paradigm, combined with the anomaly that gives rise to the perceived need for a new one, which inducts us into the revised mode of perceiving reality that we utilize in informed faith.[16]

The Third Condition: Informed Faith

As noted above, informed faith is the mode in which ideas achieved in fulfilled faith are allowed to inform or shape our understanding of new experiences in deductive acts of reasoning about those experiences. Strictly speaking, these acts of reasoning are not simply deductive but demonstrative, since they appeal to the genus or nature of a thing in order to explain some aspect or the entirety of its being. In addition to helping us evaluate new objects of experience, the ideas acquired in fulfilled faith may inform our understanding of ideas that already exist in the intellectual memory as well as images in the sense memory that have yet to be scrutinized.

When a new idea comes into contact with such pre-existing ideas and images, it is likely to give rise to new questions concerning them, which must be addressed in the order of priority or urgency in which they present themselves. For example, it may reveal that some images, which formerly fell under our old definition, do not fit under the new one and need to be re-categorized. Other images that were relegated to the depths of the sense memory may suddenly seem to call for further investigation. In these ways and others, the implications of a new idea for our pre-existing knowledge need and wait to be extrapolated.

As a new idea not only calls for us to delineate these implications but also gives us the resources for doing so, it fills us with the potential to 'know more than we know.'[17] Until this potential is actualized with respect to the pre-existing body of our knowledge, there may be contradictions in our knowledge as a result of the introduction of a new idea that frames things differently than we may have understood them previously.[18] To expunge these contradictions until all our views are once again consistent—to avoid error—is one of the tasks of informed faith.[19]

Once accomplished, this task—which is more or less arduous and time-consuming depending on the extent to which a new idea is fundamental to our thinking about other things—affords the optimal position from which to allow a new idea to shape our assessment of further objects of experience. Precisely because we cannot help but see these objects in terms of our pre-existing concepts in the context of informed faith—that is, because we see the objects secondarily or indirectly rather than primarily and directly, as in expectant faith—it is especially crucial at this phase to guard against committing the fallacy of presumption, whereby a concept is projected on to some object as an explanation of it that may not in fact be relevant to rendering the object intelligible.[20]

When the implications of a new idea are extrapolated in a more cautious or unassuming manner, we not only gather understanding of new objects of knowledge, but also fill out the concept by which we understand them. As I will demonstrate in what follows, the concept that enables us to understand our experiences is one we become better able to define and comprehend through those very experiences. In that sense, informed faith is twofold. Through it, a given definition informs our understanding of objects of experience. At the same time, however, our experiences help us to elaborate the definition itself, such that our understanding of both our experiences and the definition grows proportionally.

With regard to the definition itself, such growth in understanding is important, because the idea acquired in fulfilled faith is initially only the idea of a genus, to which differentia must be added if a full-blown definition is to be procured. The process of identifying differentia turns upon employing a concept to inform our understanding of empirical objects in demonstrative syllogisms. By these means, we acquire knowledge of what might be described as the explanatory powers or 'effects' of our concept.[21]

Although the knowledge of a concept's effects naturally does not constitute direct knowledge of a genus' differentia, since it only entails indirect knowledge of its explanatory powers, it cumulatively provides a basis for identifying differentia. As in expectant faith, so in this context, the aforementioned demonstrations produce conclusions that can be reduced to first-figure EAE (universal/negative) or AII (universal/particular) syllogisms, which respectively indicate what a differentia is not or some aspect of what it involves.

As in expectant faith, the accumulation of such 'negative' or indirect insights into a genus' features, which is mediated by those things that the genus renders intelligible or 'demonstrates,' may eventually afford sufficient grounds for drawing an inductive conclusion about one or more of the differentia that should be attached to the genus. Though informed faith is primarily characterized by demonstrative reasoning, consequently, it intermittently employs inductive reasoning for its ends, just as expectant faith, which primarily functions in the inductive mode, routinely uses the powers of demonstration to test hypotheses.

This suggests that informed like expectant faith involves its own sort of dialectical interplay between deductive and inductive reasoning. Through inductive reasoning, for instance, the differences are derived that allow us to offer the fullest possible definition of a thing. Through deductive, or better, demonstrative reasoning, conversely, the definition we have developed is actually brought to bear in understanding particular entities. In this connection, it is worth noting that while definitions can demonstrate the nature of other objects, they cannot be demonstrated themselves. Precisely because they are the means by which other things are demonstrated, they are not the objects of demonstrative but inductive reasoning.[22]

Once the difference of a genus has been identified by the means described above, it becomes possible to test the more elaborate definition that results as an explanation or demonstration of the things that it defines. While demonstrations in general may take the form of any figure, they must assume the form of an AAA-1 syllogism that is universal and affirmative on all counts in this case, that is, if they are to confirm the legitimacy of the differences we have proposed to add to a definition. After all, definitions apply to all instances of the thing defined, and only AAA demonstrations refer to all such instances.

In adding a difference to a genus and testing it as an explanation of particulars along these lines, we engage in the process that Aristotle calls 'increasing' or 'thickening' the middle term of the demonstration in question. The middle terms that are added or increased through this process are interchangeable with the differences that are added to the genus.[23] As noted in Chapter 3, the process of thickening the middle term may go on as long as differences remain to be discovered, or details about the nature of the object of definition wait to be elaborated, in the inductive manner described above.

As mentioned in the same chapter, the middle term is fully thickened when every single step or middle term that mediates between the genus and the class of particulars has been delineated, that is, when the class of particulars has been rendered completely intelligible or defined in the fullest sense of the term. In syllogistic form, a fully thickened demonstration might be outlined as follows:

All A is B
All B is C
All C is D
All D is E
All E is A

In the above, the terms B, C, D, and E each represent one of the differences that might be attached to a definition in order to complete it. According to the rules for formulating definitions set out in the last chapter, the difference that comes first should include those that follow, which do not in turn entail the difference that entails them. Where the scope of A and E is wide, and there are many middle terms intervening between these two terms, it bears re-iterating that it can take a long time to thicken the middle term. For it presumably takes time to discover each term, which in turn presupposes the time involved in accumulating enough knowledge of a definition's effects to induce that term.

The thickening process can be further prolonged insofar as it is possible to come to the realization, ordinarily on identifying a new difference, that differences previously identified are improperly ordered. When middle terms are affirmed in a premature or belated manner, for example, the nature of the reality in question cannot help but be misconstrued in some respect. On realizing this error, consequently, it is essential to initiate a process of trial and error, inserting the middle terms or known differences in different premises of the sorites, until determining exactly where they logically or immediately follow and are followed. As I showed in Chapter 3, the accuracy of a definition hangs heavily on the proper ordering of its differential properties.

Another hindrance to the successful completion of the thickening process may arise when a particular term is discovered not to belong within a sorites and thus the definition overall. This can happen when an accidental or even essential property is confused with a differential one. Insofar as we neglect to remove these misplaced terms and reconfigure the sorites accordingly, we will not only be unable to identify the terms that remain to be inserted between A and E, but we may also posit additional middle terms that do not actually intervene between A and E in reality; in short, we may fabricate an imaginary reality. Despite the challenges inherent in thickening the middle term, however, the process is not impossible to complete and cannot go on interminably.[24] For A and E again set boundaries on the scope of the inquiry that limit the number of differentia that must be identified.[25]

Although it is possible to complete the project of thickening the middle term, it should not be assumed that knowledge is attained by these means that is true once and for all. At any moment, new evidence may be encountered that overthrows old assumptions, however firmly established, thus resetting the very terms or boundaries of our thinking. By confirming that the middle term may be fully thickened, therefore, I only suggest that a demonstration or definition may be developed that is as thorough as it possibly could be according to the terms of our present thinking. As I mentioned already, this is all that can be required of us when it comes to testifying to the truth, namely, that we do the best we can with the information that is available to us at a given time, remaining open to adjusting our ideas as soon as we receive new information.

On achieving a fully thickened middle term, we simultaneously acquire a full-blown definition of the type of object the demonstration in question demonstrates. As I have suggested, the process of obtaining such a fully elaborated demonstration or definition turns from beginning to end on efforts to allow the definition to inform our understanding of particular objects. These efforts fill out our definition, which in turn gives us a better understanding of particulars, such that the accuracy of both the demonstration and the definition increase in proportion.

Since the process of defining involves the repeated use of a concept, a persistent habit or skill of thinking about reality in the light of this definition can hardly help but be cultivated in the course of pursuing the definition in its final form.[26] Similar to any skill, that of demonstrating is one we can generally only perform rather falteringly at first—particularly since the definition by which we demonstrate has yet to be elaborated fully—but at which we improve with practice, which again fills out the very definition that enables us to improve our demonstrations.[27]

As we cultivate a habit of employing a particular definition or truth to unify our experiences—and so elevate it to an ever more unifying role in our knowing, where it informs most if not all of our cognitive operations—we are bound to gain a greater sense of the relevance or goodness of that truth to our cognitive concerns.[28] In that sense, the ongoing use of a concept is an indicator of its perceived usefulness for knowing the things we want to know. Put differently, it is a sign of our certainty regarding that truth's power or value for unifying or making sense of our experiences, that is, rendering them intelligible.[29]

While the definitions we continually use are the ones we ultimately memorize how to use, such that they automatically inform our knowledge of all things, we often ultimately lose the concepts we do not regularly use, in much the same way that we tend to forfeit skills we neglect to employ on a regular basis. Since those truths we do not use and in which we consequently place little confidence practically fall out of usage and so on some level fall out of existence altogether, there is a sense in which truth simply consists in the perceived value of an idea, which corresponds to its actual level of usage. That is by no means to imply that truth is subjective, or that all truths are equally viable.

By this account, truth is subjective or relative precisely because some truths are not as viable as others relative to efforts on the part of particular individuals or societies at particular places and times to account for a given state of affairs. For this reason, it is necessary in every situation to exercise judgment as to which truth best serves to explain or resolve a specific state of affairs. The truths that do this less effectively are less true in the circumstances. This does not mean that the truths that prove irrelevant in immediate circumstances are completely useless or untrue, however. For the law of non-contradiction only indicates that one and the same tenet cannot hold both true and false at the same time, and in the same respect.

On these grounds, the potential truth or utility of concepts that are not immediately true for us can be affirmed for other persons or at other places and times. All the same, the verification of truth in the immediate circumstances can be said to consist in the extent of a truth's use to understand other objects. Thus, the truths that are most true and certain—the ones in which we place the greatest degree of informed faith—are the ones that automatically inform everything we do, such that everything we do reinforces our understanding of those truths. Ironically, then, the truths about which we are most informed are the ones we no longer need to think about consciously, insofar as we apply them as a matter of habit.

Informed vs Uninformed Faith

There are two ways to 'work without thinking' about the truths in light of which we think, or the definitions by which we demonstrate. One way involves obtaining definitions of our own accord in expectant and fulfilled faith and elaborating them fully by using them in informed faith, to the point that it is no longer necessary to think about them consciously in order to use them. The other way is that of what I call 'uninformed faith,' in which we bypass the phases of expectant and fulfilled faith and simply appropriate our definitions from others, imitating how they use those definitions without really understanding the meaning or significance of what we do.[30]

In both informed and uninformed faith, we lack direct vision of the definitions by which we know, insofar as we use them to draw deductive conclusions about other objects of inquiry. That is to say, our faith is blind. In the case of informed faith, however, knowledge or vision is presupposed. On account of our previous efforts to acquire a definition, we possess what Aristotle calls 'knowledge-what' it is that we know, which is accompanied by 'knowledge-why' it is the way it is. In uninformed faith, by contrast, we possess only 'knowledge-that' something is the case, which does not entail the other two forms of knowledge. For this reason, uninformed lines of reasoning cannot strictly speaking be referred to as demonstrations; they are mere deductions.

The difference between knowledge-what/why and knowledge-that—or between informed and uninformed faith—is the difference between what Chapter 3 referred to as real and nominal definitions. As I explained in that context, we all start out to some extent with uninformed faith—or nominal definitions—as new learners of a language or indeed as novices in any field of inquiry. While the acquisition of such definitions is a necessary condition for obtaining real definitions, it is not a sufficient condition. The problem is that nominal definitions can seem deceptively similar to real definitions. This similarity can lead to the mistaken conclusion that we have completed our defining work as soon as we have acquired nominal definitions, when in fact we have only been conditioned to react to or think about the world in conventional ways, such that our intellectual lives are more a matter of trained instinct than conscious deliberation.

As suggested previously, the search for real definitions is important, insofar as it transforms knowledge-that into knowledge-what, accidental into necessary truths, nominal into real definitions, which have been arrived at through our own efforts. The reason it is crucial to do our own work along these lines is that the question whether or not we have done so bears directly on whether and how we are able to use our knowledge.

In this section, my purpose is to explain the significant difference it makes to be informed or uninformed about our definitions—to know what we are talking about. Aquinas identifies eight respects in which something like informed faith enhances knowledge.[31] These pertain to the use of reason, the acquisition of insights, to memory, foresight, shrewdness, or a capacity for self-instruction, docility or receptivity to teaching and correction, circumspection, or sensitivity to the demands that circumstances place on the way we use our knowledge, and caution with respect to the truth claims we advance and accept. In what follows, I will contrast informed and uninformed faith in these respects.

The notion of 'using reason' to which Aquinas refers in the first place underlines the fact that informed faith trades on definitions we have obtained through our own intellectual labor in expectant faith. The use of reason therefore entails the 'acquisition of insights' in fulfilled faith.[32] The 'memory' that the use of reason to achieve insight forms in our minds as to how we obtained the insight in the first place is extremely important. For the ability to demonstrate how we gained knowledge by retaining a memory of the process that generated it not only predisposes us to repeat that process in other situations but also to apply our knowledge under new conditions, in which variables may have changed.

In this connection, memory instills 'foresight,' through which we are prepared to recognize when new and unfamiliar circumstances call for an as yet untried and perhaps more complicated application of a definition.[33] In turn, foresight fosters 'shrewdness,' or a disposition independently to acquire new understanding.[34] On account of this disposition, we possess the conceptual resources needed to inquire into and comprehend new fields of study. Indeed, a shrewd mind can often grasp the layout of a subject area and identify how to navigate it efficiently and effectively, even in the absence of formal training.[35]

Though informed faith enables us to teach ourselves, it also instills in us a teachable or 'docile' spirit. In fact, the independence of mind associated with shrewdness is frequently attributable to a willingness to be corrected by others or through new encounters with reality.[36] For the informed, therefore, the impossibility of capturing all truth is far from a cause for living in denial of this impossibility or for despairing of the very possibility of knowledge. Rather, it represents a reason for remaining open to new discoveries and thereby maintaining a sense of wonder at the world, the knowledge of which can seemingly never be exhausted.

A teachable spirit not only disposes us to discern where our ideas need to be adjusted if we are to keep apace of new developments or discoveries. It also helps us to teach or communicate ideas to others operating in different contexts. The art of being adaptable along these lines entails 'circumspection.'[37] In the first place, the ability to be taught is a necessary condition for teaching, because it renders us sensitive to the needs and interests of others, thus enabling us to perceive how to instruct or convey lines of argumentation to them in ways with which they can identify and which they may find compelling.

According to Aristotle, the persuasiveness of an argument is dependent upon three factors: the character and credentials of the speaker (*ethos*); the psychology and concerns/emotions of the audience (*pathos*); and the coherence of the argument itself (*logos*).[38] In order to capture the imagination of an audience, consequently, we must adjust the manner in which we present our arguments and indeed our own self-presentation in order to ensure that our listeners have no reason related to the aforementioned factors not to embrace sound lines of reasoning.

In addition to fostering effective teaching, circumspection enables us to mediate between individuals or parties that may find it difficult to communicate with one another. As indicated in the last chapter, there are in theory many different ways of referring to one and the same concept, and one and the same word can be assigned different meanings in different contexts. Under these circumstances, the ability quickly to adapt to the way different parties use language can help us perceive the real definitions they presuppose and consequently discern where they do and do not disagree about different issues.

Although the open-mindedness fostered by docility and circumspection is crucial to informed faith, it must be counterbalanced by due 'caution' with respect to what is true.[39] There are three main ways of falling short in this regard. The first way turns on a presumption of entitlement to fabricate ideas as to what is true, which may lead to throwing off any responsibility to respond to reality. The second is to adhere dogmatically to narrow-minded notions about the truth. While this approach may not appear incautious at first glance, closed-mindedness nonetheless severs ties with the truth insofar as it prevents the recognition of challenges to personal opinions, not to mention the truth of other perspectives. In short, it is in-cautious with respect to what is true because it is over-cautious regarding what is true.

The third way trades on the conclusion that there is no way to know what is true, given the existence of diverse and even conflicting truth claims and the way the knowledge of truth develops at both the individual and collective levels. On these grounds, the further conclusion is often drawn that all ideas of truth are equal, such that all persons should be permitted to believe what they like. As mentioned above, the problem with this perspective is that ideas of truth do not all exhibit the same degree of truth, or any truth at all, relative to particular states of affairs.

Those that promote tolerance for all truths therefore undercut the possibility of discriminating amongst competing ideas about what is true and so render it impossible to discern what is most true relative to the circumstances. Although their excessive tolerance may seem compatible at first glance with authentic open-mindedness, it ultimately generates an attitude of closed-mindedness towards all views of truth except the one according to which there can be no view about what is true.

By contrast to the three approaches or attitudes mentioned above, true open-mindedness entails a commitment to the ongoing task of adjudicating as to what is true in every single instance. This commitment turns on a refusal to affirm that there is truth where truth is lacking, or to deny that there is truth, where truth can be found. It requires that we live constantly in the uncomfortable throes of expectant, fulfilled, and informed faith through which our understanding of what is true is continually revised.

Because the search for truth is arduous and ongoing, it should come as no surprise that many try to circumnavigate it in one of the three ways described above. In those who are prepared to rise to the challenge of pursuing truth, however, caution counterbalances any inordinate desire to be persuasive or self-promoting, preventing docility and circumspection from overtaking the effort to advance sound arguments that are the product of using reason to gain insights which are stored in the memory, where they foster foresight and shrewdness. As such, caution acts as the guarantor of the other seven features of informed faith.

By this point in the argument, it should be fairly plain to see why these eight aspects of informed faith tend to be lacking in uninformed faith. After all, using reason is precisely what we fail to do when we adopt our definitions unquestionably and even unwittingly, simply by being inducted into a whole way of doing things—and a language—which is perhaps imposed upon us or modeled before us by others, on whose authority we base our lives.

Though we may possess knowledge-that 'this is the way things are done' in uninformed faith, we can scarcely be said to have acquired true insight into the objects of our knowledge and their importance. For we lack a memory of the patterns of reasoning that led to our conclusions concerning them, which can only be acquired through personal efforts exerted in expectant and fulfilled faith. Insofar as we bypass these efforts, any claims we make which successfully describe the nature or importance of things can only be described as accidentally true.[40]

When we lack the standard of right reasoning, which consists in a memorized pattern of reasoning, we may additionally find it difficult to reproduce our conclusions, particularly if we are forced to work independently. Moreover, we may prove deficient in the foresight that is needed to determine how to apply ideas in new and perhaps more challenging cases. Where all the normal variables are not in place, we may not even recognize a situation as one that calls for the application of a particular concept. Because our ideas are the product of indoctrination rather than conscious deliberation, we may also find it difficult to teach ourselves new subjects, which is quite a different skill from that of accumulating information to bolster preconceived notions that have been uncritically adopted.

Though uninformed faith generally renders us adept at this skill, it is precisely by exercising it that we tend to cultivate the mindset that our way of thinking is the only right way. This attitude renders us unreceptive to teaching and correction, even, or especially, albeit ironically, where there are shortcomings in our own outlook. As a result of this attitude, consequently, we may go so far as to block out information that challenges our preconceived notions or fabricate evidence that corroborates them.

The resistance to instruction that results from uninformed faith further fosters an unwillingness or inability to teach others effectively. After all, we cannot explain the rationale behind our conclusions if we lack an understanding of that rationale. We can only impress upon others conclusions we ourselves have been indoctrinated to affirm, without explaining why they are warranted or how they have been reached, thus perpetuating our own dogmatism.

In cases where we are called upon to communicate with those who may not share our views or who may speak about shared views in different forms of words, uninformed faith additionally prevents us from understanding the ideas of others and explaining our own ideas on their terms. Thus, it hinders our ability to discern whether or not we agree with our interlocutors on fundamental issues and resultantly polarizes individuals or groups in ways that often terminate in the total breakdown of communication. As this confirms, communication difficulties do not normally arise because other minds are in principle inaccessible. Rather, they are the consequence of unwillingness on the part of one person or party to learn the terms on which other persons or parties communicate, and engage with them accordingly.

Because we tend as rational animals to desire to be able to give reasons for our beliefs, uninformed faith further renders us susceptible to devising reasons for our conclusions that do not strictly speaking count as reasons at all. In this connection, we may turn by default to one of the logically fallacious forms of reasoning I mentioned in the last chapter, and especially to one or another of the fallacies of relevance, such as appeals to popular opinion, authority, emotions, force, and so on, or to the fallacies of presumption, which include begging the question, circular reasoning, and so forth.

While uninformed faith may lead us to offer such 'reasons' in support of our claims, it also renders us vulnerable to accept these reasons as grounds for assenting to the claims of others. In short, uninformed faith produces naïve and uncritical thinkers, who accept the truth of arguments for reasons that have nothing to do with their truth, even reasons to do with the validity or logical rigor of arguments. As this suggests, uninformed faith renders us deficient in the caution that is needed to know the truth. In order to avoid the pitfalls of uninformed faith, consequently, it is necessary to delineate the conditions that make it possible to sustain the pursuit of truth through expectant, fulfilled and informed faith. This will be the task of the following chapter.

Endnotes

¹   S.H. Mellone makes a similar albeit less fully-developed argument in his *Elements of Modern Logic* (London: University Tutorial Press, 1945), iii: 'the syllogism, the distinctive form of inference derived by Aristotle from his analysis of propositions, is [quoting W.E. Johnson] "practically important" because it represents the form in which persons unschooled in logical technique are continually arguing; it is theoretically important because it exhibits in their simplest guise the fundamental principles which underlie all demonstration whether inductive or deductive.' As Mellone re-affirms later in his work, 'the syllogism is a form in which we actually do reason' (178).

²   As Peter Geach writes in *Reason and Argument* (Oxford: Blackwell, 1976), xi: 'the discipline of thought ... is attainable in practice only by using a modicum of formal logic.'

³   On the three stages of inquiry as Aristotle describes them, see David Charles, *Aristotle on Meaning and Essence* (Oxford: Oxford University Press, 2003).

⁴   On tacit knowledge, see Michael Polanyi, *Personal Knowledge: A Post-Critical Philosophy* (Chicago: University of Chicago Press, 1974). See also Polanyi's *The Tacit Dimension* (Chicago: University of Chicago Press, repr. 2009).

⁵   Alasdair MacIntyre, 'Truth as a Good: A Reflection on *Fides et Ratio*,' in *The Tasks of Philosophy* (Cambridge: Cambridge University Press, 2006), 206: Aquinas has 'a conception of the mind as standing in more or less adequate relationships to those realities about which it judges.'

⁶   *ST* 1.85.5.

⁷   In *APo.* II.1–2, Aristotle refers to four possible kinds of question: if something is, that it is, what it is, and why it is.

⁸   By appealing to expectant faith, consequently, we can resolve the paradox presented in Plato's *Meno* 80e; cf. *APo.* I.1, 71a25–30. According to this paradox, we cannot search either for what we know or for what we do not know. We cannot search for what we know, because there is no need to search for knowledge we already possess. Conversely, we cannot search for what we do not know, because we do not know that for which we are looking.

⁹   See Plato's *Thaetetus* and Augustine's *Confessions*, book 10.

¹⁰   On conversion, obversion, and contraposition, see note 12 in Chapter 3.

¹¹   Here, I am roughly following the seven steps of the scientific method that Aristotle outlines in *Prior Analytics*: 1. Identify a problem; 2. Formulate a preliminary hypothesis or tentative solution; 3. Collect additional relevant facts; 4. Formulate another explanatory hypothesis; 5. Deduce its consequences; 6. Test its consequences; 7. Provided the test is successful, apply the theory.

¹² On what it means to 'save the appearances,' see G.E.L. Owen, *'Tithenai ta phainomena,'* in *Logic, Science, and Dialectic* (London: Duckworth, 1986), 239–51.

¹³ See a relevant article by Alasdair MacIntyre, entitled, 'First Principles, Final Ends, and Contemporary Philosophical Issues,' *The Tasks of Philosophy* (Cambridge: Cambridge University Press, 2006), 167: MacIntyre reconfirms that the question regarding what is true can never be closed in time, both on account of changes in circumstances and the developing nature of our knowledge of circumstances.

¹⁴ Patrick Byrne, *Analysis and Science in Aristotle* (Albany: State University of New York Press, 1997), 121: at the initial moment of intuiting a principle—the moment of fulfilled faith—we 'hit upon a single, undifferentiated middle that intelligibly connects A to B.'

¹⁵ On this point, see Alasdair MacIntyre, *Whose Justice, Which Rationality* (London: Duckworth, 1998), 356.

¹⁶ Alsadair MacIntyre, 'Epistemological Crises, Dramatic Narrative, and the Philosophy of Science,' *The Tasks of Philosophy* (Cambridge: Cambridge University Press, 2006), 5.

¹⁷ *APo.* I.1, 71a; cf. *ST* 1.85.3.

¹⁸ *ST* 1.85.6. See also Peter Geach, *Reason and Argument*, 6, in a chapter on 'Consistency' (pages 6–10): 'if we tolerate inconsistency in the thought we harbor and pass on to others, some of those thoughts will be false—will be at odds with the way things are in the world.'

¹⁹ According to William James, avoiding error is just one of two different 'ways of looking at our duty in the matter of opinion—ways entirely different, and yet ways about whose difference the theory of knowledge seems hitherto to have shown very little concern.' On James' account, these two approaches do not represent identical means of seeking knowledge. Rather, they are two separable methods, 'and by choosing between them, we may end by coloring differently our whole intellectual life. We may regard the chase for truth as paramount, and the avoidance of error as secondary; or we may, on the other hand, treat the avoidance of error as more imperative, and let truth take its chance.' Although efforts to avoid error which are proper to informed faith are essential and are rightly given priority in many circumstances, James writes that there are other cases in which 'the risk of being in error is a very small matter when compared with the blessings of real knowledge, [such that we should] be ready to be duped many times in our investigation rather than postpone indefinitely the chance of guessing true,' through the pursuit of what the present chapter terms 'expectant faith.' See William James, 'The Will to Believe,' in *Pragmatism and Other Writings* (London: Penguin, 2000), section VII.

²⁰ *SE* I.5.

²¹ *ST* 1.12.11.

²² *APo.* II.3ff.

23   Ibid.

24   *APo.* I.20.

25   *APo.* I.22. In *The Arts of the Beautiful* (Dalkey, 2009), medievalist Etienne Gilson outlines a number of criteria for determining when a work of art has been completed, which might also be employed in an analogous way to identify when a middle term has been fully thickened. On Gilson's account, a 'work is finished when it has completely annulled in the artist the need to produce it' (103). As Gilson elaborates, this point is reached not only when the artist stops thinking of features to add to the work of art but also when attempts to improve or alter it only seem to detract from its beauty. That said, he acknowledges that it can take time for an artist to realize that the product of ongoing efforts does in fact satisfy an original desire to produce a work of art. At the moment of completion, for example, the artist may not be completely satisfied with the work or may sense that there is more that could be done to it, or that it could have been done differently. This sense of dissatisfaction may motivate attempts to undertake the project anew. As Gilson notes, however, the artist who has fulfilled an initial creative desire will find that these attempts do not improve the work. Thus, the creative process terminates when the artist or author realizes that it 'really was that work and no other that he wanted to create' (104). On reflecting on this work in the last analysis, consequently, the artist comes to feel 'not necessarily that it is a masterpiece but that after all it is such as he wished it to be, but, for whatever it may be worth, the work is done' (104).

26   Since the search for a definition is 'largely promoted by an acquaintance with its properties' (*DA* I.1, 402b22; cf. *ST* 1.85.4) as Aristotle puts it, such a definition ultimately makes us 'able to give an account conformable to the experience of all or most of the properties of a substance … [and thus to be] in the most favorable position to say something worth saying about the essential nature of that subject' (*DA* I.1, 402b22–25).

27   As Aristotle writes, 'the things we have to learn before we can do, we learn by doing' (*EN* II.1, 1103a32). According to Aquinas, a habit of acting in a certain way subsists midway between a power and an act not only because habits must be formed by actions but also because the only evidence for the existence of a habit can be derived from its actualization (ST 1.2.49).

28   *De Veritate* 21.3.

29   As Aquinas notes in *De Veritate* 21.1, being, truth, and goodness, not to mention unity, are convertible concepts, which are only distinguished conceptually. In the intellectual context, the knowledge of truth is the good of the intellect, which presupposes the unifying capacity of the intellect.

30   The distinction between informed and uninformed faith corresponds roughly to Aristotle's distinction between 'science' and 'opinion' (*APo.* I.33).

31   Aquinas refers to these as the eight 'integral parts' of prudence.

32   *ST* 2.2.49.1, 2, 5.

33 *ST* 2.2.49.6.

34 *ST* 2.2.49.4.

35 Dorothy Sayers, *The Lost Tools of Learning* (London: Meuthen, 1948): 'the tools of learning are the same, in any and every subject; and the person who knows how to use them will, at any age, get the mastery of a new subject in half the time and with a quarter of the effort expended by the person who has not the tools at his command. To learn six subjects without remembering how they were learnt does nothing to ease the approach to a seventh; to have learnt and remembered the art of learning makes the approach to every subject an open door.'

36 *ST* 2.2.49.3.

37 *ST* 2.2.49.7.

38 See Aristotle's *Rhet.* I.2, 1356a.

39 *ST* 2.2.49.8.

40 *APo.* I.9, 76a4–5: 'we understand a thing non-accidentally when we know it in virtue of that in virtue of which it belongs, from the principles of that thing as a thing.'

Chapter 5

Rationality

In Chapter 4, I argued that human understanding remains constantly subject to development through expectant, fulfilled, and informed faith. Since it is consequently impossible to formulate concepts that are true for all persons, at all places, at all times, it would also seem to be impossible to meet the standard of rationality or objectivity that has predominated in many schools of modern thought. In this chapter, therefore, my purpose will be to explain the sense in which knowledge as previously described is compatible with human rationality. In offering this explanation, I will discuss rationality in a way that emphasizes the essential role the will plays in the work of the mind or intellect.

As I will show in the first section of this chapter, the will cooperates with the intellect at each of the three phases of inquiry, motivating the intellect to do whatever it takes to testify to the truth at a given time. The collaboration of intellect and will along these lines is signaled by the concept of faith, inasmuch as faith implies the involvement of both the mind that pursues knowledge and the will that desires to possess knowledge. In order to accomplish the joint purpose of intellect and will, namely, to testify to the truth as it is accessible though experience, it is necessary to explain the conditions that allow for the possibility of sensory experience, that is, to give an account of the embodied nature of human knowledge.

This account can be provided by appealing to what Aquinas and other pre-modern thinkers called the 'passions' (from the Latin *passio*). Though we tend today to speak more commonly of 'feelings' or 'emotions' than of 'passions,' it bears noting that the terms are not entirely interchangeable. Whereas feelings and emotions tend to be conceived as irrational inner forces, the passions represent 'judgments of value'[1] about the objects of experience that register the significance of those objects to the purposes of the intellect and will and are in that sense wholly compatible with, and indeed indispensable to, human rationality.[2]

Although the purpose of the passions is to induct the intellect and will into the truth, the passions may also undermine the pursuit of truth and foster various 'intellectual vices,' or logically fallacious patterns of reasoning. In this perverted form, I contend, the passions are more accurately referred to as 'dis-passions.'[3]

In order to counteract the intellectual vices such dis-passions produce, I subsequently argue that the intellect, will, and passions require a resource for remaining responsible in the pursuit of truth.

In a development of Aquinas' famous discussion of the four cardinal virtues—which is at once a contribution to contemporary literature on 'virtue epistemology'—I submit that these virtues of prudence, justice, fortitude, and temperance can be construed as the means through which the three aforementioned faculties are held accountable to the truth; in short, they can be characterized as intellectual as well as moral virtues.[4] These four intellectual virtues can be distinguished from the three intellectual virtues of wisdom, science, and art, which I mentioned in Chapter 2, insofar as the former facilitate the pursuit of knowledge while the latter represent types of ability for pursuing knowledge. Thus, I will refer to wisdom, science, and art as the 'knowledge-type intellectual virtues,' by contrast to prudence, justice, fortitude, and temperance, which I describe as 'knowledge-generating intellectual virtues.'

Together, the four knowledge-generating virtues render us rational in the three contexts of wisdom, science, or art—in ways that will be explored at the end of the chapter—inasmuch as they predispose the intellect, will, and passions to account for our experiences and adapt our views in ways that may become necessary as a result of new experiences. At an initial level, for example, prudence holds the intellect accountable to testify to the nature of reality, insofar as it is accessible to our knowledge. The justice of the will motivates the intellect to do exactly this, such that prudence and justice, while logically distinguishable, operate as interdependently as the intellect and will themselves. They accomplish their joint task of facilitating the collaborative effort of the intellect and will to pursue truth through the aid of two further virtues associated with the passions. The first of these virtues, fortitude, is the virtue that gives us the strength to face the challenges involved in prioritizing the pursuit of truth over all other considerations. Implicitly, then, fortitude helps us overcome the difficulties that might keep us from doing this.

The second virtue, temperance, teaches us to derive pleasure primarily from ordering our passions towards the pursuit of truth. In this way, it prevents the passions from becoming excessively preoccupied with interests that are not particularly relevant to the pursuit of truth and which would therefore detract from that pursuit. To sum up: fortitude and temperance enable us to follow through on the purposes of prudence and justice as they respectively fill us with the courage and discipline to do just this. Insofar as they enable the work of prudence and justice, I will argue that these virtues of the passions, which are not intellectual virtues strictly speaking, may be described as intellectual virtues 'by participation.'

Although the aforementioned intellectual virtues do not render us rational in the sense that they enable us to capture thoughts of things that are universally and infallibly true, it is worth noting that such thoughts would in any case be impossible to formulate, precisely because our knowledge is embodied and therefore subject to the diversity that characterizes different embodied beings and to the developments that become necessary as a result of embodied experience and embodied life.[5] In that light, any conception of rationality that denies the exigencies of embodied knowing might seem implicitly to construe rationality as merely a matter of the intellect that achieves understanding in fulfilled faith, rather than an effort of the intellect that is guided by the will in expectant and informed faith to formulate thoughts in keeping with input provided by the passions, which fluctuate with persons and experience.

By re-construing rationality in terms of the intellectually virtuous intellect, will, and passions, in contrast, the account developed in this chapter defensibly provides a more 'rational' definition of rationality. This definition is consistent with the essence of the reality being defined, namely, the human being that is both rational and animal, to wit, embodied. Though such a 'faculty psychology,' which appeals to the intellect, will, and passions, has been accused of positing a 'ghost in the machine,' that is, a set of mental equipment that operates over and above the life of the rational animal, my summary of this chapter in the introduction, as well as the chapter itself, establish that the three faculties are not real or independently existing entities which call into question the embodied nature of the mind's work. To the contrary, they are logical constructions, which enable us to explain the conditions for the possibility of pursuing knowledge in the context of embodied life.

In an ultimate sense, however, the intellectual virtues that sustain rationality as I construe it are moral virtues first and foremost. Thus, I will contend in concluding this chapter that human rationality culminates when the intellectual virtues are cultivated for the sake of cultivating moral virtue, that is, when knowledge is pursued for purposes that are compatible with rather than contrary to our being and becoming what we are as 'rational animals.' Though there is obviously a degree of rationality to be achieved at the purely epistemological level, namely through intellectual virtue, it is only when moral virtue is achieved that we can be described as 'rational' in the fullest sense in the term.[6] On these grounds, I conclude that moral virtue is the final arbiter of rationality—a claim I will develop in Chapter 7.

Intellect and Will

In the two preceding chapters I focused on describing the work of the intellect—also called mind or in some cases 'theoretical' or 'speculative' reason.[7] As a result, I may have given the impression that the intellect carries out the process of cognition entirely on its own. In this section, however, I will demonstrate that the will plays a vital role in facilitating the intellect's operation.[8] At the outset of this discussion, I will briefly review Chapter 3's account of the way the intellect operates when it engages in inductive and deductive acts of reasoning. When reasoning inductively, for instance, the mind seeks insight or understanding in the form of complex apprehensions; in reasoning deductively, by contrast, it employs such apprehensions to draw conclusions about various objects of knowledge.[9] In both cases, it pursues and ultimately perceives truth that is the product of a valid line of reasoning. As such, the first principle of the intellect's work is the law of non-contradiction, which posits that a conclusion cannot be both true and untrue at the same time.

As mentioned previously, a prolonged effort is often required in order to acquire understanding in induction and to apply it in deduction. In this light, it would appear that the success of reason's work presupposes the operation of yet another faculty, which propels the mind to acquire and apply knowledge over the course of time. This faculty is the will or 'intellectual appetite.'[10] Whereas the intellect is concerned with ends, or the conclusions that result from inquiry, the will is preoccupied with devising appropriate means to the end of achieving or applying the knowledge of truth.[11] Thus, its work concerns 'things-to-be-done' to the end of achieving understanding as opposed to 'things thought,' as is the case with the intellect.[12]

Although the will is the means, that is, middle term, finding faculty of the rational animal, it nevertheless has access to the results of inductive and deductive reasoning in virtue of its cooperation with the intellect.[13] While the intellect alone can perform the actual work of reasoning in both ways, consequently the conclusions or universal concepts the intellect seeks to generate or has generated respectively give the will an end to aim for in induction—a motivation, as it were—as well as a basis for drawing conclusions in deduction. When it comes to exercising rationality at the epistemological level, in summary, the will and the intellect are mutually interdependent.[14]

Because the role of the will is to find means to the ends of inquiry, it is primarily concerned with the particular entities that are needed to devise ways of acquiring or applying principles. In fact, the whole purpose of the will in this context is to compel the intellect to account for such particulars by forming ideas about them in induction or applying ideas to gain understanding of particulars in deduction. Thus, we will see later in the chapter that the will or intellectual appetite is closely linked with the passions, which register the relevance or significance of particular objects to our cognitive purposes, thus informing the will how to direct the intellect in accordance with those purposes.

An account of the will's role in motivating the intellect to testify to the truth can be helpfully elaborated with reference to the notion of natural law. As I have noted, this law requires all beings, including human beings, to strive for the good, or, better, the best, and avoid evil or the privation of the good in accordance with their abilities.[15] Just as the proper object of the intellect is the truth, so, consequently, the proper object of the will is the good. Though the notion of a natural law is most obviously relevant in the ontological, moral, and legal spheres, it can also be said to sustain the will's search for the best possible means to accounting for the truth, which is itself captured by the intellect. So construed, the natural law is the will's counterpart to reason's law of non-contradiction.

In many medieval accounts, including that of Aquinas, a disposition called *synderesis* holds the will accountable to fulfill the natural law.[16] According to Aquinas, *synderesis* is an instinctual or habitual disposition, which cannot as such be altogether lost.[17] Though this habit prevents the will from erring or failing to strive for the highest good, which is the truth in cases concerning human knowledge, it is not inconceivable for the will to grow confused as to that in which the good of knowing truth consists, such that it opts for a lesser good, which may not prove to be good at all—or true—in a given situation.[18] This confusion occurs at the level of the conscience, which applies the universal stricture of *synderesis* to particular cases, binding the will to perform certain acts, accusing the will or filling it with remorse when it commits misguided acts, or defending the will when its acts, however appropriate, are called into question.[19]

There are two ways in which the conscience can err about what is genuinely good or right to do with respect to the pursuit of truth.[20] Since the universal mandate of *synderesis* to achieve what is best can only be applied in particular cases through some more specific universal judgment about what it means to do what is best in those cases, it is possible to make a mistake about the more specific universal that applies to a particular case. It is also possible to fail to see that certain particulars fall under a given universal judgment; this failure can lead to regarding privations of the good that is the knowledge of truth as good. Because it is possible for the conscience to become detached from *synderesis* in these ways, *synderesis* may be inhibited until it is ultimately obliterated in practice.[21]

When the will habitually answers to *synderesis*, by contrast, it motivates the intellect to offer the best available account of the truth. In thus following the natural law, the will places the intellect in the optimal position to adhere to the law of non-contradiction and indeed prevents reason from breaking that law. This is something reason is naturally liable to do, since it is primarily concerned with drawing conclusions through inductive and deductive acts of reasoning and, as such, tends to rest content with existing understanding, to the point of refusing to alter that understanding to accommodate new information. By motivating the mind to keep its understanding up to date, and to relinquish ideas whenever they become irrelevant or obsolete, consequently the will ensures that the mind consistently aims for the highest *good* that is attainable in human knowledge, which is the most universal (*one*) or encompassing account of what is *true*.[22]

In order to demonstrate specifically how the will performs its role as the guarantor of the intellect's knowledge of truth, it may be helpful to return to a discussion of the three distinct phases in which Aquinas, following Aristotle, claims that reason accomplishes its work, showing how the will facilitates this work at every stage.[23] The first stage involves deliberating—researching, inquiring, and seeking counsel—as to the best means to the end of identifying what is true. During this phase of expectant faith, the will alerts us to the fact that we have not accounted for some significant object in our experience; it consequently fills us with the desire to overcome the deficiency in our understanding, motivating us to undertake the inductive cognitive efforts that are relevant to this end, and preventing us from settling for any solution that fails fully to satisfy our desire for knowledge.

In the second phase, which I have described in terms of fulfilled faith, the will signals that we have achieved the desired understanding, identifying the middle term that reconciles the object in question with an account of what it is.[24] In the same instance, the mind obtains the conclusion of the inductive argument that produced the middle term. The third phase of informed faith finds the will commanding or directing further deductive or demonstrative acts of knowing on the basis of the conclusions acquired in inductive reasoning. In this case, the will recommends to the intellect the middle term on account of which a universal principle may be employed to render a new object of experience intelligible. At the very moment the will suggests this term, the intellect is once again enabled to draw a conclusion about the nature of its object.

As the discussion above suggests, the capacity to acquire knowledge through the process outlined in the last chapter is in point of fact a capacity to employ the intellect together with the will. In that sense, the human essence, existence, and life can be further defined in terms the intellect, its knowledge, and the will.[25] Since we all possess in varying ways and degrees the intellectual—and volitional—capacities, which predispose us to pursue wisdom, science, or art, there is a further sense in which acquiring knowledge by employing the intellect and will is a matter of learning to use our talents or abilities, that is, our 'knowledge-type intellectual' virtues. In sum, the triad of intellect, knowledge, and will is most fundamentally a triad of 'talent, learning, and use.'[26]

Passions

As noted above, the work of intellect and will presupposes a means by which both faculties come into contact with specific realities, which in turn necessitates an account of the embodied nature of our knowledge.[27] In Chapter 2, I explained how the intellect draws the external world into its purview by means of images formed in perception. These images provide the raw data for the mind's formation of universal concepts. The passions represent the will's counterpart to the intellect's images.

As the name suggests, the passions are signs of our passivity, even vulnerability, to the impact of our own bodily states and external realities and experiences in the world.[28] In fact, the whole role of the passions is to form value judgments about such objects of perception, which register those objects as helpful or inimical for our purposes.[29] In the very moment of perception, these judgments—or passions—become attached to the images of the objects about which they are formed.

While the so-called 'natural appetite' generates our concern for the 'goods of the body,' including health, nourishment, and reproduction, the 'sense appetite'[30] oversees our interests regarding the 'external goods' of the world and our circumstances.[31] Although we share these two appetites with non-human animals, whose highest appetite is the sense appetite, the higher, intellectual appetite that we also, exclusively, possess renders unique the way in which we experience the 'lower' appetites.[32]

Whereas non-human animals primarily engage the sense objects of the body and the external world for the sake of satisfying the natural appetite to find food and mates and avoid predators, the natural and sense appetites of human beings are or ought to be ordered towards and governed by the intellectual appetite. In other words, human efforts to satisfy desires for the goods of the body and the external world should be incorporated into and facilitate a larger effort to pursue the 'goods of the soul,' which are both intellectual and moral, and so to help others do the same, thus fostering a distinctly human society.[33]

Although an account of the appropriate relationship between the natural and intellectual appetites falls outside the scope of the current project, the more focused purpose of the present chapter is to explain how the sense and intellectual appetites ought to relate in the context of achieving the knowledge of truth and to discuss the intellectual vices that arise when they fail in this regard. In chapters 6 and 7, respectively, I will explore how the two appetites inappropriately and appropriately relate in the moral context.

As these statements suggest, therefore, the passions produced as a result of such appetites are ambivalent; they may serve or stymie the intellect and the will in the intellectual, to say nothing of the moral context. In that sense, neither the passions nor their objects are intrinsically beneficial or detrimental. Rather, they become so in virtue of the ways in which they are used either to promote or undermine the pursuit of truth. In the subsequent discussion, I will explain how the passions may be employed to either end, depending on whether or not reason is fixed in its proper purpose of pursuing truth by a will that holds fast to this purpose.[34]

*   *   *

At the start of this discussion, it will be helpful to offer a taxonomy of the passions, which can be divided into four general categories. In these categories, there are passions that have to do with 1. immediate (present) goods/pleasures, 2. immediate evils/pains, 3. imminent or anticipated (future) goods/pleasures, and 4. imminent evils/pains. These categories can be further reduced to two broader categories.[35] The first category includes the so-called 'concupiscible passions,' which pertain to immediate pleasures and pains.[36] The passions that register immediate pleasures include love and joy or contentment, which fill us with an overall feeling of *elevation*. The passions that signal immediate pain are hatred and sorrow or distress, which fill us with feelings of *depression*.

The second category includes the 'irascible passions,' which pertain to imminent pleasures and pains.[37] The purpose of the irascible passions is to overcome obstacles to obtaining the objects of the elevating or concupiscible passions, or to eliminate the cause of the depressive concupiscible passions. After all, we undertake challenges so that we can live without them. In that sense, the irascible passions are motivated by and culminate in the concupiscible passions; they are derivative thereof.

The irascible passions that pertain to pleasure include hope and confidence, which are accompanied by a general sense of *expansion* in the face of an object of desire. The irascible passions that concern pains include despair and fear, on account of which a feeling of *contraction* occurs in the presence of an object of aversion. Another irascible passion is anger, which readies us to deal with an already present difficulty.[38] Aquinas sees anger 'as the most reasonable of the (irascible) emotions in that it excites us to act for an (apparent) reason,'[39] namely on account of an injury already suffered. By contrast to hope and despair, and confidence and fear, anger has no opposite, because there is nothing arduous about the attempt to obtain a good that is already accessible.

For every internal sense of elevation/depression or expansion/contraction that a passion causes us to experience, there is a corresponding *physical* elevation/ depression or expansion/contraction, which Aquinas calls the *transmutatio corporalis*, or 'change of the body.'[40] In the presence of a desired object, for example, we literally 'expand' physically in various ways in order to receive or indicate our willingness to receive that object. These ways include standing up, leaning in, opening the mouth or eyes, undergoing the dilation of pupils or the blushing of cheeks, stretching out the arms, raising brows, and so on.

When we encounter an object of aversion, by contrast, we ostensibly 'contract' physically, backing away or recoiling from a threat, bending over, clenching fists and teeth, covering the face or eyes, going pale, and so on. While feelings of elevation are typically signaled physically by some upward-turning gesture—a smile, a deep breath, the lifting of the head—depression is evidenced by sinking or downward movements, such as a frown, a sigh, closed eyes, or the hanging of the head.

These types of physical reaction generally occur involuntarily on encountering an object of passion. An exception to this rule can be identified in the case of objectless moods, in which we do not so much fixate on an actual object of pleasure or pain, whether apparent or anticipated, but sense that some such object is missing in our experience. Such moods notwithstanding, the absence of any physical reaction signifies that a passion is one we have either been trained to control or that has already been processed by the will and so transformed into the mere memory of a passion that has been experienced in the past. Thus restrained, the passions in question are strictly speaking affections of the intellectual appetite or will, such as I will describe further below.[41]

Though the *transmutatio corporalis* is essential to any given passion, I have hinted that it is just one of two components. One is the material component that is represented by the physical movement towards a perceived good or away from a perceived evil. The other, formal, component, which 'Aquinas identifies with the internal movement itself of the sensitive appetite,'[42] involves an alteration in the inner state or disposition of the person who undergoes the passion.[43] Since both components are essential to the constitution of a passion, the passions are ultimately 'body-soul phenomena, or psycho-physiological states.'[44]

For this very reason, they cannot be reduced either to the sorts of physiological or behavioral reactions described above, nor to the psychological states like hope and fear that those reactions generate, in the manner of many modern philosophies of psychology. After all, the inner feeling a bodily or external stimulus evokes would not arise without a reaction to this stimulus, which would not in turn be registered apart from the inner feeling.[45] The logical corollary of this analysis is that feelings ineluctably arise in the same moment reactions occur, which is the very same moment stimuli are encountered in perception.[46]

As explained in Chapter 2, acts of perception, like passions, also turn on the coincidence of physiological and cognitive or material and formal components, which respectively involve the impression of a sensible object upon a sense organ, and the production of a mental image of that impression. Since passions and perceptions are registered at the same time, as part of a single sensory event in which the sense image highlights a reality and the passion forms a judgment of value about it, the material and formal components of any given act of perception immediately correspond to the material and formal components of any associated passion.

Insofar as the images formed in perception are cognitive or at least pre-cognitive in that they provide a basis for the intellect's efforts to abstract concepts, there is a sense in which the passions that are always attached to these images also entail a cognitive dimension. Far from the irrational states they are often believed to be, they become cognitive in the full sense of the term whenever the sense images with which they are associated are selected by the intellect at the direction of the will, itself informed by the passions, for the sake of abstracting a universal concept. That is to say, the passions take on a role in cognition when they participate in the work of reason and will, which is in turn made possible by the passions, to say nothing of sense perception, in the ways I will describe below.

*   *   *

As indicated above, the passions put the will or intellectual appetite in touch with the particular realities it must pursue or avoid in order to carry out the intellect's plans, just as the images formed in perception provide the raw material the intellect needs to construct concepts. In fact, it is in registering the effect of bodily or external goods upon us that the passions implicitly make recommendations to the will as to how to act in line with certain intellectual goals. Though the passions represent predispositions to be acted upon in certain ways, consequently they at once represent predispositions to act, albeit at the direction of the will.[47]

That stated, it can take time for the will to deliberate about how to act.[48] The passions the will eventually deems conducive to reason's goal of seeking truth are the aforementioned affections of the will.[49] These affections are the only passions we ultimately allow ourselves to 'feel' in the sense that we follow their lead through the phases of expectant, fulfilled, and informed faith.[50] The passions of fear, hope, or anger, for example, which might be aroused in us as a result of certain experiences, but which we do not permit to guide our actions, cannot be construed as affections of the will. In what follows, therefore, I will enumerate some of the ways the passions guide the will through the aforementioned phases, such that they are transformed into affections of the will.

In expectant faith, the passions signal to the will that we are unable to explain a matter that we are predisposed to desire to explain. They thereby alert the will to the need to undertake an inductive investigation, sensitizing it to the particular objects of knowledge that are relevant to conducting the investigation and simultaneously desensitizing it to those that are irrelevant. At every point in an inquiry, the passions indicate to the will what is most urgent, important, or immediately in need of the mind's attention. By focusing our attentions along these lines, the passions do not stymie our perspective on the truth but put us in the optimal position to find the truth we are seeking. They do likewise when they signal to the will that the mind simply needs to rest from inquiring.

While the irascible passions give us the strength we need to engage in the often arduous process of induction, thereby preventing us from glossing over details that are relevant to our investigation, the concupiscible passions give us the resolve to follow through on deductive lines of reasoning until we achieve a fully satisfactory solution to the problem under investigation. In doing this, they stop us from settling for an inadequate solution to the problem or indeed from abandoning the search for a solution prematurely.

As such a search makes progress, the passions not only alert us when particulars needed to gain the understanding we are pursuing are not in place or are out of place; they also notify us when the relevant particulars are beginning to fall into place and so increasingly attune the will to the nature of the intellect's goal, which was bound to be somewhat obscure at the start of the search. As we approximate discovery, the passions heighten our anticipation for the arrival of new understanding, with the irascible passions giving us a final surge of intellectual energy we require to seek and receive it.

At last, the concupiscible passions let us know when we have arrived at a resolution: when our faith for knowledge has been fulfilled. Subsequently, the passions continue to offer guidance by showing us how to apply our new knowledge most fruitfully to gain further understanding in informed faith. At every step in the cognitive process, in summary, the passions compel us in the most specific of terms to show preference for the highest good or the most relevant account of the truth we can attain under the circumstances.[51]

In addition, they help us know how to communicate our understanding to a wider audience by sensitizing us to the concerns—or passions—of others, which we must take into consideration in order to reach them in a relevant and intelligible way. By the same token, the passions enable us to recognize when others may be trying to manipulate our own passions and so persuade us to accept unsound arguments. Through these means and others, the passions—or better, affections—inform the will as to how to accomplish the work of the intellect and thus participate in the activities of intellect and will. They become rational by participation, insofar as the intellect and will accomplish their tasks by means of the contact the will maintains with the passions.[52]

Although I have focused so far on explaining the way the passions inform the will as to how the intellect should operate, it is worth noting in concluding this section that the passions play another role in human knowing, in that they shape the intellect's very capacity for operating in accordance with one of the knowledge-type intellectual virtues of wisdom, science, or art. Whereas the question *whether* knowledge is obtained concerns the degree to which the will is strengthened by appropriate passions, the question *what* is known—which is determined by the type and level of the mind's intellectual abilities—pertains to the nature and extent of its ability to be affected by certain fields of inquiry.[53]

Put differently, knowledge-type intellectual virtues turn on a fine sense of touch or natural feel for certain objects of investigation. This sensitivity to or better passion for a particular area of inquiry enables us to orientate ourselves to that area in an exceptionally efficient way. Subsequently, it equips us to navigate or 'feel our way' with great effectiveness towards solutions to particular problems that arise in the field. Though there is no way of discovering our knowledge-type intellectual virtues apart from the passions that inform the will and thus the intellect as to the nature of those virtues, the foregoing observations suggest that the aptitudes or knowledge-type intellectual virtues themselves are nothing more than 'intellectual passions,' which predispose us to explore and order the world in certain ways.[54]

When the passions put us in touch with reality—including the reality of our own aptitudes in the areas of wisdom, science, and art—and give us the energy to do justice both to the truth and our aptitudes for knowing it, they simultaneously prevent us from committing the intellectual vices that would inhibit our testimony concerning the truth. As I have already suggested, the passions may hinder as much as help us in the search for truth, insofar as they fail to perform their proper function of pointing the will and thus the intellect towards what is true in actual reality. In the section that follows, I will explain how the passions, which are here better described as 'dis-passions,' do this in ways that cause us to perpetuate the intellectual vices that manifest themselves in various forms of logically fallacious reasoning.

Intellectual Vices

Though the affections are the only passions the will ultimately allows itself to be guided by and so strictly speaking to feel, the will cannot help but be affected on some level even by the passions it decides not to pursue. Certain philosophers have differentiated between the initial arousal of our passions and the influence they exert on us once sanctioned by the will—or transformed into 'affections'—by distinguishing between the 'first' and 'second' movements of the will.[55] While the first movements are involuntary and bodily or passionate, the second movements are or should be the product of considered reflection and are in that sense 'affectionate.'

Many of the passions that can be classified as first movements of the will afford considerable pleasure, for example the pleasure of discovery or achievement. Others cause significant pain, such as the pain of realizing that one of our accomplishments has been superseded, or that there is a significant, even fatal, flaw in one of our arguments. When we undergo such passions, our responsibility to testify to the truth requires that we relinquish the immediate pleasure of success and withstand the immediate pain of failure for the sake of inquiring anew into the way things are. In other words, we must allow the affections of the will to override passions of pleasure and pain so that we may continue to strive towards the larger and more significant goal of sustaining a commitment to the pursuit of truth.

As mentioned, the will frequently needs time to decide which passions to permit or forbid to guide the work of reason, and thus to count amongst its affections. Ironically, the space for deliberation that is inherent in the tensed process of reasoning and that allows for the very possibility of a conscious decision in favor of the truth—to wit, the highest good in knowledge—at once creates an opportunity to opt instead for a lesser good, like the advancement of a particular theory that may not actually be optimally true but in which a great deal of time and energy has perhaps been invested and on which a personal or professional reputation may have been staked.

When these or other significant concerns related to self-preservation are at issue, the temptation to take advantage of the opportunity to reduce the truth to an idea that is inadequate to it—to disown the truth precisely in taking undue ownership of it—is bound to be strong. While this urge for instant gratification, as it were, that is, to seek immediate personal relief, security, or pleasure, and avoid immediate personal disrepute, loss of time and energy, or pain, may prove helpful when bare physical survival is at stake, it can prove destructive when it is allowed to influence the intellectual, to say nothing of the moral, life.

Since the goals set in these contexts almost always take time and sustained effort to achieve, they require a delay in the gratification that comes from understanding what is true, as well as a willingness to admit our own ignorance so long as we are still inquiring after the truth. In the case of those who prove unwilling to tolerate the discomfort that is inevitably associated with this admission, the will's desire for truth cannot help but be replaced by a desire for intellectual self-promotion, which utterly transforms the will's way of being informed by the passions.

Whereas the will to pursue truth enables reason to discriminate amongst the passions that are or are not relevant to this end, and, in that sense, to govern them, the will to promote a private intellectual agenda leaves the mind completely at the mercy of the passions or, better, 'dis-passions' for self-promotion. These dis-passions not only render the will susceptible to the influence of only those passions that promote a personal intellectual agenda, however contrived or fallacious it may be, thus leading the mind to over-emphasize or even fabricate information that supports this agenda.[56] They simultaneously de-sensitize the will to information that challenges its agenda, such that the mind suppresses or modifies information that contests its assumptions, even if it promotes the knowledge of authentic truth.

By means such as these, the dis-passions give way to the intellectual vices I enumerated in Chapter 3. These vices prompt us either to oppose the truth altogether or to fall short of it in crucial respects.[57] In other words, they impel us to advance lines of reasoning that are either mendacious or nonsensical, in the sense that they fail to communicate anything that bears meaningfully on the nature of reality.[58] The longer the will is ruled by the dis-passions that generate such false or senseless beliefs, the further the mind is bound to be driven and to drive others into logically fallacious patterns of reasoning that increasingly attenuate any memory, individual or collective, of what it means to testify to the truth.[59] In order to avoid becoming disconnected from reality in these ways,

I will argue below that we must cultivate the intellectual virtues that have the power to curb our intellectual vices and keep the intellect, will, and passions honest in the pursuit of truth.

Rationality as Intellectual Virtue

Amongst contemporary philosophers, there is a growing interest in what has come to be called 'virtue epistemology,' or theories of knowledge that emphasize the important role that certain epistemic character qualities play in facilitating successful acts of knowing and so in sustaining rationality. A variety of different virtue epistemologies have been proposed, some of which draw insights from ancient philosophers like Aristotle, but many of which have little or no basis in the historical-philosophical tradition.[60] Since Aquinas' theory of the four cardinal virtues offers the mature refinement of earlier virtue theories, it arguably represents the ideal resource for developing a virtue epistemology.[61]

In what follows, I will show how each of these four virtues orders the faculty with which it is associated towards the pursuit of truth, such that the virtues taken together act as the regulators of human rationality. While prudence holds the intellect accountable to maintain contact with reality, I will demonstrate that justice rectifies the will for the purpose of motivating the intellect thus to 'do justice' to the truth about reality. Fortitude gives us the strength or stamina to confront the challenges involved in doing this, particularly those inherent in inductive reasoning; and temperance instills in us the discipline to pursue the highest good of truth, without succumbing to the distractions posed by lesser goods. It thereby enables us to be as thorough as possible when it comes to delineating deductive lines of reasoning.

In order to help us maintain contact with the truth, prudence compels us to prioritize the advancement of truth over that of any self-promoting intellectual agenda. In doing precisely this, prudence helps us to navigate any inquiry and the information that comes to our attention in the course of it in a way that ultimately leads us to the truest possible conclusions. As mentioned, prudence accomplishes its purpose on account of the justice of the will, which motivates us to act in an intellectually fitting manner.

In addition to keeping us apace of the truth in this way, the justice of the will raises our awareness of those areas relevant to our knowledge where we lack the resources or skills to make contact with reality. In other words, it discloses where we may need to seek out and rely upon others if we are to know the truth that it concerns us to know. When we turn to others in this way, we adopt their rationality vicariously, allowing our own intellectual efforts to be informed by it, as in a sort of 'informed' uninformed faith.[62] Such mature intellectual interdependence differs qualitatively from the uninformed faith in which we tend to accept others' ideas unquestioningly. After all, our decisions about whom to depend upon, and how, are guided by knowledge we have acquired of our own accord. At base, they are informed decisions, designed to help us do justice to the way things are in reality.

While our ability to discriminate amongst views about what is true may compel us to appropriate ideas from others in some cases, it may also lead us in others to endorse views that drastically diverge from common opinion. However innovative our views may be, it is important to acknowledge that they are still in some sense indebted to wider assumptions, insofar as they derive their intelligibility from the intellectual background these assumptions provide. In cases where we neglect to recognize this, our ideas of truth simply will not bear on the thought of our contemporaries and will therefore fail to do justice to our intellectual situation, even by rectifying it, and thus to prove true. In casting our testimony to the truth as part of a larger, communal search for truth, which began before our time and will continue long after we are gone, by contrast, we make our ideas available where they can affect the dialectical development of ideas about truth over time.

In the context of this dialectic, our own way of conceiving truth may represent any given step in the threefold cognitive process of expectant, fulfilled, and informed faith, writ large across history and society. In other words, our conception of truth may set the stage for a great discovery, even by another, as in expectant faith. It may constitute discovery itself, fulfilling the intellectual expectations of earlier thinkers. Or it may extrapolate the implications of others' findings, as in informed faith. In expectant and informed faith especially, the truths we articulate may be rendered obsolete after or even within our own lifetimes. Alternatively, they may be among the truths that are tried and found true across time. Whether or not they are eventually superseded, however, our views may represent indispensable stages in the dialectical search for truth, to the extent that they give full expression to the truth that is accessible at the time.

Since prudence and justice enable us to offer the best available account of what is true, it follows that they also predispose us to adapt our understanding of the truth as efficiently as possible in the light of new experiences or discoveries. Though these intellectual virtues cannot render us rational on the terms of the seemingly unrealistic definition of rationality according to which our ideas must hold true for all persons at all places and at all times, consequently they have the power to make us rational by the more realistic standard which simply requires that we articulate the truth insofar as it is accessible through experience.

As I have already suggested, the operation of the prudent intellect and the just will to the end of sustaining the knowledge of truth—and thereby rationality—is empowered by the passions, which put the will and thereby the intellect in touch with the resources needed for their work. This brings us to the two further virtues associated with the passions, namely, fortitude and temperance, which enable us to be affected by or passionate about particular objects of experience only in ways that facilitate our efforts to uphold the truth and so exhibit prudence and justice.

Since fortitude is the virtue that deals with feelings of pain, it is especially accustomed to dealing with the irascible passions, though it is also involved in managing the more painful concupiscible passions, like sorrow. When it comes to knowledge, consequently, fortitude is the virtue that gives us the strength to persevere through the oftentimes arduous and prolonged process of achieving understanding, particularly through inductive lines of reasoning. Temperance is the virtue that pertains to pleasure and which is largely concerned with the governance of the positive concupiscible passions like joy, love, desire, and so on. The primary purpose of this virtue in the intellectual context is to teach us to take pleasure in pursuing truth above all else and to articulate it as thoroughly as we are able. As such, temperance is the virtue proper to deduction.

In fulfilling their primary purpose of ensuring that we have the passions we need to testify to the truth, the virtues of fortitude and temperance seemingly accomplish a second task, which is to curb the dis-passions that would prevent the intellect and will from being prudent and just, respectively. For example, fortitude counteracts the weakness and despair we sometimes feel in the face of large and challenging inductive tasks.[63] In its own turn, temperance disciplines us to focus on our tasks, particularly those associated with deduction, when other interests threaten to distract us.

In these ways and others, fortitude and temperance ensure that we have the passions we need to fulfill the purposes of prudence and justice and check the dis-passions, which would prevent us from accomplishing those purposes. When they enable the passions to participate in the work of prudence and justice along these lines, I have noted, the virtues of the passions may be counted amongst the intellectual virtues. As it is on the strength of the virtues of the passions and so implicitly the passions themselves that the tasks of the intellect and will are carried out with prudence and justice, respectively, conversely, it is possible to conclude that intellectual virtue is fundamentally a matter of what might be described as 'intellectual passion.'

Since the passions that help rather than hinder the work of the intellect and will are rational by participation in the work of those faculties, it follows that human rationality ultimately consists in the collaboration not only of the intellect and will but also of the passions. As I have argued, these three components of rationality can only properly perform their functions with respect to the pursuit of truth when they are informed by the intellectual virtues of prudence, justice, fortitude, and temperance. In that sense, human rationality is ultimately a matter of the intellectual virtues

As mentioned previously, the four cardinal intellectual virtues are moral virtues first and foremost. This suggests that our intellectual efforts to testify to the truth through the exercise of our aptitudes are or should be part of a larger moral or personal effort fully to realize our personal potential. After all, the human capacity to acquire knowledge through the exercise of the intellect, will, and passions is a capacity human beings possess for the sake of fostering a distinctly human style of life and community. In that sense, self-actualization is the proper cause of or context for the pursuit of knowledge.[64]

Because the highest degree of rationality—informed as opposed to uninformed faith—is achieved when we possess a rationale for whatever we do, it could be argued that we are rational in the full sense of the term when we exhibit the four cardinal *intellectual* virtues with a view to cultivating the *moral* virtues that enable us to realize our potential as individuals.[65] Of course, it is entirely possible to be intellectually and not morally virtuous and vice versa—a matter to which I will return in Chapter 7.[66] In ideal circumstances, however, human rationality paradigmatically entails intellectual and moral—or intellectual *for* moral—virtue.

In the following chapter, I will delineate the conditions under which we become deficient for the purpose of cultivating the morally virtuous life in which our intellectual efforts are consummated, before going on to describe that life—and the arbiter of rationality—itself. In the concluding section of this chapter, however, I will offer some brief remarks on how rationality at the level of intellectual virtue seemingly plays out in the fields of wisdom, science, and art.

Rationality in Wisdom, Science, and Art

Thus far, my account of human rationality has mainly considered the way that rationality plays out in the sciences, that is, the fields of inquiry that are organized around particular objects of inquiry. Some examples of sciences include the biological and life sciences, and the humane sciences, including history, language and culture studies, and so on. As I have indicated, rationality in any such area of inquiry turns on accounting for the nature of the objects the science treats in a manner that is consistent with the way those objects actually present themselves in reality.

Although I have demonstrated how to do this in the account of rationality I have provided thus far, I have not considered what it would mean to exercise rationality in the fields of art and wisdom, or philosophy. Although I cannot explore this topic at length in the present context, it seems essential to the end of offering a complete account of rationality to call attention at very least to the different ways that rationality can and should play out in these other contexts. Thus, I will discuss in turn what Aristotle calls *techne* (craft knowledge, arts, or skills), and *sophia* (wisdom).

The most pragmatic of the knowledge-type intellectual virtues, *techne*, encompasses a wide range of activities, including the practical and productive arts as well as the creative arts (literature, poetry), performing arts (music, dance, drama), and visual arts (painting, drawing, sculpting, etc.). When it comes to practical or productive arts—ranging from architecture, medicine, business, politics, engineering, industry, and farming, to the culinary arts—rationality is not merely a matter of theory but also, and ultimately, of practice, for it entails and necessitates the practical application of understanding.

In that sense, the architect who designs a structure that is less than maximally efficient with respect to its purposes, or which is subject to structural weakness, can be described as deficient in rationality, as can the medical doctor who is inexcusably unschooled in the symptoms of certain common diseases and therefore misdiagnoses and mistreats patients, or at least fails to provide them with the most effective treatment available. In both cases, rationality is hindered not only by a deficiency in theoretical knowledge but also by a corresponding inability to apply that knowledge practically.

While rationality in the aforementioned instances involves directing passions to the end of thinking in ways that are true to reality, whether in theory only or in theory through practice, the pursuit of passions in the creative, performing, and visual arts is primarily ordered towards the expression or evocation of the passions themselves. Though art is not therefore directly concerned with cognition or volition, the feelings it evokes can or seemingly should be nonetheless related in some way to the purposes of the intellect and the will; they should inspire us to fulfill those purposes; and they ought to instill in us a profound sense of all that we would forfeit in neglecting to do so.

Thus we might say that art is rational in the way that is proper to art—and therefore intrinsically valuable or beautiful—the more clearly and closely related it is to the aforementioned purposes; the more important or universal are the purposes to which it is related, the more powerfully it evokes feelings of pleasure or even pain related to the accomplishment or failure to accomplish those purposes, respectively; and the more realistic or authentic, as well as common or accessible, are the feelings it evokes in these respects.[67] In sum, art is more rational the more universally and profoundly it arouses us to the pursuit of the most universal and profound things.

From these extremely cursory comments on *techne*, I turn to the question what rationality involves in the case of wisdom, which I defined in Chapter 2 as the highest science, in which the object of knowledge is the whole nature of reality, or ontology, including the nature of human knowledge of reality, and, finally, the nature of human life. As such a second-order field of inquiry, it falls to philosophy to describe the way things are, the way we know, and the way we should live, in a manner that is consistent with the dynamic or developing nature of realities, knowledge, and human life.

Above all, philosophy must illustrate and establish that the disciplines of ontology and epistemology are ordered towards describing a functional and fulfilling or morally virtuous life. Since a description of this sort is at once a prescription, it follows that the consummation of philosophy consists not merely in its attendant inquiries but in a life led according to philosophy's prescriptions concerning the love of wisdom or the highest good. Stated otherwise, the truly rational philosopher is not only able to offer a rational account of reality and especially the reality of an ethical human life but also serves as an example of the moral way of life I will describe in Chapter 7.[68]

Endnotes

[1]   On passions as 'judgments of value,' see Martha Nussbaum, *Upheavals of Thought: The Intelligence of the Emotions* (Cambridge: Cambridge University Press, 2001), 1–4, 19, 22, ff.

[2]   See Peter King, 'Aquinas on the Passions,' in *Aquinas' Moral Theory* (Ithaca: Cornell, 1999), 101–32. See also, Thomas Dixon, *From Passions to Emotions: The Creation of a Secular Psychological Category* (Cambridge: Cambridge University Press, 2003). See also Augustine's account of the passions in *De civitate Dei*, books 9, 14.

[3]   On passions versus pseudo-passions, see chapter 2 on 'The Definition of Passion,' in Robert Miner, *Thomas Aquinas on the Passions* (Cambridge: Cambridge University Press, 2009).

[4]   Of course, there are many other virtues besides the four cardinal virtues of prudence, justice, fortitude, and temperance, some of which Aristotle discusses in his

EN. By the time of Aquinas, however, virtue accounts had been refined to foreground the four mentioned above. These virtues are described as 'cardinal' (from the Latin *cardo* or hinge), in the sense that they are the basic virtues upon which all other virtues depend or from which they proceed.

5   As Aristotle writes in *EN* I.3, 1094b12–13: 'our discussion will be adequate if it has as much clearness as the subject-matter admits of; for precision is not to be sought for alike in all discussions.'

6   My distinction between rationality at the intellectual and moral levels bears some resemblance to Paul Tillich's distinction between 'technical reason' and 'ontological reason' in his *Systematic Theology*, vol. 1 (Chicago: University of Chicago Press), 73ff.

7   Josef Pieper writes that, 'Thomas did not establish any definite fixed terms which he planned to use in a consistent manner. On the contrary, he was fond of employing several synonymous expressions side by side (or in different contexts) ... Not only is this his practice, but it is intentionally so. Thomas wanted it that way. It was not a mere chance matter of temperament but the product of a definite, clearly formulated principle. Thomas was careful to avoid making exact precise definitions of such fundamental concepts as cognition or truth. For Thomas was convinced that an absolutely adequate name, completely and exhaustively defining a given subject or situation so that all alternatives are excluded and that name alone can be employed, simply cannot exist.' Josef Pieper, *Guide to Thomas Aquinas* (San Francisco: Ignatius, 1962), 112–13, citing F.A. Blanche, 'Sur la langue technique de Saint Thomas d'Aquin,' *Revue de Philosophie*, vol. 30 (Paris, 1930).

8   On the mind, practical reason (will) and the other 'knowledge-type intellectual virtues' that Aquinas and Aristotle discuss, see *ST* 2.1.57; cf. EN VI.

9   *APo.* II.19.

10   Paul Griffiths, *Intellectual Appetite* (Washington, DC: The Catholic University of America Press, 2009).

11   Though I have here effectively conflated Aquinas' theory of the will with Aristotle's account of *phronesis* (and Aristotle's *nous* with Aquinas' 'intellect'), this move admittedly flies in the face of the common scholarly contention that Aristotle himself had no theory of the will, which many believe to have been originally devised by Augustine. In a study entitled *Aristotle's Theory of the Will*, however, Anthony Kenny sheds light on the appetitive and volitional nature of the functions performed by *phronesis* or practical reason, arguing that Aristotle did possess an idea of a faculty that performs operations akin to those of the will, even though he did not generally use the term 'will' in discussing the work of practical reason. On Aquinas' integration of Aristotle's notion of practical rationality and Augustine's theory of the will, see also Alasdair MacIntyre, *Whose Justice? Which Rationality?* (London: Duckworth, 1988), 184. On page 164, MacIntyre develops a related argument that Aquinas' account of practical rationality should not be abstracted

in piecemeal fashion and treated 'in too great isolation from the context supplied by his overall point of view and method. The degree of interdependence between Aquinas' treatment of one set of topics and issues and his treatment of others does of course vary, but sometimes the relationships are, to modern readers at least, unexpected.'

12   See again *ST* 2.1.57 and EN VI on intellectual virtues.

13   *ST* 2.2.47.1–7.

14   Herbert McCabe, 'Action, Deliberation, and Decision,' in *On Aquinas* (London: Burns and Oates, 2008), 81: 'but we must not think of two instants, one the operation of the intellect presenting something attractive and the next an operation of the will being attracted. It is a single, complex operation involving both will and intellect, for of course you will not actively attend to some aspect of (say) having a drink if you don't want to; so the understanding bit presupposes the will as well.'

15   On the will's tendency towards the good, see *De Veritate* 22. On Aquinas' privation theory of evil, see *ST* 1.48–9.

16   *ST* 2.1.94.2; cf. *De Veritate* 16.

17   *De Veritate* 16.1.

18   *De Veritate* 16.2.

19   *De Veritate* 17.1.

20   *De Veritate* 17.2.

21   *De Veritate* 16.3.

22   Here, I allude to the three transcendentals (*unum, bonum, verum*) that were often referred to by medieval thinkers like Aquinas.

23   *ST* 2.2.51; *EN* VI 9–11.

24   *ST* 2.2.51.3.

25   See Lydia Schumacher, *Divine Illumination: The History and Future of Augustine's Theory of Knowledge* (Oxford: Wiley-Blackwell), 42.

26   Ibid., 48–9.

27   *EN* II.5: on the passions.

28   Nicholas E. Lombardo, *The Logic of Desire: Aquinas on Emotion* (Washington, DC: The Catholic University of America Press, 2010), 36: the primary feature of passions is receptivity.

29   On the relationship between the imagination and the passions, see chapter 3 on 'The Activation of Passion,' in Robert Miner, *Thomas Aquinas on the Passions*. See also, Martha Nussbaum, *Upheavals of Thought*, 65, where the author discusses the connection between the emotions and the imagination. See also her introduction and chapter 1, which argues that the emotions highlight objects that are relevant to our purposes and projects.

30   On the sensitive appetite, see chapter 1, 'The Sensitive Appetite,' in Robert Miner, *Thomas Aquinas on the Passions*; see also *ST* 1.2.17.7, 1.2.22.3.

[31] *ST* 2.1.22.2–3; cf. *EN* I.8, 1098: on the goods of the body, the external world, and the soul.

[32] *ST* 2.1.4; Nicholas E. Lombardo, *The Logic of Desire*, 31: on the three kinds of appetite.

[33] Martha Nussbaum, *Upheavals of Thought*, 12; see also her *Fragility of Goodness: Luck and Ethics in Greek Tragedy and Philosophy* (Cambridge: Cambridge University Press, 2001); cf. Alasdair MacIntyre, *Dependent Rational Animals* (London: Duckworth, 1999).

[34] *ST* 2.1.24.

[35] *EN* II.5; cf. *Rhet.* II: Aristotle on the passions: feelings pertaining to pleasure and pain include appetite, anger, fear, joy, love, hate, longing, pity, jealousy.

[36] *ST* 2.1.23.1; on irascible/concupiscible passions, see also Evagrius Ponticus, *Praktikos: Chapters on Prayer* (Cistercian Publications, 2006), 86. Also consult Nicholas Lombardo's chapter on the irascible and concupiscible passions, namely, 'The Structure of the Passions,' in *The Logic of Desire*, 49–74. For another extensive taxonomy of the passions as Aquinas discusses them, see Robert Miner, *Aquinas on the Passions*, and Peter King, 'Aquinas on the Passions,' 1–20.

[37] *ST* 2.1.23.2.

[38] *ST* 2.1.23.3.

[39] Herbert McCabe, 'Emotions and Inclinations,' in *On Aquinas*, 78.

[40] Paul Gondreau, 'The Passions and the Moral Life: Appreciating the Originality of Aquinas,' *The Thomist* 71 (2007), 419–50, at 423: 'Aquinas points out how an emotion involves in every case some kind of change in the body such as an increased heart rate, trembling of the hands, flushing of the face, hormonal and biochemical changes. The bodily alteration of a passion accounts for why biochemical and neurological phenomena are so intimately bound up with the emotions (and why today psychopharmacology and neuropsychology can be of therapeutic benefit in certain cases of emotional imbalance). In point of fact, the *transmutatio corporalis* is so essential to every movement of passion that we could not even undergo emotion if we did not have bodies (which explains why God and the angels are not subject to emotion, only intellect and will).'

[41] Nicholas Lombardo, *The Logic of Desire*, 47: according to Aquinas, 'the body expresses and resembles on a physical level the experience of the soul' (citing *ST* 1.2.17.7 ad 2, 46,5, 51.1, 63.1, 82.4 ad. 1; 2.2.35.1 ad 2, 1.2.64.2, 661). According to Aquinas, consequently, the question whether and how individuals react to stimuli is a function of personality type or temperament; conversely, temperament is often closely linked to features of an individual's physiology. The extent to which persons express passions also has much to do with cultural norms for expressing emotion.

[42] Paul Gondreau, 'The Passions and the Moral Life: Appreciating the Originality of Aquinas,' 424.

⁴³   Ibid.

⁴⁴   Ibid.

⁴⁵   *DA* I.1. Richard Sorabji, *Emotion and Peace of Mind: From Stoic Agitation to Christian Temptation* (Oxford: Oxford University Press, 2000), 25.

⁴⁶   William W. Fortenbaugh, *Aristotle on Emotion* (London: Duckworth, 1975); Herbert McCabe, 'Emotions and Inclinations,' in *On Aquinas*, 71–8.

⁴⁷   L.A. Kosman, 'Being Properly Affected: Virtues and Feelings in Aristotle's Ethics,' *Essays on Aristotle's Ethics* (Berkeley: University of California Press, 1980), 103–16. Nicholas E. Lombardo, *The Logic of Desire*, 38: passions are passive and active; they receive input and guide the will. Richard Sorabji, *Emotion and Peace of Mind*, 29: passions involve two distinctive value judgments, regarding a good or bad at hand; and how it is appropriate to react to the object evaluated by the passions.

⁴⁸   *ST* 2.1.13–14. See also, Herbert McCabe, 'Deliberative Reasoning,' in *On Aquinas*, 87–100.

⁴⁹   Thomas Dixon, 'Passions and Affections in Augustine and Aquinas,' *From Passions to Emotions*, 26–62. Nicholas E. Lombardo, 'The Affections of the Will,' in *The Logic of Desire*, 75–93. See also Augustine's *Confessiones* X on 'affections.'

⁵⁰   On the intentions or the will's tendencies to lead the intellect to act, see again *ST* 2.1.12 and G.E.M. Anscombe, *Intention* (Cambridge, MA: Harvard University Press, 2000). See also Herbert McCabe, 'Action, Deliberation and Decision,' in *On Aquinas*, 79–86.

⁵¹   *De Veritate* 1.

⁵²   Nicholas Lombardo, 'Passion, Reason and Virtue,' in *The Logic of Desire*, 94–117. The author argues that when the passions participate in the work of reason and will, they are rational by participation; equally, however, they can become irrational when they fail thus to participate in the work of the intellect and the will.

⁵³   *ST* 1.76.5.

⁵⁴   On intellectual passions, see Michael Polanyi, *Personal Knowledge: Towards a Post-Critical Philosophy* (Chicago: University of Chicago Press, 1974).

⁵⁵   Keith Oatley, 'Two Movements in Emotions: Communication and Reflection,' *Emotion Review* 2 (January 2010), 29–35. Richard Sorabji, *Emotion and Peace of Mind*, 376: on the two phases of emotion.

⁵⁶   *ST* 2.1.75.1; cf. 77.1. The cause of vice is the sensitive appetite or the grasp of some apparent good together with reason going after that good.

⁵⁷   See Paul J. Griffiths, 'Owning,' in *Intellectual Appetite: A Theological Grammar*, 139–62. See also Griffiths, *Lying: An Augustinian Theology of Duplicity* (Eugene: Wipf and Stock, 2004), especially on 'Disowning,' 85–100.

⁵⁸   Harry G. Frankfurt, *On Bullshit* (Princeton: Princeton University Press, 2005). Josef Pieper, *The Abuse of Language* (San Francisco: Ignatius Press, 1992). Pieper

describes nonsensical claims as 'an abuse of language,' since language is meant to facilitate the communication of meaningful or truthful thoughts. See also Robert Sokolowski, *Introduction to Phenomenology* (Cambridge: Cambridge University Press, 2000), 105: 'the human power of speech makes it possible for us to seem to be thinking when we really are not. This is a specifically human way of failing to be what we should be, and it is very important in human affairs. What occurs in thoughtless speech is that the categorical activity that should accompany the speech is not adequately achieved. There is some categorical activity, but it is not up to the issues being discussed and asserted ... If I speak vaguely someone who listens to me and who is more thoughtful than I am will usually find as time goes on that what I am saying makes no sense.'

[59]   *ST* 2.2.53–4.

[60]   Linda Zagzebski, *Virtues of the Mind* (Cambridge: Cambridge University Press, 1990). In this work, Zagzebski, an analytic philosopher, draws on the work of Aristotle to develop a virtue epistemology that stresses the internal aspect of decision-making—that we are personally responsible for our choices as opposed to reliant in this regard upon some external decision-making mechanism. Her account seems highly compatible with the one developed here, both in terms of content and historical orientation.

[61]   Aquinas himself emphasizes the importance to acts of knowing of a rightly ordered will; see *ST* 1.82.

[62]   *ST* 2.1.14. This is what Aquinas refers to as 'counsel' (*consilium*).

[63]   Nicholas Lombardo, *The Logic of Desire*, 178ff.: on the primary/secondary operations of fortitude and temperance.

[64]   See Alasdair MacIntyre, 'The Virtues, the Unity of Human Life, and the Concept of a Tradition,' in *Why Narrative? Readings in Narrative Theology*, eds Stanley Hauerwas and L. Gregory Jones (Grand Rapids: Eerdman's, 1989), 89ff. In this context, MacIntyre contends that human beings need a sense of where their activities fit with respect to the grander narrative of their personal lives, and even how those activities are enfolded into the larger story of human history, in order to determine how to act appropriately and thus derive a sense of flourishing from life.

[65]   Pierre Rousselot develops a similar argument with respect to Aquinas in *The Intellectualism of Saint Thomas*, trans. James E. O'Mahoney (London: Sheed and Ward, 1935); see for example page 199, where Rousselot argues that the answer to the question, 'What is the value of an idea? Is in practice reducible to this other question: to what extent is the idea a force for action? And to what extent does it bring about good conduct?'

[66]   *EN* VI.7, 1141b. Here, Aristotle notes that individuals may possess wisdom or an understanding of the causes of things but still lack prudence when it comes to determining what is best for themselves.

[67]   See Etienne Gilson, *The Arts of the Beautiful* (Dalkey, 2000).

[68]   See Pierre Hadot, *Philosophy as a Way of Life* (Oxford: Blackwell, 1995).

PART II
Sufficient Conditions for Pro-Theology Philosophy

Chapter 6
Deficient Conditions for Pro-Theology Philosophy

Towards the end of the previous chapter, I affirmed that the ultimate guarantor of rationality consists in a commitment to sustaining what might be described as a personal orientation towards the highest good, or moral virtue. In the next chapter, I will delineate the conditions that allow for following through on this commitment, thus outlining the sufficient conditions for pro-theology philosophy. These conditions include the four cardinal virtues of prudence, justice, fortitude, and temperance.

Before delving into the discussion of the virtues, however, I must treat what I would describe as the 'deficient conditions' for a virtuous existence, namely, the conditions under which it is difficult or even impossible to serve the highest good by engaging fully in self-actualization. I will outline these conditions in terms of the seven capital vices of pride, greed, envy, apathy, anger, lust, and gluttony. This list of vices was codified early on in the development of Christian thought, in the work of thinkers like Evagrius Ponticus, John Cassian, and Gregory the Great.[1] It was upheld and arguably developed most fully in medieval accounts, above all that of Aquinas, whom I will take as my guide in the present context, supplementing my discussion as Aquinas did with references to Aristotle, as relevant. The aforementioned vices are called 'capital' (from the Latin *caput*, for 'head') because all further manifestations of vice arguably stem from them.[2]

In the first section of the chapter on 'passion and vice,' I will demonstrate that the moral vices arise when 'dis-passionate' tendencies become ingrained dispositions, at the moral by contrast to the intellectual level. The tendency to fall prey to dis-passions is one to which we are especially susceptible in the moral context, for reasons I will explain in this section. By discussing these reasons, I do not mean to deny that the passions, properly channeled, have just as indispensable a role to play in self-actualization as they do in furthering intellectual pursuits.

As I will elaborate in the next chapter, the passions perform a vital function in fostering moral as well as intellectual virtue.[3] In the perverted form under consideration here, however, the passions deceive us into believing that our good consists in something other than self-actualization, thus hindering us from striving towards this end. On account of them, we become entrenched in one of the dis-passionate dispositions I have identified with the seven capital vices, which transform us into the worst rather than the best possible versions of ourselves.

After delineating the nature of each of these vices in a section on 'the seven capital vices,' I will proceed in the final section of the chapter on 'vice versus virtue' to explain the condition that must be met in order for us to hold the dis-passions in check and curb our vicious tendencies, thus satisfying what I call the 'precondition' for fulfilling the sufficient conditions for pro-theology philosophy. This precondition is met when we realize that self-actualization is our proper end as human beings and come to grasp what self-actualization actually involves. Although prudence normally operates as the intellectual virtue that helps appoint the means to any end, I will show why this virtue is uniquely suited in the ethical context to remind us of the true nature of our end.

While we lack the resources to curtail the vices in the absence of knowledge of our end, the prudence that raises our awareness of that end positions us to deliberate subsequently about the best possible means to the end of self-actualization. The means in question are also appointed by prudence, working through the moral virtues of justice, fortitude, and temperance. By explaining how prudence appoints our end, consequently, the concluding section sets the stage for the next chapter's treatment of the four cardinal virtues, through which we work towards that end and satisfy the sufficient conditions for pro-theology philosophy.

Passion and Vice

In the previous chapter, I explained the conditions that make it possible to give in to an urge for instant gratification when engaged in the pursuit of truth, thus disowning the truth. In this section, I will elaborate on two reasons why this sort of surrender to the passions might occur still more readily in the moral context of striving to actualize personal potential. After discussing these reasons, I will show how the passions actually operate to hinder self-actualization, thus allowing for the development of dis-passionate habits, or vices.

The first reason why it is especially easy to succumb to dis-passions in the moral context has to do with the fact that self-actualization is the most long-term, indeed lifelong, goal imaginable. As I suggested in earlier chapters, it often takes a significant amount of time to achieve any given goal, whether intellectual or moral; and in striving towards a goal, it is frequently necessary to work for extended periods of time without knowing whether efforts will come to fruition. Since larger goals take longer to meet, the faith that motivates attempts to strive towards such goals needs to be stronger than the faith required to complete ordinary tasks. This long-suffering faith can prove particularly difficult to maintain, precisely because there is rarely any clear end in sight in the case of long-term goals.

As a lifelong process, self-actualization is the goal with the most distant and indeterminate terminus, namely, the hour of death. Because most people do not enjoy and actually tend to avoid contemplating this moment, it can be easy to forget that there are limits on human life, such that it is essential to make the most of the available time. As a result, it becomes virtually impossible to avoid excessive preoccupations with immediate interests, which may be irrelevant or even inimical to the effort to make the most of life, and thus to fall short of engaging in activities that conduce to self-actualization or the personal pursuit of the highest good.

The second reason why the dis-passions become particularly irresistible in the moral context concerns the difficulty associated with specifying exactly what the goal of self-actualization entails. Though the purpose of all human beings is to strive for self-actualization, I noted in chapter two that every human being is characterized by highly individualized abilities, which can be realized in an indeterminable number of ways, depending upon circumstances.[4] For these reasons, each person must pursue the goal of realizing personal potential in accordance with personal aptitudes and circumstances. Since these vary from person to person, self-actualization will almost certainly play out in highly individualized ways, such that there will be virtually innumerable ways to engage in this activity.[5]

In this connection, it is worth noting that the open-ended nature of the goal of self-actualization accounts for the difference between moral and intellectual efforts—or the exercise of what has been traditionally called practical as opposed to theoretical reason.[6] For the most part, intellectual pursuits involve definite activities, which are dictated by the relevant objects of inquiry. In order to learn a language, for example, it is necessary to learn the rules of its grammar, syntax, and pronunciation.

Although self-actualization cannot be conducted apart from specific activities, even language learning, that are appropriate for the individuals engaging in the process, it differs from the pursuit of knowledge of, say, a language, because it cannot ultimately be reduced to any one activity or set of activities, such as those involved in learning a language. After all, the object of self-actualization is the realization of human potential, which means different things for different persons and even for a single person at different points in life. For this reason, the nature of the largely indefinable goal of self-actualization can only be specified in terms of 'bearing well' whatever intellectual aptitudes, opportunities, resources, circumstances, or challenges present themselves to be borne at a particular time by an individual or, for that matter, by a community.

As the proper goal or end of human existence and thus the arbiter of human flourishing, it stands to reason that the self-actualizing activity of bearing life well is at once the source of human happiness.[7] Happiness is the most 'objective' life objective there is, not only because it is a goal all human beings share in common, but also, and especially, because it is the objective that determines the other objectives human beings set.[8] In point of fact, individuals do not aim at happiness in order to obtain things other than happiness, but rather aim at things other than happiness in order to secure happiness. Since happiness rightly construed consists in the activity of bearing things well, and there are many ways to do this, it follows that there are many ways to be happy.

These points can prove difficult to remember for the two reasons I have mentioned. Because we can only engage in self-actualization in individual ways, for instance, we may be inclined to conflate self-actualization with our own way of engaging in it—or with the ways with which we are familiar on account of social conventions. Moreover, the time-bound nature of our existence may lead us to believe that self-actualization consists in the attainment of whatever goods we perceive as compatible with our happiness in the immediate sense. The goods in question may include any goods of the body (health, beauty, fitness), goods of the external world (power, relationships, fame, reputation, institutions, education), or even goods of the soul (such as political or religious causes, ideals, or the pursuit of knowledge).

By reducing the locus of our flourishing to the attainment of any one of these goods, we not only overestimate the power such goods possess in terms of affording happiness, thus setting ourselves up for disappointment; we also underestimate the scope of the activities that are conducive to self-actualization. To sum up, we limit or restrict the whole idea of self-actualization in accordance with our own present or personal understanding of happiness, and therefore overlook the fact that happiness consists in self-actualization, or the activity of bearing all things well. As a result, we become liable to undermine self-actualization in our own lives to say nothing of others.[9]

The blame for the reductive mindset mentioned above lies with the will, which becomes entranced by a dis-passion for a particular good and so allows reason to think our ultimate good consists in something less than self-actualization, such that reason's work comes to be ruled not by the goal of engaging in self-actualization but by the passions associated with the attainment or loss of whatever we take to be the source of our happiness. There are two ways in which the passions can come to rule reason.

First, the will can fail to give reason the chance to deliberate about how appropriately to deal with particular objects or circumstances that arouse certain passions, thus allowing the relevant passions to influence reason prematurely in its decision as to how to act, in what might be called a 'crime of passion.' Although such crimes are clearly blameworthy, those that commit them may make seemingly legitimate excuses for their behavior by claiming to have acted out of the necessity of the moment or with a view to seizing what seemed in the circumstances like a fleeting opportunity to achieve some beneficial end.

The passions can also overtake reason when the will allows them to undermine reason's prior knowledge of the right way to act in certain situations. While such cases of 'weakness of will' may entail a simple and cognizant failure to do what is obviously right, they still more frequently turn on negligence in the area of accessing and applying moral knowledge.[10] By managing attentions in ways that obscure the connection between a particular act and its vicious character and consequences, the weak of will find ways to explain or justify why it is acceptable or even appropriate for them to commit evil deeds in particular cases. That is to say, they delude or deceive themselves and others regarding what is good or right for them to do.[11]

Whether through self-deception or appeals to the necessity of action on impulse, I have hinted that those who exhibit weakness of will or commit crimes of passion bear their circumstances badly, yet do so in relatively good conscience. As this suggests, human beings do not normally promote evil for its own sake. More commonly, they commit wrong acts under the auspices of accomplishing a good end, which is not in fact good, or at least the greatest good. This is one upshot of the privation theory of evil, which Aquinas and many other pre-modern authors generally espoused.[12]

According to this theory, evil consists in the absence or privation of the good and is parasitic upon it. That is not to imply that evil lacks detrimental effects but to draw attention to the fact that its effects consist in the loss of opportunities, time, life, or an overall sense of flourishing: the introduction of disorder where there should be order and discord where there should be peace. Both crimes of passion and of weaknesses of will turn on a privation of the good—the former, by giving rein to feelings that should not be permitted to influence decisions, the latter, through an absence of the passions that would recognize wrongdoing as such.

Because the passions in both cases undermine rather than accomplish the purpose of bearing things well, they are not genuine passions but rather dis-passions, which are present when they should be absent or absent when they should be present, such that they denote a privation of due passion. This privation is what renders us unfit to engage in self-actualization. After all, we cannot be ruled by the dis-passions associated with some particular good which we believe can secure our happiness, even in just one respect or for a particular purpose, and at the same time be governed by the passions that compel us to bear our lives well. Put differently, we cannot regard the various and variable means to our end as ends in their own right and simultaneously strive towards our proper end. For the pursuit of the lesser and the higher goods involve mutually exclusive methods for dealing with immediate pleasures and pains, that is, the passions aroused by our experiences in the world.[13]

While the quest for particular goods is predicated on following urges for instant gratification, I have shown that an overarching concern for self-actualization entails resignation to a delay in gratification. In fact, a determination to bear life well instills a kind of tolerance for the postponement of certain satisfactions and a capacity to cope with the sacrifices and challenges that may comprise part of the process of following through on this determination. Although a decision to bear life well consequently liberates us on some level from the difficult passions that cannot help but be aroused when we are called upon to forego some pleasure or withstand some pain to this end, bearing our lives well by no means necessitates the extirpation of the passions.

Rather, it is contingent upon cultivating the passions that promote the pursuit of our own best interests and so enable us to become passionate in the true or life-promoting sense of the term. Though we must check the dis-passions that would cause us to counteract our own thriving in the course of this pursuit, I would nevertheless affirm the importance of acknowledging such dis-passions, whether pleasurable or painful, provisionally entertaining and allowing the will to be affected by them. Arguably, it is by coming to terms along these lines with the immediate pains we must undergo and the immediate pleasures we must forego in order to cultivate true passions—as opposed to suppressing or denying the dis-passions—that we strengthen our sense of where our good lies and our determination to act in accordance with it.

When we allow ourselves to be impacted by the feelings that might hinder self-actualization, for example, we embrace the fact that they do not serve our purposes and thereby diffuse them. In the same instance, we recognize what we are willing to give up or go through in order to pursue the greater goal of bearing things well. This recognition reinforces our feeling that our overarching goal is worthwhile and thus corroborates our passion to strive for it, even at the expense of pursuing lesser albeit more immediately satisfying goods.[14] While every pursuit entails some tasks about which we are bound not to feel very passionate, and we cannot escape the mundane and toilsome nature of much of our work, the assurance we thus derive as to the ultimate significance of our efforts reminds us of the deeper passion, or better affection, for self-actualization, which gives us the motivation we need to complete menial tasks and even see the greater value in doing so.

In addition to acknowledging the pleasures we are willing to forego and the pains we are willing to tolerate in order to realize our human potential, we should also give ourselves the space to celebrate successes and mourn the pain of failures. In other words, we must recognize the feelings that directed us towards or away from our overarching goal, respectively. Inevitably, we can learn a great deal from both our successes and our mistakes. When we identify how a course of action proved effective, for instance, we affirm the passions that led us to take it and set ourselves up for similar successes in the future. As soon as we come to terms with the feelings that caused us to make a mistake, conversely, we catch the mistake at its dis-passionate source and thus identify how to rectify our approach and avoid making a similar mistake again.

When we acknowledge all the feelings that arise in the course of working towards our proper end—even those we ultimately choose to override or correct—in summary, we reinforce both reason's sense of purpose and the will's determination to execute it, situating ourselves in the optimal position to cultivate the passions that support the joint effort of reason and will to bear things well. If we stake our hopes for happiness on the attainment of specific goods or circumstances, on the other hand, we will inevitably succumb to the pleasures we would have to forgo and resist the pains we would have to suffer in order to bear our lives well. In other words, we will be led by dis-passions to delight in things that prevent us from bearing things well and to be repulsed by things that enable us to bear things well, such that we become unable to respond to stimuli in a manner that conduces to our flourishing.

Whereas we organize our lives around accomplishing our personal best in all situations when we bear things well, we are governed in the aforementioned circumstances by the impulses associated with obtaining the particular things we love and avoiding the particular things we hate.[15] Rather than conforming our lives around what is good, consequently, we become functions of our fixations and aversions, often developing what might be regarded as obsessive, addictive, or otherwise pathological tendencies. Although we may believe that we act in accordance with our own happiness when we operate on the basis of these desires and aversions, the paradoxical reality is that we do just the opposite.[16]

After all, happiness hinges on bearing things well.[17] Because limited ideas about happiness inhibit our ability to engage in this activity, they place our happiness at the mercy of circumstances, which determine whether or not we obtain the finite and fleeting objects of our desire. When we pursue goods that are not the arbiters of happiness on the assumption that they can secure our happiness, consequently, we invite not only unhappiness but also considerable perplexity as to the cause thereof. Though we may attain in some cases the things we thought would make us happy, the fact remains that we will not obtain happiness unless we cultivate the simple habit of bearing things well or making the best of what we have, which is the actual guarantor of happiness.

When the disordered passions—which lead us to love the things we ought not to love and not to love the things we ought to love—become fixed dispositions, they are transformed into vices, which are deficient dispositions on the part of the will to react to and act on the basis of stimuli.[18] In fact, vices and virtues simply represent two divergent approaches to reckoning with the passions—one that controls them and one that is controlled by them. The question whether we achieve our personal best or our personal worst—virtue or vice—thus comes down to which of these approaches we choose to employ. In what follows, I will outline the consequences of a choice in favor of what is not strictly speaking favorable, namely, vice, through a discussion of the seven capital vices.

The Seven Capital Vices

In the ethical account Thomas Aquinas creatively appropriates from Aristotle, every virtue represents the mean or perfect balance between a state of excess and one of deficiency.[19] The vices are perpetuated at the site of those two extremes. In what follows, I will elaborate on seven different pairs of extremes, each of which can be associated with one of the seven capital vices of pride, greed, envy, apathy, anger, lust, and gluttony.

The first of the capital vices is pride, the excessive and deficient forms of which are hubris and false humility, respectively.[20] Hubris entails an inflated self-image or self-love that is accompanied by an exaggerated sense of personal entitlement. When individuals thus regard themselves more highly than is appropriate, they deny their human limitations and so ironically betray some degree of shame over the physical and intellectual limitations that characterize all human beings.

By contrast to hubris, false humility turns on a deflated self-image or self-love. Whereas the hubristic deny personal limitations and inadequacies in the attempt surpass them, the falsely humble reduce their existence to those limitations. As a result, they perceive themselves as incompetent, undeserving, and worthless in one, many, or even all respects. Though false humility may be a matter of personal disposition, it is worth noting that it may also be imposed upon individuals, normally on account of some feature such as sex, race, or class, which is assumed to justify their manipulation or exploitation.

Either way, both the hubristic and the falsely humble self-assessments fail accurately to reflect the reality of the human situation.[21] Contrary to the hubristic presumption, for example, human beings are subject to limitations and do not therefore deserve to be revered as supremely authoritative beings, even in one particular arena. Nevertheless, all persons possess more restricted capabilities and seemingly deserve the right to develop them, however atypical they may be in relation to the conventional division of labor.[22] For the reasons just stated, therefore, hubris represents an excess while false humility constitutes a deficiency with respect to pride, while both bespeak an undue preoccupation with and false image of the self.[23]

Where pride fosters an excessive or deficient self-image, the second vice of greed actually directs human actions in accordance with that image. As Aquinas puts it, pride is the root of all vice when it comes to the intentions, which provide the impetus behind human actions, but greed takes priority when it comes to executing prideful actions.[24] Similar to pride, greed manifests in two extremes. Aristotle describes these in terms of extravagance and insensibility with respect to pleasures and pains, respectively.[25]

Since hubris generates the type of greed that is extravagant in terms of its thirst for pleasure and its resistance to pain, those characterized by hubris tend to assume entitlement to the fulfillment of their desires and to the avoidance of all they find unpleasant or distasteful. By contrast, the falsely humble are generally insensible to their own pain, including pain they should not tolerate and do not deserve to suffer. This is because they tend to think that they do not have the right to expect respect or appreciation, and that others alone deserve to enjoy pleasure and avoid pain, even at the expense of the basic human right of the falsely humble themselves to acquire and preserve the goods that are relevant to survival, to say nothing of cultivating personal capabilities.

Whereas hubris is marked by greed for pleasure and resistance to pain, in summary, false humility is defined by a 'greed for pain' and reluctance to accept pleasures, even including basic human rights. As I have already hinted, these extravagant and deficient tendencies play out in very practical ways when it comes to treating the objects of greed. On account of an inflated sense of entitlement, for example, the hubristic manipulate other persons, objects, and circumstances for personal ends, without regard for the damage or sheer loss of opportunity for self-actualization that may be incurred by the victims of their greed in the process.

Because the falsely humble effectively refuse to regard themselves as agents or subjects in their own right, by contrast, they make themselves available to be treated as objects to accomplish the purposes and fulfill the desires of others, even if these are vicious. Since the falsely humble generally perceive personal identity as derivative of or dependent upon that of others, moreover, they tend to seek approval for all their decisions from others, to whom they may even defer the authority to direct their lives. While pride leads persons to think of themselves as more or less than they really are, consequently, greed compels them to attribute greater or lesser significance to persons and objects than is warranted.

In one way or another, all the remaining five vices—envy, apathy, wrath, lust, and gluttony—derive from pride, in one of its forms, through greed, in a corresponding form. These further vices are the means through which individuals direct themselves towards different and mutually exclusive ends, in accordance with the objects of their greed. These ends bring them into conflict with one another, where virtue unites persons with diverse objectives under the overarching purpose of 'bearing things well.'

According to Aquinas, the order in which the remaining vices are commonly listed does not necessarily determine the order in which they are committed.[26] Furthermore, it does not bespeak any intrinsic connection between the vices. While certain vices may be present together in some cases or in some persons, this is completely a matter of contingency. Beyond pride and greed, all persons and parties are characterized by their own peculiar combination of vices, in whatever extreme. In Aquinas' account, in fact, the order in which the vices are listed merely traces a progression from more intensely spiritual to physical vices.[27] The spiritual vices, including pride, greed, envy, and apathy, are described as 'cold-hearted' or reputable, because they are indirect and thus covert or relatively easy to hide. By contrast, the physical vices of wrath, lust, and gluttony are referred to as 'warm-hearted' (i.e. 'carnal'), because they are direct, overt, obvious, and, to put it bluntly, childish.[28]

In ways on which I will elaborate below, the cold-hearted vices thrive on a failure to do what ought to be done and/or a tendency to take up tasks other than the ones that are most important. Though others are harmed by both means, this can be difficult to prove, precisely because no deed is strictly speaking done in the first place, while other potentially beneficial efforts are undertaken in the second. Though the harm done in these cases may not be directly intended, consequently, the perpetrators of cold-hearted vices are nonetheless blameworthy. For in the event they extrapolated the implications of their primary intentions to commit or refrain from committing certain acts, their culpability for the consequences of their actions would become obvious. Thus, it is by neglecting—and that culpably—to consider the consequences of their actions that the cold-hearted may succeed in exonerating themselves of vicious behavior in their own eyes and even in the eyes of others. In short, they succeed at self-deception.

Since vices can be disguised as virtues through self-deception, human acts must be understood to derive their virtuousness or viciousness from the ends towards which the acts are ordered—directly or indirectly—in a particular context. For example, politeness and charm can be employed to manipulate persons to make themselves available for abuse or exploitation, and to make them feel guilty or fearful if they fail to do so. As this example suggests, it takes acute sensitivity in every situation to what Aquinas calls the 'circumstances' of an action (who did what to whom, when, where, why, and how) in order to detect the intention behind an action and so decide whether it counts as an instance of a particular vice.

A related principle applies when it comes to determining whether certain ostensibly vicious acts are actually virtuous or at least acceptable in particular circumstances. While it seems possible and necessary to declare that acts like murder, theft, and lying are universally wrong, for example, it can be difficult to lay down hard and fast rules for determining when particular actions fall under such universal categories.[29] Indeed, it is sometimes ambiguous whether certain acts are virtuous or vicious, and discernment regarding circumstances is again required in order to tell the difference.[30]

By contrast to the cold-hearted vices, I have mentioned that the warm-hearted vices are not very easily concealed. The harm inflicted by the perpetration of such vices tends to be obvious, such that it is not normally difficult to cast blame for a wrong deed done. Though the physical or practical damage these vices cause can be very serious, it is arguably less grave than the harm done by the cold-hearted vices, not only because it is detectable and therefore correctable, which is often not the case with cold-hearted vices, but especially because it generally undermines the goods of the body and the world more than the higher goods of the soul, namely, intellectual and moral flourishing.

The first and arguably most sinister of the reputable vices is envy, which can be defined in terms of the despair that arises when an individual realizes that they lack something that another possesses.[31] So construed, an envious disposition is the result of a tendency to compare oneself to others as opposed to being content with one's own lot. While envy sometimes entails covetousness concerning another person's belongings, however, it does not always presuppose an actual desire for or interest in another's possessions, which may not after all be desirous or interesting to oneself. It can also entail a rather more base desire to eradicate evidence that others possess property, achievements, capabilities, or even personal qualities that differ from one's own. Thus, it can entail a desire to eliminate differences, which serve as an unwelcome reminder of personal limitations.

In the case of those characterized by hubristic envy, the desire to demolish difference tends to manifest in indirect or covert attempts to prevent others from exhibiting qualities the envious do not themselves possess or from succeeding in areas where the envious themselves wish to succeed. Generally, these attempts involve withholding due credit, support, or protection from those envied.[32] To cover up these subtle attempts to marginalize, exclude and generally deny those envied their due, the envious may show favoritism towards individuals who may not be deserving or at least not supremely deserving of assistance or honor—those who most closely resemble themselves—thus making it impossible for those envied to advance in a given area.[33]

By contrast, the falsely humble aim in envy to eliminate the differences they themselves exhibit, so as to blend in with the majority and thus benefit from the solidarity and protection of the *status quo*. In some cases, the envy of the falsely humble may express itself through flattery and servility.[34] By such means, the falsely humble self-deprecatingly misrepresent or indebt themselves to others, disingenuously affirming the primacy of those they flatter with a view to manipulating the same to overlook their differences and regard them as equals.[35] In the case of both extremes, the vice committed is indirect and covert and thus cold-hearted, precisely because envy is disguised in the form of assisting or praising other persons. For this very reason, I have noted, the envious may persuade others and even themselves that their vicious acts are virtuous.

While hubris generates excess and false humility deficiency in the case of most vices, the situation is exceptionally reversed when it comes to the next vice of apathy. The deficient form of this vice, which is proper to hubris, consists in lethargy, laziness or lack of ambition, while the excessive form associated with false humility entails rash or reckless behavior.[36] Either way, apathy is marked by a sense of purposelessness or a lack of the willpower to follow through on a given purpose.

In the case of this vice, hubris manifests in a refusal to take risks or countenance unknown or potentially challenging situations. After all, hubris precludes the recognition of personal deficiencies and consequently compels the apathetic to avoid situations where they might fail or be found wanting. Frequently, the hubristic form of apathy also entails meanness, or an unwillingness to spend time, energy, or other resources to accomplish some worthwhile end.[37] Ironically, then, the excessive form of the vice in question engenders cowardice, the form of indirect action in which individuals refuse to do what they can and ought to do on account of their fear of being exposed as ignorant or incapable in some respect.

This immobilizing fear often leads the lethargic to fill their time with idle, non-threatening pursuits that can easily be mastered. It gives way to what Aquinas calls *curiositas*: the pursuit of activities, knowledge or hobbies that have no particular purpose, and do not even count as 'leisure' activity, which strictly speaking serves the purpose of rejuvenating the mind and body for work.[38] In certain cases, some of the other vices are called upon here to pass time. While hubristic envy undermines or excludes others, wrath overtly sabotages their plans. By contrast, lust and gluttony turn to sex or food—not for genuine intimacy or nourishment—but simply to secure fleeting satisfaction for an empty, restless heart.[39]

Though such activities may consume a considerable amount of time and energy, they merely serve as a substitute for any real activity, directed towards a purpose or end compatible with self-actualization. They represent attempts to evade boredom. By these means, of course, the apathetic neglect their duties, presumably on the assumption that they are 'above' dealing with any tedious or onerous tasks. Through their negligence, consequently, they shift the burden of their responsibilities on to others, whose time is unjustly regarded as less important.

Since the falsely humble in their turn tend to lack a sense of purpose or at least the self-confidence and willpower to follow through on their purposes, they are particularly prone to assuming these abandoned responsibilities. In fact, the falsely humble are recognizably reckless or rash because they remain perpetually ready to desert their own purposes and projects in order to re-organize their plans around the demands of others, even in cases where they are not explicitly asked to do so.[40] Since the need to be needed effectively substitutes for any real sense of purpose in their situation, the falsely humble may insist on sacrificing what they need or want to give to others, even if this is not what others need or want to receive. They thus control and manipulate those for whom they feel responsible in ways that can actually prove detrimental to the objects of their so-called affection.[41]

The ironic and largely counterproductive motivation behind such behavior is in many cases a vainglorious craving for praise, attention, and approval—apart from which the falsely humble cannot normally sustain any sense of self-worth.[42] This need for approval may also render the rash susceptible to perfectionism and excessive tenacity, or a headstrong preoccupation with details that are of little consequence, and a corresponding habit of nagging others about those details, especially those who are apathetic in the deficient sense.[43] By virtue of being so quick to take up all the tasks the lethargic fail to complete satisfactorily or even leave undone, however, the reckless merely establish their hubristic counterparts more firmly in a passive frame of mind and invite upon themselves an ever-increasing burden of responsibility.

Since it is scarcely possible to bear this burden well, the reluctance of the rash to lay down principles by which to prioritize activities, decline requests, and respond to needs—whether real or perceived—tends to launch them into a flurry of trivial and diffuse activities, which prevent them not only from maximizing personal potential but also from perceiving wherein that potential truly lies. Because they are constantly distracted, scattered, rattled, rushed, and thrown off course, they do a thousand things and nothing, such that they may eventually lose all sense of self, or even self-destruct.

While the cold-hearted vices largely turn on indirect action, I have intimated that the warm-hearted vices of wrath, lust and gluttony are mainly matters of direct action, which is why they are more easily detectable and thus less 'reputable.'[44] In its hubristic form, the first of these vices, namely, wrath, lashes out in a long list of ways, which on Aquinas' account includes robbery;[45] cheating;[46] murder;[47] injury;[48] derision;[49] defamation of character;[50] discord or contrariety of wills;[51] contention or contrariety of speech;[52] strife or contrariety of actions;[53] schism;[54] and so on.

In its falsely humble form, wrath entails a deficiency in due anger, that is, an over-willingness to reconcile with or remain subjected to the harmful influence of oppressors.[55] Both excessive wrath and its opposite, which might be defined in terms of over-submissiveness or over-compliance, evidently proceed from an urge towards self-protection. For the hubristic, this urge motivates hostile attempts at self-defense; by contrast, it renders the falsely humble reluctant to stand up for themselves in threatening situations, since they may be penalized by the powerful for resisting their own mistreatment or exploitation.

The excessive form of the next vice, namely lust, is shamelessness with regard to sexual fixations, perversion, or the sexual exploitation of others. The deficient form involves shamefulness or unwarranted disgust at personal sexuality.[56] Such prudishness can be distinguished from chastity, wherein an individual or a couple abstains from sex for the sake of accomplishing some specific purpose, and not out of repulsion at sex itself.[57]

In addition to manifesting their own characteristic vices, there are numerous ways in which both the shameless and the shameful may participate in and thus perpetuate each other's lustful habits. Through certain forms of promiscuity or immodesty, for example, the shame-faced may implicate themselves in the activities of the shameless by enabling those activities, which are an especially sad manifestation of the self-loathing that is inherent in false humility.[58]

On the other hand, the shameless may participate in and exacerbate the prudishness of the shame-faced by failing to treat sex as the sign of a committed and mutually empowering relationship between two people. In fact, the shameful may develop disgust at their own sexuality on account of having been treated by so-called lovers as objects to be used for the satisfaction of lustful desires rather than as subjects worthy of being loved and supported on their own terms.

Though lust is normally considered to be a vice that is specifically related to human sexuality, I would argue that it can also be more generally defined in terms of an overpowering desire for or resistance to any particular good: not merely personal relationships, but also fame, power, wealth, and so on. Arguably, lust can also have as its object some of the goods of the soul, such as knowledge, causes, and so on. In short, any good that becomes an obsession can be said to be an object of lust.

A similar principle applies to the last vice of gluttony, which concerns the goods of the body by contrast to those of the external world. Though gluttony is ordinarily supposed to manifest in any inordinate—self-indulgent or self-depriving, excessive or deficient—desire for food or drink, it might also be said to express itself in the pursuit or avoidance of any substance or activity that is relevant to the physical needs—life, health, hygiene—of the body.[59]

The Extremes of Vice

Thus far, the seven capital vices have been shown to manifest in both excessive and deficient forms. Although I will elaborate in the next chapter on the way the four cardinal virtues strike the mean between these extremes, I would briefly note here that the mean between the extreme forms of pride and greed, respectively, seems to involve an accurate self-image and image of other things, that is, the virtue of prudence; the mean between the extreme forms of both envy and wrath entails justice; apathy, fortitude; lust and gluttony, temperance.

In this section, my purpose is to demonstrate how the two extreme forms of vice tend by default to obscure the existence of one of the extremes, normally the one associated with false humility. I will explain how the one-sided perspective that results enables perpetrators of both extremes to avoid acknowledging their vices and even to regard those vices as virtues. Indeed, I will argue that the vices subsisting at both extremes cannot be fully conquered until the very existence of the two extremes is recognized.

On Aristotle's account, the aforementioned bias towards the hubristic vices is attributable to the fact that the majority is prone to lapse into precisely these vices.[60] Thus, persons are more liable in his view to be extravagant than insensible; to sabotage than to flatter; to be lazy than reckless; to be wrathful than over-willing to reconcile with oppressors; to act shamefully than prudishly; and to over-indulge than subject themselves to deprivation.

According to Aristotle, the reason for the human tendency to exhibit these vicious proclivities sometimes pertains to human nature itself, namely, where human beings have a particularly common weakness to, say, indulge, rather than deprive themselves, on account of their animal orientation towards self-preservation or survival.[61] In other cases, the reason for human leanings towards specific vices has more to do with the nature of the vice and corresponding virtue in question. When one of the extremes is especially closely related to the relevant virtue, as in the case of rashness and bravery, for example, it is easy to overlook the fact that recklessness is a vice and simply oppose bravery and cowardice.

Though Aristotle could scarcely help but perceive the hubristic vices as normative, given the patriarchal structure of his society, his efforts to develop an account of virtue as the mean between extreme forms of vice positioned him to overcome the hegemony of the hubristic vices and elaborate on the vices that are more common from the standpoint of false humility: vices that play out altogether differently from those proceeding from hubris and must therefore be corrected by correspondingly distinct methods.[62]

In addition to the plausible reasons Aristotle offers as to why a one-sided conception of vice tends to prevail, I have suggested that the very nature of the extremes themselves allows for the eclipse of one by the other. Where the hubristic conception of pride is considered standard, for example, the falsely humble tend to perceive even appropriate attempts to assert personal rights as expressions of pride. As a result, they find themselves guilty of vices they do not actually exhibit and in the same instance exacerbate their own vicious habit of acting in overly-submissive and compliant ways, whereby they enable the exploitative tendencies of the hubristic.

Since this arrangement works in their favor, the hubristic are generally not inclined to correct the vices of the falsely humble. Instead, they usually do everything in their power to keep the falsely humble in a subjected state of mind. To this end, they may accuse their vicious counterparts of the very vices they themselves exhibit, in order to disguise the fact that they exhibit them, in what is an exemplification of, or at least closely related to, the phenomenon known in modern theorization as 'psychological projection.'[63]

In such cases, the hubristic may accuse the falsely humble of insubordination for appropriate attempts to resist authoritarian control; or of excessive self-interest or self-indulgence for requesting help that is needed and deserved. According to Aristotle, the hubristic may even go so far as to accuse those who are virtuous of vices opposed to their own in order to detract attention from their personal faults. Thus, the cowardly call the brave 'rash' in order to cast cowardice in an acceptable light; gluttons accuse moderate eaters of self-deprivation in order to excuse their own over-indulgence; and the lazy charge those who are appropriately ambitious and industrious with working to an excessive and even unhealthy degree in order to render their own lack of purpose and drive unproblematic.

Such tactics are bound to enjoy a high rate of success, not only because the falsely humble are predisposed to demean rather than defend themselves, but also insofar as the hubristic tend to penalize those who resist their authority in ways that make it impossible to do so, particularly in cases where individuals or classes are falsely humble by coercion rather than disposition. In this light, it emerges that the correction of false humility requires not only a commitment on the part of the falsely humble to overcome their own reluctance to challenge the hegemony of hubris, but also a willingness on the part of the hubristic to be receptive to confrontation and indeed to exercise restraint when it comes to assuming entitlement to privilege or authority.

For these purposes, however, an awareness of the very existence of the two forms of vice is clearly required. In the absence of such an awareness, the falsely humble can hardly help but proceed by correcting vices stemming from hubris which they do not actually possess, while the hubristic, enabled by the falsely humble, carry on committing their characteristic vices without consequences and thus on the assumption that their vices are not vicious at all. Under the auspices of a one-sided conception of vice, in summary, perpetrators of both forms of vice may successfully manage to commit their respective vices on the assumption that they are actually living rightly and well.

The Degrees of Vice

The last point brings us to a discussion of the various degrees of vice. In this connection, I will consider both the degrees to which individuals may be entrenched in vicious habits and the degree of gravity that may be attributed to vicious acts.[64] When it comes to the first of the aforementioned ways of analyzing the degrees of vice, there are three main levels of vice, namely, incontinence, intemperance, and systemic intemperance.[65] Although the incontinent are fully aware that they are in the wrong when they act viciously, they nevertheless act against their better judgment, whether through crimes of passion or weakness of will.

As noted previously, a crime of passion results from a failure on reason's part to think through an appropriate course of action in particular circumstances.[66] Such neglect leaves room for reason to get 'caught up in' or 'carried away by' feelings associated with those circumstances.[67] By contrast, weakness of will springs from a failure to access and act on the knowledge of what is right.[68] Although the incontinent circumnavigate reason in these ways, their wrongdoings nonetheless accord implicitly with decision, insofar as they retain recourse to the knowledge of what is right which accuses them or could in principle accuse them of the wrong they have done.

While the incontinent may be prevented by external circumstances, restraints or even sheer willpower from acting in line with evil intentions, the intentions are nonetheless problematic, because they are bound to engender vicious acts as soon as circumstances or a loss of self-control allow.[69] Thus, incontinence—actual or intentional—creates a rather slippery slope in that every one-off or occasional vicious act or desire to commit a vicious act sets the stage for further vicious acts and makes it more difficult not only to choose virtue but also to perceive the problems with vice. In this regard, incontinence anticipates although it does not necessarily terminate in intemperance.

At the stage of intemperance, the vicious become unable even to recognize their vices as such, because they sever completely their ties with the moral sense that alerts them or can in principle alert them to the base nature of their actions.[70] By thus eradicating their moral sensibilities or conscience, they come by some twisted logic to believe that wrongdoing is in their best interests and those of others. On adjusting desires accordingly, they come to want to do what is wrong and to delight in doing it, where the incontinent would feel guilty about their behavior on some level. As a result, the intemperate feel no remorse or regret over their wrongdoings. While it may have been open to them at one point to reacquire virtue, the ongoing tendency to opt for vice eventually brings them to the point where they are effectively unable to break the vicious habits they have formed. At this advanced phase, they can only be corrected, if at all, through external efforts to break a completely contorted will.

A third degree of vice sets in when intemperance infiltrates the very structures or institutions of society. This presumably occurs when society or groups within it lose sight of the viciousness of a particular method of operating, such that wrongdoing is normalized or institutionalized and thus rendered right within a given context. When intemperance is writ large in this manner, contesting the oppressive or destructive structures, systems or institutions that supposedly facilitate society's functioning, itself comes to be regarded as an offense. Under these circumstances, it is arguable that vice cannot be conquered until awareness is raised of the extremes of vice, the oversight of which allows for the systematization of intemperance in the first place.

The degree of severity attributable to vicious acts at any of the three aforementioned levels may be further exacerbated by what Aquinas calls the 'circumstances' of an action, which concern who committed the act, the nature of the act, and against whom, where, when, and how it was committed.[71] In this connection, I have noted that a cold-hearted act is in many respects more serious than a warm-hearted one.[72] Moreover, a vice that is habitual is more problematic than a one-off or occasional mistake.[73] An evil deed committed by an individual with a great deal of authority is worse than one committed by a person with little influence.[74]

Conversely, an attack directed against someone with wide-reaching influence is graver than an attack on a person with little or no influence.[75] That stated, harm done to someone with little or no means of defending themselves is more culpable than wronging a person who has means of self-protection. A vice that affects a large number of people is more serious than one that affects only a few.[76] Similarly, a vice that causes greater harm or destruction is more blameworthy than one that affects only a minor upset; murder, for example, is significantly worse than a slap on the face.[77]

In addition to all these factors, which increase the severity of any given vicious act, the gravity of vice may be intensified in accordance with the degree to which it is committed voluntarily.[78] In cases where a vice is committed involuntarily, that is, unconsciously or unintentionally, the severity of the vice is diminished, to such an extent that the offender can in some cases be exonerated of responsibility altogether.[79] An exception to this rule consists in cases where the offender could or should have known better than to commit a vicious act but was hindered in this regard by the influence of alcohol, for example, sleep-deprivation, or some other inhibited state of mind.[80] In such instances of what Aquinas calls 'non-voluntary' action, the offense in question is blameworthy, precisely because it would have been possible to avoid acting in or to avoid altogether the state of being which impaired the ability to discern the difference between right and wrong.[81]

In cases where individuals are forced to participate in vicious social structures—as slaves or otherwise exploited parties, for example—they cannot by contrast be held responsible for the situation into which they are compelled, unless they enter into it willingly. That stated, there are certain situations in which it is arguably better to suffer punishment or even death than to comply with evil forces, in particular when individuals are compelled not only to subject themselves to those forces but even to contribute to and thus consent to them.[82]

These cases aside, Aquinas further refers to actions that proceed from 'mixed' motives, which are part voluntary, part involuntary, in that they would not normally be committed by choice but become necessary under certain circumstances. While a ship's captain would not willingly waste his cargo, for instance, he might instruct his crew to throw it overboard when doing so means saving the lives of passengers during a severe storm at sea.[83] Since human beings are inevitably caught in a network of relationships involving diverse and sometimes conflicting considerations, pressures, expectations, desires, and fears that have to be weighed against one another, there is a sense in which many choices are likely to proceed from mixed motives. However they are motivated, human actions are vicious and culpable in accordance with the degree to which they are consensual.

Vice vs Virtue

In the first part of this chapter, I demonstrated how vicious tendencies are formed when the greatest 'good of the soul,' namely self-actualization, which is the cause of flourishing and happiness, is reduced to any other good of the soul, the external world, or the body. When our proper end is thus confused with one that is inferior to it, I showed that our energies tend to be invested in the pursuit of purposes that are inconsistent with our own happiness, or flourishing. In the most paradoxical cases, we may actually undermine our own thriving in our very efforts to promote it. As this suggests, and as I now wish to argue, it is necessary to grasp that in which happiness truly consists in order to obtain it. Apart from the knowledge of our real purpose or end, it is impossible to pursue our best interests, let alone recognize them, even if they are manifestly obvious.

Although reason is generally the faculty that appoints ends or objects of pursuit for human beings, while the will deliberates about the most effective means to these ends, the task of determining an appropriate end falls exceptionally to the will in the moral context of self-actualization. This is because there is no fixity in moral by contrast to intellectual matters, as Aristotle suggests, and as I noted in the section on 'passion and vice.' In other words, there is not 'one way' to be a human being. Rather, there are virtually as many ways to engage in the moral project of self-actualization as there are human beings.[84]

Since there is considerable flexibility concerning ends when it comes to choosing a course in human life, the will must deliberate prudently about what counts as an appropriate end in the first place.[85] When it does so, it clarifies our basic human purpose to engage in self-actualization in what Aquinas calls the 'order of intention,' so that it can subsequently fulfill this purpose in the 'order of execution,' or with regard to the virtuous use of our aptitudes and resources as means to the end of being and becoming what we are.[86]

The way the prudent will performs its function in the moral sphere parallels while remaining distinct from its mode of operation in the intellectual context. In intellectual endeavors, the rightly functioning will alerts us when we say more or less than is true of a given state of affairs, or when we claim more or less than we validly can on the basis of available evidence.[87] It accomplishes both feats by identifying the middle term that unites two extreme terms, such that nothing irrelevant is included and nothing relevant is excluded in the conclusion of a final argument or syllogism.

In the moral context, similarly, the will helps us discern when we are aiming for more or less than is appropriate for us as human beings. It thereby strikes upon the moral counterpart to the middle term, which Aristotle and Aquinas have famously called the 'mean' between the excessive and deficient extremes of vice.[88] As I have followed Aristotle in emphasizing, this mean is relative to individual persons and to what Aquinas calls the circumstances of any given action. What is appropriate for one person or in one context may not therefore be right for another person in another situation.

As regards the end of self-actualization, I have intimated that prudence appoints the mean between excess and deficiency by teaching us simply to bear to the best of our abilities whatever we have to bear in terms of intellectual and other resources.[89] To do anything less, through false humility, would be to fall short of our humanity. To try to do more, on account of hubris, would be to attempt to escape the human condition. By striking the intermediate between the extremes of hubris and false humility, consequently, the prudent will focuses our sights on our proper end, namely, that of bearing things well, enabling us to make the most of the human lives we actually possess.

In this respect, the will safeguards reason from the passions that might lead us to mistake our proper end for some other end, thus preventing us from moving towards our end. More specifically, the will gives reason the chance to respond appropriately to conflicting emotions, without rushing into a crime of passion, or to make recourse to knowledge of what is right when there might be a temptation to neglect it out of weakness of will. By these means, the prudent will prevents the mind from being controlled by the passions aroused by immediate pleasures and pains, giving it the chance to exercise control over the passions and properly manage its responses to them instead.

Since it belongs to us as rational beings to maintain such control over the one matter that is subject to our direction, namely, our ability to bear things well, this activity of responding rightly to situations can arguably be described as operation 'in accord with (human) nature' and therefore in 'accord with reason.'[90] By operating along these lines, we observe the mean or identify what an appropriately balanced, as opposed to excessive or deficient, response to any situation would involve. Thus, appointing the mean is precisely the way that we as rational animals actualize our distinctive potential to the best of our abilities, fulfilling the natural law, inasmuch as it pertains to our species.[91]

As I showed in Chapter 2, the natural law entails a single mandate to seek what is best and avoid what is bad in all cases, continually striking the mean between excess and deficiency.[92] In that sense, as I argued in Chapter 5, observing the natural law as a human being involves answering to the natural habit of *synderesis*, which motivates us always to strive to achieve our personal best.[93] Arguably, further applications of the natural law—which might be described as laws in themselves—may be derived from the one natural law to promote the highest good.

In the case of human beings, for example, it might be said that all have a purpose to fulfill, with the help of prudence, though that purpose must be specified on an individual basis. As a rule, this purpose renders persons responsible to contribute in some way to the welfare of others, that is, to administer justice. Moreover, doing so requires fortitude or endurance in the face of the challenges that often arise in the course of efforts to accomplish the ends of prudence through justice, as well as the temperance to take pleasure in performing prudent and just tasks above all else, and so avoid the distractions posed by other attractive prospects.[94]

So construed, the rules pertaining to the four cardinal moral virtues serve the purpose of making it possible to fulfill the single natural law. As this implies, an ethic of virtue is not incompatible with the natural law, as some have supposed.[95] After all, the natural law simply requires that we strive by means of cultivating the moral virtues to achieve the highest good of bearing things well at all times.[96] Precisely because the fulfillment of this law is convertible with habituation in moral virtue, that law and its implications in the spheres of prudence, justice, fortitude, and temperance are formal rather than substantial by this account.[97] In other words, they offer indications of the kinds of activities that are appropriate for human persons, without necessarily specifying those activities exactly.

In espousing this conception of the natural law, the present account diverges from the interpretation of many historical and recent natural lawyers, according to whom the natural law and any further laws inferred from it prescribe the way all persons should act.[98] Arguably, this interpretation of the natural law not only overlooks the variations amongst persons and circumstances that call for equally varied interpretations of the natural law to 'bear things well,' but also proffers a version of the law which has rightly been identified as incompatible with the ethic of virtue to which the natural law is evidently reconciled in Aquinas' own understanding.

Such an interpretation notwithstanding, it is impossible to delineate universally applicable rules that exonerate human beings from the task of exercising discretion, or prudence, regarding what exactly it means to bear things well in every situation. As I have insisted, the success of such deliberations turns on the cultivation of the moral virtues, which attune us to the overarching natural law to operate for the highest good and enable us to fulfill it. The acquisition of these virtues is essential, precisely because human beings bear a daily responsibility for identifying by means of moral virtue what satisfying the natural law, operating in accordance with human nature, or maximizing human potential would involve in individual cases.

In that sense, any attempt to find a way around exerting ourselves along these lines in any and every situation would seem to entail an attempt to evade the human condition and thus to denigrate the human form of life.[99] Because the process of deciding how to apply the natural law in any situation requires deliberation and thus a reasoning process akin to the one outlined in Chapter 4, preparing ourselves to discern how to act rightly in circumstances that arise is clearly not merely a matter of establishing certain rules or laws concerning correct forms of behavior. Above all, it is a matter of being personally predisposed by moral virtue to detect if, where, when, and how rules ought to be applied: to be predisposed to bear situations well and thus fulfill the natural law in the way that is relevant for human beings, namely through the exercise of moral virtue.[100] Though all circumstances in life are subject to change, nothing can ever rob us of this ability.[101] Thus, we can never be robbed of our happiness, which consists in the activity of bearing things well.

As this suggests, happiness as I have defined it is a state we can enjoy even when we are overwhelmed by the unpleasant feelings that often accompany the challenges inherent in opting for the greater over lesser goods. As noted previously, we cannot help but feel many discomforting passions—such as fear, anger, confusion, and worry—when circumstances arouse these feelings in us. On this showing, however, happiness is not contingent upon the total extirpation of such passions. In fact, I have argued that our thriving actually depends on facing and on some level allowing ourselves to feel every passion experience arouses, however dispassionate, or even to admit when we have lost the passion or drive to take up the tasks for which we are responsible.

By acknowledging these passions or problematic deficiencies in due passion, we acquire the opportunity to decide whether the passion in question or lack thereof will help or hinder our work to fulfill our greatest passion of bearing things well and thus to decide whether and how to let it affect us. That is to say, we obtain the chance to cultivate passion in the true sense of the term, to wit, affection. Though the emotions we feel when we strive to bear things well may prove difficult, consequently, facing them, though not always allowing our actions to be altered by them, promotes and sustains the overriding and supremely satisfying feeling that bearing things well is worth our while.

Of course, this feeling may not come easily at first. But the more we find through practice that our happiness lies where we have chosen to believe it lies, namely, in bearing things well, the less likely we are to think of the things we formerly regarded as decisive for happiness as essential to achieving that state. The more we stake our hopes for happiness in the only thing we can control, which is our way of dealing with our circumstances, in summary, the less the circumstances we face will have the power to evoke difficult feelings in us. This is the force of the maxim that 'virtue is its own reward,' namely, that the reward for a life of virtue is simply to be untroubled by things that might otherwise trouble us greatly. Thus unimpeded by emotions that might crush us or subject us to various compulsions, we discover what it means to be human—to be happy—by discovering a freedom to flourish or find the good in all things by bearing them well.[102]

Once a prudent will has orientated reason towards its proper end along the lines described above, a position is obtained from which to follow through on our commitment to work towards this end. As I have demonstrated, it falls to prudence not only to rectify the will and thus give us an aptitude or intention to perform our proper functions but also to direct actions in accordance with this basic intention.[103] Since securing this intention satisfies the precondition for such actions, it sets the stage for fulfilling the sufficient conditions for pro-theological philosophy, that is, for exercising prudence as the virtue that identifies means to the end of bearing things well in specific situations.

As I will demonstrate in the following chapter, prudence, as both an intellectual and a moral virtue, accomplishes this feat by helping us observe the due order of circumstances, that is, by leading us to do the right thing to the right person or object, by the right means, with the right approach, at the right place, at the right time, and for the right reason.[104] By acting in ways that are appropriate not only for us but also in our circumstances, therefore, we bear our circumstances prudently, or well. In this connection, I will show in the next chapter that prudence is supported by the other three cardinal virtues, which are purely moral. The second cardinal virtue of justice is chief amongst these moral virtues because it extrapolates and executes the consequences of prudence for human relationships and in this capacity perfects the will.[105]

While justice strikes the mean between the extremes associated with envy and wrath, fortitude reinforces the purposes of prudence through justice by giving us the courage or irascible passions we need to follow through on them in the face of challenges. By operating in this primary sense, fortitude simultaneously works in a secondary sense, curbing apathy in both its extreme forms of lethargy and rashness, thus checking the irascible passions that would hinder us in the pursuit of our proper end.

Finally, temperance carries out the ends of prudence and justice in the midst of distractions and temptations to do otherwise by filling us with the concupiscible passions that are relevant to reaching those ends. In performing this primary task, it secondarily curbs lust and gluttony, whereby passions for things other than our primary ends are allowed to exceed our passion for those ends and thus to prevent us from reaching them. Together, then, the virtues of fortitude and temperance, which perfect the passions, fill us with the energy we need to do the work of prudence and justice. Whereas the vices enslave us to our desires for and aversions to particular things, these two along with the other virtues collectively relax our attitude towards the fleeting pains and pleasures of this world. In doing so, they remove the inhibitions on account of which we might forfeit the greatest pleasure of all, which is the pleasure of expressing ourselves without hindrance through the activity of bearing things well.

Endnotes

[1]   See Vivian Boland in *Eight Deadly Sins* (London: Catholic Truth Society, 2007). See also Dorothy Sayers, 'The Other Six Deadly Sins,' in *Letters to a Diminished Church: Passionate Arguments for the Relevance of Christian Doctrine* (Dallas: Thomas Nelson, 2004).

[2]   See Aristotle's extensive enumeration of vices at *EE* II.3, 1220b-1221a. This list is useful for present purposes, since Aristotle there isolates what can be identified as the extreme forms of many different vices.

3   In her influential article titled, 'Modern Moral Philosophy' (*Philosophy* 33:124, January 1958), G.E.M. Anscombe maintains that 'moral philosophy ... should be laid aside ... until we have an adequate philosophy of psychology, in which we are conspicuously lacking.' One of my purposes in this chapter is to provide the account of the philosophy of psychology—or human passions—that is an essential precursor to accounts of human knowledge and morality.

4   *ST* 2.1.1.7.

5   The open-endedness of human nature is precisely what distinguishes rational animals from other kinds of animals. In the case of non-human animals, there can only ever be one right way to be. This is because each species possesses only one proper end. Since members of these species move towards their proper ends by force of nature, they cannot really be said to know their ends and direct themselves towards those ends of their own accord; they possess what Aquinas calls imperfect knowledge of their ends, in which ends are not known as ends. While other animals are carried along by instinct towards ends they do not determine for themselves, reacting to their environment accordingly, human beings set their own ends and move themselves towards them under the impetus of free will (*ST* 2.1.1.1–2). Uniquely, humans are self-determining and self-moving (*ST* 2.1.6.1–2); and that is why there are innumerable possible ways for human beings to engage in self-actualization.

6   See Peter Geach, *Reason and Argument* (Oxford: Blackwell, 1976), 96–9.

7   *EN* I.7, 1098a13–19: if we affirm 'the function of man to be a certain kind of life, and this to be an activity or actions of the soul implying a rational principle, and the function of a good man to be the good and noble performance of these ... human good turns out to be activity of soul in conformity with excellence, and if there is more than one excellence, in conformity with the best and most complete.'

8   *EN* I.4.

9   *ST* 2.1.75.4. According to Aquinas, vices arise when the sensitive appetite grasps some apparent good, and the will encourages reason to pursue this good in a way that undermines its orientation towards its proper end.

10   For Aquinas, weakness of will entails a failure of what he calls 'higher reason,' which governs the operation of the intellect, precisely because it involves some level of consent to an evil act. By contrast, crimes of passion are attributed to 'lower reason,' which governs the senses and imagination, because they are not premeditated; cf. *De Veritate* 15.3.

11   Herbert McCabe, 'Prudentia,' in *On Aquinas* (London: Burns and Oates, 2008).

12   *ST* 2.1.78.1. While good may exist without evil, evil cannot exist unless in contrast with the good.

13   *ST* 2.1.1.5.

¹⁴   *EN* X.5. According to Aristotle, some pleasures are intrinsically good, but are nonetheless not worth pursuing, when they undermine efforts to prioritize more important activities, particularly those that conduce to self-actualization.

¹⁵   *EN* II.3; Martha Nussbaum, *The Therapy of Desire: Theory and Practice in Hellenistic Ethics* (Princeton: Princeton University Press, 2009). According to Nussbaum, different cultures vary in terms of the ways they teach children to cope with pleasures and pains. In this connection, Nussbaum rightly notes that many societies impart to children conventions for managing feelings that actually preclude their proper or healthy management. On her account, whole social groups or social orders may come to sanction specific surges towards instant gratification, making it socially unacceptable to break with accepted, albeit problematic, patterns of emotional reaction, since doing so challenges the legitimacy of social norms.

¹⁶   *ST* 2.1.29.4.

¹⁷   Nicholas Lombardo, *The Logic of Desire: Aquinas on Emotion* (Washington, DC: The Catholic University of America Press, 2010), 84–6: the supreme pleasure (joy) of human life consists in self-actualization, while the greatest pain (sorrow) is constituted by a failure to realize personal potential.

¹⁸   *ST* 2.1.71.1–2.

¹⁹   *EN* II.8.

²⁰   *ST* 2.2.162.

²¹   *ST* 2.1.77.4. Inordinate self-love is the cause of every vice.

²²   See Martha Nussbaum, *Creating Capabilities: The Human Development Approach* (Harvard: Harvard University Press, 2010).

²³   Valerie Saiving Goldstein, 'The Human Situation: A Feminine View,' *The Journal of Religion* 40:2 (April 1960), 100–112. Many feminist thinkers like Goldstein have called attention to the fact that women tend to fall short of their personal best in a way that differs from and is even opposed to the typical male way of doing so. Indeed, the account of vice I have been developing in terms of extremes of excess and deficiency seems to lend itself to a 'gendered' taxonomy of the vices according to which there seem to be distinctly 'male' and 'female' ways of falling short when it comes to bearing things well, ways are characterized by hubris and false humility, respectively. To affirm this is by no means to suggest that only members of the male sex can commit the male or excessive vices, and members of the female sex the female or deficient vices. Since dispositions of any kind are arguably not determined by the body but the soul, male and female vices can arguably characterize persons regardless of sex.

²⁴   *ST* 2.1.84.1–2: pride vs greed as the origin of every sin.

²⁵   *EE* II.3, 1221a2.

²⁶   *ST* 2.1.73.1.

²⁷   *ST* 2.1.72.2.

28   *ST* 2.2.142.2.

29   Jean Porter, *Moral Action and Christian Ethics* (Cambridge: Cambridge University Press, 1995), 46: 'the meaning of our concept of the moral must therefore be given first of all in terms of the concepts of kinds of actions that exemplify immoral behavior, for example, murder, theft, lying, adultery, and fraud.' See also, 38: 'if a serious question has been raised about the legitimacy of a given kind of action then what is at issue is precisely whether this kind of action should count as (for example) murder.'

30   *ST* 2.1.94.3, reply 3: 'for it is owing to the various conditions of men, that certain acts are virtuous for some, as being proportionate and becoming to them, while they are vicious for others, as being out of proportion to them.'

31   *ST* 2.2.36.1.

32   *ST* 2.1.71.5.

33   *ST* 2.2.63.

34   *ST* 2.2.115.

35   *ST* 2.2.111, 113.

36   *ST* 2.2.125–7.

37   *ST* 2.2.135.1.

38   *ST* 2.2.167.1, see Paul Griffiths, 'Curiositas,' in *Intellectual Appetite: A Theological Grammar* (Washington, DC: The Catholic University of America Press, 2009). Josef Pieper, *Leisure: The Basis of Culture* (Ignatius, 2009).

39   Dorothy Sayers, 'The Other Six Deadly Sins,' 104.

40   *ST* 2.2.130.1.

41   In fostering this 'need to be needed,' the rash oppose the principle stated by C.S. Lewis in *The Four Loves* (London: Harcourt, 1988), 50, according to which, 'the proper aim of giving is to put the recipient in a state where he no longer needs our gift ... Thus a heavy task is laid upon this gift-love. It must work towards its own abdication ... The [giving] instinct desires the good of its object, but not simply—only the good it can itself give.'

42   *ST* 2.2.132.

43   *ST* 2.2.138.2.

44   *ST* 2.2.158.6.

45   *ST* 2.2.66.

46   *ST* 2.2.77–8.

47   *ST* 2.2.64.

48   *ST* 2.2.65.

49   *ST* 2.2.75.

50   *ST* 2.2.67–8, 72–7.

51   *ST* 2.2.37.

52   *ST* 2.2.38.1.

53   *ST* 2.2.41.

54   *ST* 2.2.39.

55   *ST* 2.2.158; cf. *EE* II.4, 122b1–4.

56   *ST* 2.2.153–4.

57   *ST* 2.2.151–2.

58   *ST* 2.2.168–9.

59   *ST* 2.2.148, 150.

60   *EE* II.5.

61   *EN* I.8.

62   More specifically, overcoming the hubristic vices would seemingly involve habituation in the secondary functions of temperance and fortitude, whereby we curb excessive desires for pleasures and resistance to pain. Conquering falsely humble vices by contrast would mean learning temperance and fortitude in the primary sense, or learning to take pleasure in the things that are actually good for us, and mustering up the strength to pursue those things. In gaining victory over their vices, therefore, those prone to hubristic vices take the necessary measures to check their concupiscible passions in order to come to terms with the right irascible passions. Conversely, those prone to falsely humble vices counter their imbalanced irascible passions in order to acquire appropriate concupiscible passions. When they counteract their vices by the proper, opposing, means, consequently, those subject to the hubristic and falsely humble vices transform their areas of weakness into areas of strength: the former stand up against evil while the latter guard the good. Thus, the vices both the hubristic and falsely humble exhibit when they lack the passions they ought to have, and have the ones they ought not to have, become their virtues when the proper passions are in place.

63   A matter brought to my attention by Martin Warner.

64   For Aristotle's discussion of (in)continence/(in)temperance, see *EN* VII. For Aquinas' account, see 2.2.141–3, 155–6. See also Josef Pieper, *The Four Cardinal Virtues* (Notre Dame: University of Notre Dame Press, 1966), 145–75.

65   *ST* 2.2.156; *EN* VII: Aristotle on continence/temperance.

66   *ST* 2.2.53.4: thoughtlessness opposes prudence; cf. *EN* VII.7, 1150b19–28: impetuousness and crimes of passion.

67   *ST* 2.2.53.3: hastiness opposes prudence.

68   *ST* 2.2.53.5: inconstancy; 2.2.54.1: negligence.

69   *ST* 2.1.74.7.

70   *ST* 2.1.75.4.

71   *ST* 2.1.7.

72   *ST* 2.1.73.4–5.

73   *ST* 2.1.71.3.

74   *ST* 2.1.73.10.

Rationality as Virtue

[75]   *ST* 2.1.73.3, 9.

[76]   *ST* 2.1.73.8.

[77]   *ST* 2.1.73.2.

[78]   *EN* III.1: on voluntary and involuntary actions.

[79]   *ST* 2.1.76.4; *EN* III.1, 1110a.

[80]   *EN* III.5, 1114a.

[81]   *ST* 2.1.6.7.

[82]   *ST* 2.1.6.5.

[83]   *ST* 2.1.6.6.

[84]   *EN* I.3, 1094b14–15: 'now fine and just actions, which political science investigates, exhibit much variety and fluctuation, so that they may be thought to exist only by convention, and not by nature.'

[85]   *ST* 2.1.59.4; cf. 2.2.47.1; see also Martha Nussbaum, *The Fragility of Goodness: Luck and Ethics in Greek Tragedy and Philosophy* (Cambridge: Cambridge University Press, 2001), 247.

[86]   *ST* 2.1.57.4.

[87]   *ST* 2.1.64.3.

[88]   *ST* 2.1.64.1: the mean; cf. *EN* II.6, 1106b: nothing need be added or taken away when the mean is struck.

[89]   *EN* I.10, 1101a1–2: the one 'who is truly good and wise, we think, bears all the chances of life becomingly and always makes the best of circumstances.'

[90]   *EN* I.7, 1098a7–8: 'the function of man is an activity of the soul in accordance with or not without rational principle.' Cf. II.6, 1106b36–1107a1–2: 'excellence, then, is a state concerned with choice, lying in a mean relative to us, this being determined by reason and in the way in which the man of practical wisdom would determine it.' Cf. VI.13,1144b22–24, excellence is 'that state which is in accordance with the right reason; now the right reason is that which is in accordance with practical wisdom.'

[91]   *ST* 2.1.94.3; Josef Pieper, *Reality and the Good* (San Francisco: Ignatius, 1989), 161: on the convertibility of natural law and virtue.

[92]   *ST* 2.1.94.5.

[93]   *ST* 1.79.12; cf. *De Veritate* 17.

[94]   *ST* 2.1.94.5: *synderesis* is innate, but according to *ST* 2.1.94.4, the ways it works out in practice may vary.

[95]   For example, Stanley Hauerwas seems to perceive natural law and virtue ethics as mutually exclusive moral systems.

[96]   *ST* 2.1.94.3: 'to the natural law belongs everything to which a man is inclined according to his nature ... Wherefore, since the rational soul is the proper form of man, there is in every man a natural inclination to act according to reason: and this is to act according to virtue. Consequently, considered thus, all acts of virtue are prescribed by

the natural law: since each one's reason naturally dictates to him to act virtuously. But if we speak of virtuous acts, considered in themselves, i.e. in their proper species, thus not all virtuous acts are prescribed by the natural law: for many things are done virtuously, to which nature does not incline at first; but which, through the inquiry of reason, have been found by men to be conducive to well-living.' *Omnes actus virtutum sunt de lege naturali, dictat enim hoc naturaliter unicuique propria ratio, ut virtuose agat. Sed si loquamur de actibus virtuosis secundum seipsos, prout scilicet in propriis speciebus considerantur, sic non omnes actus virtuosi sunt de lege naturae. Multa enim secundum virtutem fiunt, ad quae natura non primo inclinat; sed per rationis inquisitionem ea homines adinvenerunt, quasi utilia ad bene vivendum.*

[97]   *ST* 2.1.61.1. Jean Porter, *The Recovery of Virtue: The Relevance of Aquinas for Christian Ethics* (Louisville: John Knox Press, 1990), 79. As Porter argues, the end of living in accord with reason/nature—which I have defined in terms of 'bearing things well'—is an 'inclusive end.' Thus, the single rule to 'bear things well' can have a wide range of applications in different lives and even over the course of one life, where all of these applications are included in and contribute to achieving the end of human life, namely, self-actualization. As a rule to guide actions, the natural law never changes, though our conception of how to apply it will almost certainly need to change with circumstances. This again is attributable to the fact that the natural law and any laws that can be inferred from it are formal, not substantial.

[98]   See for example the work of so-called 'new natural lawyers' like John Finnes and Germain Grisez. See also Jean Porter's response to these lawyers in her *Nature as Reason: A Thomistic Theory of the Natural Law* (Grand Rapids: Eerdman's, 2004).

[99]   Jean Porter, *Moral Action and Christian Ethics* (Cambridge: Cambridge University Press, 1995), 98: 'there is no determinate way to move from rational principles of human action to a specific choice of concrete action.' See also Herbert McCabe, *Law, Love and Language* (London: Continuum, 2003).

[100]   Jean Porter, *Moral Action and Christian Ethics*, 48: 'what it means to apply a rule against (certain) actions we can only determine on coming to a problem, that is, the application of moral rules is analogical, rather than analytical. As such, the unity of the concept of morality must be discovered through speculation, in this case, inspection of the basic moral notions on the basis of which we arrive at a grasp of the formal element or focal meaning in virtue of which all these count as exemplifications of one more general concept. Correlatively, the formal notion underlying the concept of morality can be articulated, but it cannot be stated in the form of an exhaustive definition understood as a definitive statement.' Provided moral rules are analogical in the way Porter describes, a wide range of activities can all be said successfully to promote the highest good, albeit in diverse ways. This is because all those activities on this account relate to one focal meaning, or accomplish one analogical good. Though it is often possible to identify the

focal meaning of a given moral concept, Porter goes on to insist that this 'does not mean that all of the correct applications of the concept of morality can be analytically derived from this focal meaning' (56). For unprecedented circumstances may always change or expand our concept of the focal meaning of a moral law, calling for new applications thereof. As this suggests, an analogical understanding of meaning allows for the possibility that the meaning of a moral concept may need to be extrapolated in new and unforeseen ways to accommodate the moral demands of unprecedented circumstances. By contrast, an analytical understanding of the moral law restricts us to a limited and static set of applications that have already been derived from that law, under past and perhaps no longer relevant moral circumstances.

[101]   With the exception of certain mental and physical disabilities.

[102]   *EN* VII.12.

[103]   *EN* VI.12, 1144a7–9: 'the function of man is achieved only in accordance with practical wisdom as well as with moral excellence; for excellence makes the aim right, and practical wisdom the things leading to it.'

[104]   *ST* 2.1.7.3. *EN* II.6, 1106b21–3: to act 'at the right times, with reference to the right objects, towards the right people, with the right aim, and in the right way is what is both intermediate and best, and this is characteristic of excellence.'

[105]   Nicholas Lombardo, *The Logic of Desire*, 170: prudence perfects the intellect, justice perfects the will, fortitude perfects the irascible passions, and temperance perfects the concupiscible passions.

Chapter 7
Sufficient Conditions for Pro-Theology Philosophy

In closing the last chapter, I argued that prudence is exceptionally well suited to appointing ends and not merely means to ends when the end in question is that of 'bearing things well.'[1] As noted previously, this activity not only conduces to achieving the end of self-actualization; it *is* self-actualization. In making us aware of our end in theory, prudence instills in us an aptitude to strive towards it in practice, that is, to cultivate the three further cardinal virtues of justice, fortitude, and temperance.[2] Below, I will treat these four virtues in turn, demonstrating the role each one plays in promoting our ability to bear things well. In doing this, I outline the sufficient conditions for a pro-theology philosophy: the conditions which, when satisfied, actualize our personal potential to promote the highest good. In the last section of the chapter, I discuss the respects in which a personal commitment to the highest good or moral virtue may be regarded as the final arbiter of human rationality.

The First Condition: Prudence

When it comes to bearing things well, our main resources consist in any intellectual abilities or virtues we may have in the areas of wisdom, science, or art. As suggested in Chapter 6, bearing these aptitudes well presupposes a preliminary assessment of their nature, degree, and scope that is neither excessive nor deficient.[3] For those prone to hubris, consequently, this assessment inevitably curbs a tendency to assume entitlement to authority, privilege, or opportunity and enables the perception and acceptance of a more limited role and limited power in the world. By contrast, it summons those susceptible to false humility to take ownership of personal aptitudes and assert the right to exercise them, despite external pressures or expectations to do otherwise.

Since self-actualization takes time, it should come as no surprise that the process through which aptitudes are evaluated and implemented with increasing effectiveness over a lifetime resembles the three-stage process of discovery.

In Chapter 4, I described these stages in terms of expectant, fulfilled, and informed faith, which respectively anticipate, achieve, and apply understanding, in this case, self-understanding. In the present, moral, context, these three stages arguably correspond to childhood, youth, and adulthood.[4]

In the first of these stages, individuals do not normally possess a clear sense of their abilities, precisely because they are in the phase of life during which the very tools needed to discover those abilities are acquired, to wit, the tools of discovery itself. For this reason, children—or novices in any new field of inquiry—might be said to live by an expectant faith, which leads them to believe they possess certain latent abilities and thus to position themselves eventually to discover those abilities.[5]

In order to make this discovery, children must be permitted to explore different life possibilities or professions. When children play in these respects, they acquire the sense that they have something to offer society, even though they may not yet know exactly what this is. Without such scope for the imagination, they might fail to acquire the confidence they will eventually need to chart a course in life. While imaginative play should consequently be encouraged, children must also be disciplined in love as necessary. By 'discipline,' I refer to correction for deviant behavior as well as the imposition of responsibility for tasks, both of which help correct the urge for instant gratification that makes it impossible to strive for worthwhile goals.

Out of love, those tasks should be assigned in proportion to each child's level of development and ability. Furthermore, correction for misbehavior should only be administered for behavior for which a child can reasonably be held accountable. Moreover, it should generally be implemented after an initial offense, certainly before the situation gets out of hand. It should be preceded by a calm and complete explanation why the punishment is being administered and should entail an appropriate form of punishment, which is not more or less severe than the offense warrants and which is relevant to curtailing the kind of offense committed, without publically shaming or embarrassing the child.[6]

When children are thus disciplined in love, they have a chance of acquiring the sense that correction is for their benefit. Through such early training, they are predisposed—if they will—not to be put off by but rather to appreciate the value of sacrificing lesser goods to gain something of greater personal value, namely, an ability to control the urge for instant gratification. Thus, the combination of discipline and love amounts to a lesson in delayed gratification, through which children eventually come to realize that they cannot play at different options and occupations forever but must identify the one for which they are best suited and apply themselves to it.[7]

In the phase of expectant faith, or childhood, consequently, prudence strikes a mean through an imposed balance between space for imaginative exploration and appropriate discipline with regard to both positive behaviors and misbehaviors. Children who benefit from this combination of space and supervision—freedom and restraint—have a good chance not only of acquiring a sense of personal purpose but also of developing the inner wherewithal to fulfill it. They become able to identify where their good lies and pursue it, without feeling subject to desires for or distractions from things that might detract from this effort.

Though most children need an environment conducive to proper development to be created for them, there are evidently exceptional children who find ways to provide space and supervision for themselves. They are naturally prudent. Thus, a lack of good upbringing need not keep children, at least extraordinary children, from self-actualization. Indeed, many children who are given every advantage when it comes to the realization of their potential fail to make the most of the opportunity and simply take it for granted. In light of this, the question whether children demonstrate the level of prudence that befits them should be treated not only as a matter of nurture but also as one of nature.[8]

Whether they have it by nature or nurture or both, children who realize through prudence that they have some purpose and develop the discipline to realize it have a foundation for the effort they must make in young adulthood to specify the direction of their lives. This is a notoriously difficult task to undertake, given that every individual is differently gifted, such that there are innumerable ways to be a human being. For this very reason, Aristotle notes, there is no such thing as absolute correctness when it comes to choosing a course in human life.[9] The only 'wrong' way is not to have a way at all, or to pursue a way that precludes bearing aptitudes and resources prudently, or well.[10]

Though advisors can certainly provide important and indeed indispensable guidance when it comes to determining how the human 'norm' of bearing things well should express itself in individual cases, decisions along these lines ultimately rest with those who have to make them.[11] However, a number of special obstacles to sound life decision making tend to present themselves in the period of young adulthood. The main obstacle concerns the lack of experience needed to make choices that are consistent with personal abilities, which young people are generally still discovering. This deficiency in experience renders youth susceptible to confusing their individual identities with roles projected upon them in keeping with various social conventions.

Although these conventions provide an important framework for human interactions and collaborations, they can also hinder human thriving when they presuppose a division of labor on the basis of various accidental features of human existence such as class, race, or sex, which have no bearing on the essential question of a person's fundamental abilities. In young adulthood, then, prudence strikes the mean between the extremes of conforming to a conventional role that is inconsistent with personal capabilities, and failing to make anything of those capabilities, by compelling individuals to consider where, if anywhere, they fit with reference to existing conventions, rather than allowing conventions to dictate their place in the world.[12]

As noted, it can prove difficult to deliberate along these lines in youth, since a certain degree of experience is needed to build a sense of personal identity and the confidence to live in accordance with it. The difficulty can be exacerbated by the fact that there is often considerable pressure at this phase to conform to conventions and the expectations of others—and even the threat of penalization for a failure to do so. Although some may disapprove or at least neglect to support unconventional decisions for malicious reasons, it is worth noting that others may do so for rather more benign but nonetheless problematic reasons. For instance, they may desire to protect young persons from struggling or failing at a challenge. Alternatively, they may wish for youth to position themselves within the confines of perceived norms because this reinforces the rest of society's commitment to living within those norms, where breaking with convention might seem like an affront to standard ways of life.

Though there is no point—or prudence—in contesting conventions and the expectations of others for its own sake, the prudence that compels us to promote the highest good at every turn reconciles us to the fact that we may have to decline the opportunities that others urge us to pursue, even in cases where we have no other prospects. Far from a sign of disdain for the highest good, the rejection of these lesser goods is an indication of commitment to it, unless the impression is deceptively given that the expectations of others will be met when there is no intention of meeting them.

By placing appropriate limits on the demands and expectations of others, therefore, the prudent strengthen their sense of identity as individuals, thus distinguishing their roles from those others might project upon them.[13] In this way, they gradually fulfill their original expectant faith to find out their purposes in this world. At the same time, they teach others who they are and how they wish to be treated—something that is more important to be able to do the more established conventions and social norms are abandoned.

Although it can be a considerable challenge thus to follow through on the decision to engage in self-actualization, it is worth emphasizing that such a decision is not really a matter of choice. After all, choice and deliberation factor into human operations only when it comes to determining the most effective means to an end;[14] or when it is necessary to prioritize different ends with respect to one another.[15] The ends themselves are given to us in virtue of our natural aptitudes, that is, in virtue of an essence or nature that is accompanied by a responsibility to respond to others and act in certain ways. In that sense, it is not possible to choose but merely to consent to being who we are and to striving towards the ends that are appropriate for us, given our capabilities.[16] That is not to say that our actions are somehow predetermined—that we are not free. To the contrary, our freedom consists in exercising the ability to be ourselves, without the hindrances to self-actualization that arise from trying be something more, less, or other than we are.

Since few of us know exactly what course our lives should take, just as soon as we become capable of deliberating on this score in young adulthood, the process of considering what it means to consent to 'becoming ourselves' invariably involves some trial and error. To engage in this process, it is necessary to follow the normal course of prudence and pursue with singleness of mind the strongest leads available, always opting for what seems like the greatest, if not the easiest, good at the time.

Though many of the approaches or activities undertaken in this connection may ultimately be outgrown, trying them out and eliminating them as long-term options affords a more refined sense of what is best for us in life and redirects efforts accordingly. Where prudence has truly attuned us to our deepest passions and thus the source of our potential, consequently, these failed attempts and alterations in course do not represent aimless wanderings or the pursuit of futile whims, as they would in the case of those who lack prudence and thus remain endlessly undecided about the direction of their lives. Rather, the changes in course that are a natural part of self-discovery instill a clearer sense of direction in life, while strengthening a commitment to follow it.

Once this mature sense of self has been achieved, the phase of personal development that corresponds to informed faith begins. At this stage, prudence manifests itself by shaping our decisions about how to act in keeping with the knowledge we have acquired as to the nature of our purposes.[17] By contrast to the run up to fulfilled faith, which is inevitably characterized by all kinds of changes in course, the eventual fulfillment of faith in informed faith enables us to translate self-knowledge immediately and decisively into action. As a result of doing this, we do not scatter but streamline our energies to achieve maximum personal effectiveness, even if we do so through a wide range of activities.

Whereas counsel from others may prove helpful when it comes to making decisions during youth, it should not be necessary at this stage to take advice in order to determine what it would mean to realize personal potential in different situations. That is not to deny that it may prove relevant, even essential, to rely on others to share expertise or experience, which is necessary for personal engagement in certain activities. Yet it is to underline that our reliance upon others for information and assistance under these conditions differs qualitatively from the normal way of depending on others in youth. For it is not a sign of immaturity but of mature interdependence, and an ability to contribute significantly to the accomplishment of major goals that require collaboration.[18]

The ultimate objective of cultivating prudence in the phase of informed faith is to become so well acquainted with our abilities as to be able on some level to forget them and simply act automatically in accordance with authentic self-knowledge.[19] By these means, our own flourishing or happiness is fostered, and, at the same time, we make the greatest possible contribution to the well-being of others. As this confirms, a prudent commitment to accomplishing our personal best—or the highest good—is convertible with a commitment to the common good, that is, the good of humanity.

As I will demonstrate further below, the two goals of individual human and humane being mutually imply one another, because prudence without justice reduces to activities that fail to meet the needs of others and therefore render the use of personal abilities irrelevant. By the same token, justice without prudence satisfies the needs of others at the expense of fulfilling the most basic human need—and responsibility—to maximize personal potential.[20] Thus, it remains to explore how prudence operates under the aspect of the common good, or in the context of interpersonal relations, through the next virtue of justice.

The Second Condition: Justice

Whereas prudence determines personal aptitudes—and limitations—or how it is appropriate or inappropriate to interact with others, the virtue of justice presupposes this basis for acting in order to discern and meet the needs of potential beneficiaries.[21] According to Aquinas, there are three species of justice, all of which operate on a principle of equality, which posits that persons and parties ought to receive assistance that is equal to their capabilities and needs.[22] This is what it means to appoint the mean with respect to justice, namely, to determine what is appropriate—neither excessive nor deficient—when it comes to giving others their due.[23]

In this connection, it is worth stressing that the principle of equality does not translate into a principle of uniformity, according to which individuals would receive the same benefits, regardless of their differences. To the contrary, it turns on the assumption that human beings differ significantly amongst themselves, such that administering justice which is equal or proportional to the needs of individuals may mean offering them very different forms of support, all of which are nonetheless ordered towards facilitating the cultivation of diverse human capabilities.[24]

The first form of justice is commutative justice, which concerns the relations of persons to one another.[25] The second is distributive justice, which deals with the relationships between institutions and their members, or authorities and those they govern. The third type of justice is legal justice, whereby the actions of individuals are ordered towards the state.[26] Since a discussion of the latter topic falls outside the compass of the current inquiry, I would refer readers to the extensive work of others on the subject.[27]

Before turning to a more detailed discussion of commutative and distributive justice, it seems fitting to offer some preliminary remarks about what it means to 'give others their due' in either context. This is an important question to address at the start of any treatment of justice, because human beings tend automatically to perceive the world in terms of their own interests and are, consequently, prone to deal with others in ways that are ultimately ordered to accomplish personal ends. Whether consciously or unwittingly, individuals who operate along these lines defeat the whole purpose of justice, which is to assist others on their own terms, as opposed to treating them as objects of greed.

There are a number of ways in which the power to administer justice may be abused in this manner. One involves treating others in ways that reinforce a sense of personal importance, fulfillment, or usefulness. When this approach is employed, assistance can actually become a hindrance to the thriving of alleged beneficiaries and prevent the actual satisfaction of their needs. This is especially true in cases where a benefactor simply does not possess the ability or resources to meet the needs of beneficiaries but is too proud to admit it and invoke the aid of individuals who might be more capable of offering the relevant assistance.[28] It is still more true when 'help' or 'advice' is designed to control, limit, or suppress activities through which individuals might challenge a certain understanding of the way things should be done or even supersede a benefactor in power.

Such forms of assistance are clearly aimed at protecting a prideful ego that is unwilling to accept personal finitude and therefore refuses in envy to recognize the validity of alternative ways of thinking and living.[29] Since efforts indirectly to enlist others in the fulfillment of personal needs or the reinforcement of personal opinions, power and approaches are bound ultimately to undermine the flourishing of beneficiaries, the feigned interest in others that motivates such efforts might be described as a 'complicated form of hatred,'[30] which can be contrasted with the overt form of hatred that motivates direct acts of injustice stemming from wrath.

For the sake of fostering justice, therefore, it seems necessary to identify and check any concern to protect or promote personal interests or satisfy personal desires at the outset of efforts to administer so-called justice. Whatever these personal concerns, projects, or affiliations may be, they are irrelevant when it comes to evaluating the needs of others on their own terms, just as the self is evaluated in prudence.[31] The greatest of these needs, of course, is that of learning to realize personal potential.

Thus, acts of justice should be tailored towards providing others with the training, resources, opportunities, or encouragement relevant to enabling them to thrive independently of any external aid or approval.[32] In other words, any help or aid offered should be of a sort which ultimately renders that help superfluous. Far from aiming to keep others under our control, in need of ongoing advice or aid, consequently, justice requires that we create the conditions and above all provide the freedom whereby they may learn to operate on their own terms, of their own accord.

By evacuating the space our beneficiaries need to exercise their humanity, we obviously relinquish the right to take credit for any success they may experience in this regard or to hold them in our debt.[33] Precisely for this reason, however, we truly do them justice. For it is only when our contribution to the thriving of others is non-specifiable, even invisible, that we can be certain that our efforts have been entirely altruistic, not tinted in any way by self-serving motives, as justice demands.[34]

With these considerations in view, I will now turn to consider how justice plays out in the contexts of commutation and distribution, respectively. As mentioned, commutative justice pertains to inter-personal relationships. Thus, it is relevant here to discuss the three different kinds of inter-personal relationship—or friendship—that Aquinas following Aristotle describes.[35] The first type of relationship, 'for the sake of utility,' unites individuals or parties who are able to help one another in a particular way. The second kind of relationship, 'for the sake of pleasure,' exists between those who enjoy the same activities or have similarities in temperament or personality.

The third kind of relationship, 'for the sake of prudence,' connects those who are governed by an overarching concern to 'bear things well.' On account of this concern, individuals in relationships for prudence are also generally concerned to bear their relationships well. As a result, their primary reason for being in relationships is not to derive something pleasurable or useful from them but to do justice to those with whom they relate and thus to help them cultivate prudence, or the ability to bear things well—a form of assistance they receive in return.

Since there is nothing more useful or pleasurable in life than to aid and be aided thus to flourish, relationships for prudence are arguably the most useful and pleasurable of all relationships, even though they often require the relinquishment of personal needs or desires for the sake of the other in the relationship. By acting in ways that always promote one another's best interests, in fact, persons in relationships for prudence may achieve a level of intimacy that far exceeds what is possible in relationships for utility or pleasure. After all, there is nothing more natural than to draw close to those who offer the freedom and support to engage in self-actualization.[36] In contrast, it is virtually impossible—and often unsafe—to draw close to those who enter into relationships in order to reinforce a prideful self-image and thus to obtain benefits for themselves. When expectations along these lines are not fulfilled, such individuals cannot help but behave in possessive and imposing ways that undermine the trust on which relationships turn.[37]

Whether a relationship exists for prudence, pleasure, or utility, it can last only so long as each party provides an equal measure of utility, pleasure, or prudence, respectively, to the other.[38] In relationships for utility and pleasure particularly, this equality is frequently thrown off by the give and take that is characteristic of all relationships. The role of commutative justice is to restore the equilibrium that upholds the relationship.[39] In this connection, it is worth noting that an equality of sorts may be maintained between parties that are strictly speaking unequal, such as employer and employee, or parent and child, insofar as the inferior offers the superior service, obedience, gratitude, or respect that represents an appropriate return for benefits or aid received.[40]

In any case, commutative justice stipulates that no more should be repaid than is owed, lest the repayment come across as ostentatious, manipulative, or sycophantic; and no less, in order to express due appreciation for the gift originally given and the relationship overall.[41] Moreover, it requires that recompense be made for a debt owed within a reasonable period of time. That stated, it is not always fitting to make an immediate return. On some occasions, justice is best served by waiting until the time or opportunity arises to offer restitution in a way that does perfect justice to the original gift. For this reason, it is incumbent upon those who are owed a debt to wait patiently for appropriate compensation and to consider discontinuing the relationship only in cases of unreasonable delay.[42]

When it becomes necessary, the dissolution of a relationship for utility or pleasure need not involve any animosity or hard feelings on the part of either party, particularly if both parties recognize the inability of one or both to meet the other's needs for utility or pleasure. The prudent do not generally struggle thus to accept the termination of a relationship, since they have the virtue needed to discern that relationships other than those for prudence cannot satisfy human social needs on a comprehensive or permanent basis. Those lacking in prudence on the other hand may prove extremely reluctant to let go of relationships that have become asymmetrical, especially if the asymmetry is owing to their own shortcomings. This reluctance is attributable to a tendency not only to resist confronting personal finitude but also to treat relationships for utility or pleasure as though they could exhibit the longevity that is only proper to relationships for prudence.

As I suggested in Chapter 6, this tendency is symptomatic of a deeper proclivity to regard whatever is most pleasurable or expedient in an immediate sense as the arbiter of happiness. Because the imprudent make decisions about relationships at the impulse of what is effectively an urge for instant gratification, they often form binding relationships—which should arguably always be based on prudence—out of a desire to unite themselves with individuals who seem in the moment like all-sufficient sources of utility or pleasure, which will inevitably prove insufficient in ways that bring about the painful deterioration of what should be interminable relationships. On account of this liability to confuse relationships for prudence with those organized around utility or pleasure, the imprudent are likely to struggle to form not only relationships for prudence but also the relationships for utility and pleasure that every prudent person possesses.

Whereas the balance in relationships for utility and pleasure is preserved through the exchange of various goods and services, it stands to reason that relationships for prudence may survive only so long as both parties remain equally committed to bearing things well.[43] In the event this commitment stays strong on both ends, relationships for prudence may endure all sorts of imbalances with regard to utility and pleasure which would spell the demise of relationships organized around these matters. Since prudence is a rare virtue that can take a lifetime to cultivate, however, it bears noting that relationships for prudence are generally quite uncommon.

This is all the more true in light of the fact that it can take a lifetime to prove that another person is really prudent. Though an individual may appear prudent for a certain period of time or in a particular context, the passage of time and changes in circumstance often reveal that relationships for prudence really only existed for the sake of utility or pleasure. For this reason, it is advisable, particularly in the impressionable period of youth, to be cautious about pronouncing relationships 'for prudence,' thus organizing life around these relationships, which may eventually turn out to be pleasurable or useful in only limited ways, and break down.

Where a relationship for prudence has been established, it remains to inquire how to discern when an insuperable inequality has arisen in such a relationship, which calls for its dissolution. This discernment is particularly difficult to exercise in this context, precisely because relationships for prudence are built on the belief that each person will act in accordance with the best interests of the other. Any legitimate suspicion to the contrary clearly undercuts the whole foundation for the relationship, summoning the offended party to extend forgiveness.

Though it is often argued that forgiveness necessitates the restoration of broken relationships, forgiveness as I understand it is only secondarily concerned with reconciliation. First and foremost, by my account, forgiveness is the means through which the forgiving party is protected from the threats of an offender and thus enabled to bear life well.[44] Of course, 'forgiving and forgetting' may involve overlooking an offense, re-embracing the offender and moving forward in a relationship, in cases where the harm one individual causes another is unintentional, incidental, or irregular: where it is readily acknowledged and not repeated.

When offensive acts are consciously and continually committed, however, extending forgiveness necessitates the withdrawal of the offender's opportunity to do damage by discontinuing the relationship itself. It requires forgetting quite literally about any past or future role the offender might play in the forgiver's life. In some situations, inevitably, there is not much that can be done to escape a harmful situation involving a particular offender. When it is impossible to escape a traumatic situation physically or practically, however, there are other ways to engage in self-protection or forgiveness, for example, by denying oppressors power over personal feelings and thus over reactions and further actions.

Because so much is at stake in relationships for prudence, it obviously takes considerable discernment to decide which form of forgiveness—acceptance or rejection—is appropriate in any given situation. The upshot of the foregoing discussion, however, is that forgiveness is always ultimately orientated towards preserving the integrity of the forgiver, and, in particular, their ability to bear things well. It is about observing the rule of equality in relationships for prudence, which sometimes requires the dissolution of a relationship that has become hopelessly imbalanced or abusive.

Whereas commutative justice concerns inter-personal relationships for utility, pleasure, or prudence, distributive justice entails the one-sided form of justice through which individuals fulfill a duty to utilize personal aptitudes for the benefit of others. In this connection, it is worth emphasizing the importance of being selective when it comes to deciding how to make the most of personal abilities to help others.[45] As Aristotle writes, just individuals 'refrain from giving to anybody and everybody that they may have something to give to the right people at the right time and where it is noble to do so.'[46] Thus, it is essential to set priorities with regard to the distribution of justice.[47]

Since relationships for prudence—presumably close family and friends—are most crucial to the thriving of all involved, they should seemingly enjoy a certain primacy in our lives.[48] Next in the order of priority stand relationships for utility, including the work-related relationships, which invariably consume a good deal of energy with regard to the commutation and distribution of justice. When it comes to these relationships, it seems consistent with the goal of maximizing the good that can be accomplished for others to prioritize helping not only those we are most able to help but also those who are most worthy or in need of our help.[49]

For some distributors of justice, maximizing the good along these lines may involve very little or highly selective interaction with other people, as in the case of a scientist or researcher who works for long hours in isolation. Given the laborious and time-consuming nature of many tasks that support the common good, it would be a mistake to assume that distributing justice always involves direct contact with human beings, particularly large groups of human beings. Though there is a risk of overlooking the common good in the absence of certain social connections, it remains nonetheless true that most need to manage interactions with others in order to do as much as possible for the good of humankind.

Arguably, relationships for pleasure fall last in the order of priority, as these relationships are largely superfluous if pleasure is derived from relationships for prudence and adequate time is invested in relationships for utility, especially in places of work. In fact, the accumulation of many relationships for pleasure may indicate a lack of prudent relationships and of prudence more generally, as well as a deficient sense of vocation or commitment to profitable work.

Although I have been trying to suggest that a personal commitment to the common good can only be fulfilled through efforts to administer justice to particular persons in a certain order of priority, it bears stressing that such efforts are the locus of this larger commitment. Where a sense of this commitment is lost, I will show below, it becomes impossible to serve others well. This loss is particularly common in the case of distributive justice, on account of its intrinsically one-sided nature, or the fact that others cannot be expected in this context to offer much or anything of substance in return for efforts on their behalf.

Because of the asymmetrical nature of relationships revolving around distributive justice, work to facilitate the self-actualization of others may not be recognized as the means through which this process is advanced in our own lives. In other words, we may not realize that our service to the common good is the source of our vocation or purpose in life and thus our main resource for achieving our own highest good. As noted above, this is the good it falls to us to serve when dealing with the limited and specific circumstances through which we serve it. When we neglect to treat particular responsibilities as mere means to the end of fulfilling this more significant responsibility, our allegiances to particular persons, parties or institutions cannot help but replace an allegiance to the common good and consequently undermine it.

In normal circumstances, of course, it can prove difficult to distinguish those who fulfill their responsibilities for the sake of the common good from those who do so merely to promote those persons, parties, or institutions that pertain to their areas of interest or responsibility. For many take considerable care to administer justice in the ways mentioned above, even though they lack a commitment to the common good. They give others their due, because doing so either provides a sense of fulfillment or is essential to securing the support and protection of society.

Although promoting the common good for the sake of surviving and thriving is a natural reason for acting, it is not strictly speaking a reason that has anything to do with the just promotion of the common good. Indeed, true motives for acting generally only come to the surface in extenuating circumstances, when serving the highest good proves incompatible with the promotion of private interests, such that it becomes necessary to choose one end over the other.

For example, a deficient commitment to the common good becomes obvious when undue and thus unjust favoritism is shown towards particular persons and projects that promote a personal agenda, while those who truly need and deserve support remain neglected.[50] A commitment to the common good is also undermined in cases where individuals or groups are excluded from society on account of breaking with convention for the sake of the common good or for some other unwarranted reason stemming from prejudices or vices that are nursed by society itself.[51] The threat to the common good in this instance is exacerbated by those who neglect to support the marginalized and oppressed out of concern for their own status in society.

On yet another level, a predisposition to betray the common good becomes evident when individuals neglect to attend to the needs and sufferings of those in the wider world, because of the discomfort that is involved in observing distant or atrocious suffering, or out of a selfish desire to spend resources exclusively on personal or local projects. In these exceptional cases and others, a lack of commitment to the common good leads to undermining the common good in the only way it can be promoted, namely, by dealing with personal, local, and even global concerns that come to our attention, with a view to a goal that transcends them.[52]

While some refuse to distribute justice in these ways, others are simply unable to do so, on account of a disability, mental or physical.[53] That is not to say that disabled individuals are incapable of participating in the distribution of justice, however. As I argued in Chapter 2, their participation simply necessitates an extra measure of determination, and oftentimes, receptivity to the help of others, which makes it possible to realize potential in ways that ultimately represent the most profound exemplifications of human being.[54] A similar principle applies in the case of those who for reasons unrelated to disability—for example, poverty or racial discrimination—lack the power personally to create conditions that are conducive to the realization of personal potential. For these, involvement in distributive justice also means seeking and making the most of appropriate forms of aid, or a special degree of determination to overcome any lack thereof, which in turn exposes the inhumane ways of a society that too often turns a blind eye to the greatest areas of human need.

As the discussion above suggests, therefore, the way individuals are treated who desperately need or deserve our aid, yet have no power to hold us accountable to administer to it, determines whether justice is at play at all. In that sense, those who need distributive justice the most supremely champion the cause of justice by summoning society most urgently and unmistakably to its defense.

The Third Condition: Fortitude

Thus far, I have explained how prudence and justice respectively determine what is fitting for individuals to do, both on their own terms and with regard to their treatment of other people.[55] In these respects, prudence and justice are concerned with human operations. The last two cardinal virtues of fortitude and temperance do not pertain to these operations as such. Rather, they are virtues that regulate the passions that enable efforts to perform the operations associated with prudence and justice.[56]

For example, fortitude is the virtue related to the passions, which affords the courage to overcome the challenges that are often involved in prudent and just projects.[57] In performing its primary function, fortitude simultaneously curbs the dis-passions on account of which the challenge of completing these projects might be avoided. As noted in Chapter 6, the dis-passionate dispositions that are most opposed to the virtue of fortitude include fear and recklessness—the extremes that accompany apathy.[58]

While fear creates a tendency to cower in the face of difficult circumstances, recklessness generally results in heedlessly rushing into them, before an adequate course of action has been planned. In either case, the vices in question are indicative of a deficiency in both prudence and justice. This is true of fear, insofar as it depletes the ambition needed to complete prudent and just tasks, and of rashness, inasmuch as this wastes the energies that ought to be spent on those tasks. Fortitude makes it possible to avoid both of these extremes by reassuring us of our purposes and reconciling us to them.[59] The steadfastness of purpose it thus affords is what enables us to confront the challenging feelings and overcome the obstacles associated with the fulfillment of those purposes.

That is not to say that courageous individuals are unaffected by challenging feelings—that they feel no fear in the face of difficult circumstances. Fortitude is distinguished from cowardice not by a lack of fear, but simply by a refusal to lapse into evil or back away from realizing the good on account of fear.[60] Provided the object of fear is truly terrifying, there is no shame in feeling fear in the face of it.[61] In fact, the absence of fear in circumstances requiring fortitude might be indicative of rashness, which disregards dangers where fortitude is conscious that challenges require courage.

By instilling a commitment to bear things well notwithstanding the risks involved in doing so, fortitude renders individuals willing to sacrifice the energy and resources needed to fight for prudence and justice.[62] Furthermore, it gives them the perseverance and patience to work until their goals in these respects are achieved.[63] Because the courageous do everything in their power to serve the good, they always enjoy the knowledge that they have borne their circumstances to the best of their abilities. Although their efforts may meet with failure for reasons beyond their control, consequently they need harbor no regrets. They can accept their failures, and negative feedback more generally, for it is part of fortitude to remain open to correction in all spheres, including the personal or moral sphere in which even the courageous may fail.

Though all human beings behave badly on occasion, vices can clearly be exacerbated when the very fact that circumstances have been borne badly is itself borne badly. While the cowardly generally do this by refusing to confront their failures to bear things well, for example, the rash simply disregard their obvious shortcomings. Because they deny their failures, albeit in different ways, both the cowardly and the rash set themselves up to make more of the same, albeit possibly more serious, mistakes in the future.

By sharp contrast, the courageous acknowledge personal failures as soon as they become aware of them and immediately seek to correct or compensate for their shortcomings. In this way, they bear even their mistakes well and thus learn from them how to bear similar circumstances better in the future. Of course, it would be incompatible with fortitude to indulge in personal vices simply for the sake of overcoming and learning from them. Nevertheless, it is consistent with fortitude to make good of personal mistakes in the way I have described above.

While the courageous keep no record of past wrongs for any other reason than to learn from them, they also resist resting on past accomplishments or indeed worrying about the future. Though they build on past achievements and plan prudently for the future, they live fully in the present. After all, this is the only context in which fortitude can exert itself. Thus, it is by acting courageously with respect to immediate concerns that those with fortitude not only overcome past failures and build on past accomplishments but also prepare for the future.

Though the description of fortitude given so far presupposes the practical possibility of setting prudent goals that are consistent with personal aptitudes and realizing them justly, it bears acknowledging that a lack of or sudden change in fortune, social injustice, or disability can deplete any power to realize personal potential that the courageous may possess. In what follows, however, I will show that such extenuating circumstances, which may deplete human potential in different ways, need not pose any ultimate hindrance to the life of virtue—let alone fortitude—through which human nature is realized. They only call for a different approach to realizing personal potential and indeed to exercising fortitude.

This difference can be underlined through the invocation of a distinction between what might be called 'imperfect' by contrast to 'perfect' happiness.[64] The former type of happiness turns on the acquisition of certain goods and resources that allow for the free exercise of personal aptitudes.[65] These goods may include money, education, a good upbringing, physical attractiveness, health, friends, family, honor, rights, sustenance, shelter, work, and so on.[66] By contrast, perfect happiness consists in needing nothing for happiness but an ability to bear things well, an ability that can be exercised even when any or all of the aforementioned goods have been lost.[67]

However it may seem, the detachment from or indifference towards the good things in life that characterizes perfect happiness does not imply that they are devalued in this context. As I affirmed previously, the goods proper to imperfect happiness are intrinsically good. So far as it is possible, consequently, it falls to the virtuous to pursue, maintain, and appreciate these goods, as appropriate. Moreover, it is incumbent upon them to seize every opportunity to cultivate and maximize personal abilities.[68] It is only by forswearing the available goods, abilities, or opportunities—whether out of a reluctance to embrace the responsibilities that accompany them or a sense of guilt regarding these privileges—that individuals denigrate those goods, and at the same time neglect the means they have to improve the lives of others or make a difference in the world.

Though the goodness of all goods must be affirmed and optimized when they are available, it is nonetheless possible to be struck by misfortunes or even to undergo sustained trials, which deprive us of some or all such goods.[69] While such misfortunes may thwart the exercise of our aptitudes, I have suggested that they do not deplete our ability to realize personal potential by bearing things well. They only alter what presents itself to be borne well, namely misfortunes instead of good fortune.

In the case of those who suffer from a debilitating illness, for example, the human task of bearing things well might be re-construed in terms of bearing the sickness well by complying with necessary treatments without complaining, requesting aid without being demanding, and so on.[70] Similarly, those who lose considerable fortune and the attendant comforts would bear poverty well by seeking new employment and curbing expenditures appropriately. As these examples confirm, the circumstances individuals are called upon to bear well are more or less irrelevant to the question whether it is possible in principle to bear things well. Whether it is necessary to bear well opportunities to exercise aptitudes or the sufferings that hinder efforts to do so, what matters is simply that circumstances are borne well.[71] That is the sum total of what it means to be human, and it is all that is required of human beings.

As indicated above, perfect happiness is the sort of happiness which is enjoyed by those who are able to bear not only good but also difficult circumstances well. To reiterate, this sort of happiness does not turn on a denigration of ordinary goods. Rather, it is indicative of an ability to appreciate these goods when they are available without failing to appreciate the gift of life itself in the face of their loss. On account of this ability, those with perfect happiness may secure the greatest good, namely, the ability to bear things well, in the midst of some of the most horrendous sufferings. This is the upshot of the maxim that 'virtue is its own reward.'[72]

Since it is difficult to obtain perfect happiness apart from the sufferings and losses that necessitate bearing difficult circumstances well, such happiness is ironically contingent upon the experience of trials. Although there is no objective difference between bearing trials or benefits well, consequently, the subjective difficulties inherent in suffering would seem to necessitate a greater measure of the fortitude that is needed to face the ordinary challenges involved in the realization of personal potential.

Because bearing things well is the arbiter of human happiness, it could be argued that the intense sufferings that call for a heightened ability to bear things well can create the most gratifying experiences in life—if they are managed with the fortitude that effectively enables individuals to bear the loss of all things. On this basis, moreover, maturity might be regarded as a function not of age but of the number and gravity of the challenges an individual has faced with fortitude. After all, a higher degree of fortitude is indicative of a stronger ability to bear things well.

This fortitude is what ultimately prepares us to face death—the ultimate loss of our lives.[73] For Aquinas, fortitude by definition involves a 'preparedness to die,' since it operates out of a determination to bear things well—or die trying.[74] That is not to say that the courageous live to die, much less that they live in fear of sudden disasters. Because they focus on the present, they do not preoccupy themselves with disasters that might unexpectedly happen, until they happen. They do not organize life around averting disaster, let alone death. Still, the courageous are prepared to face either disaster or death when these events strike, because they habitually ready themselves to bear whatever they are called upon to bear well, to the point of and thus including death itself.

The Fourth Condition: Temperance

While fortitude provides the strength to follow through on prudent and just purposes, temperance teaches us to take pleasure in or be supremely passionate about doing just this. In the process, it curbs the passions that might entice us in other directions.[75] Whereas fortitude helps us reckon with feelings that spring from the fear of death, consequently temperance regulates passions that accompany our natural desire to preserve and continue life. Though sex and food are the paradigmatic examples of life-perpetuating goods, the purview of temperance is not limited to these. As I argued when treating lust and gluttony in the last chapter, the goods in question can include any goods of the external world—such as possessions, relationships, knowledge, honor, fame—or goods of the body—like beauty or health—that might be regarded as essential to personal survival and thriving.

Although it is both natural and appropriate to engage in self-preservation through the procurement of such goods, I have shown that these goods, which serve the purposes of life, can prove inimical to human life where desires for them grow excessive or deficient. Since the tendency to pursue various goods as ends in themselves as opposed to means to the end of bearing life well destroys their life-giving power, these desires, which are otherwise natural, become unnatural when they come to control us rather than the other way around.

As a counterbalance to such unnatural desires, temperance gives us the discipline to pursue only the goods that are needed to sustain life, in exactly the quantity they are needed for this purpose.[76] In this way, temperance follows through on the directives of prudence, which often conflict with bodily desires for instant gratification. In thus eliminating the inner tension or conflict between soul and body and creating harmony between the two, temperance aligns our desires for pleasure with the true sources thereof. As such, it acts as the arbiter of the functionality and flourishing of rational animals, and in that sense, of the other moral virtues.

By disciplining us to take pleasure where we ought to do so, and not where we ought not to do so, temperance by no means obliterates the passions we have for various goods of the body and the external world. Instead, it fosters the only true enjoyment of these life-giving gifts that is available to us as human beings. Temperance allows us to be passionate about these gifts in the true sense of the term, because it attunes us to our deepest passion for our own thriving, and disciplines us to chase only the desires that advance the pursuit of this passion.

As it focuses all our energies or passions on the project of self-actualization, temperance maximizes the energy and thus the passion we have for whatever we do, which would be diffused and dampened were it not thus directed.[77] Far from compelling us to denigrate bodily or external goods, consequently, temperance helps us to use these goods in ways that promote rather than undermine our thriving, within our limitations. Without the discipline it affords, the dis-passions that are irrelevant or inimical to our flourishing would inevitably overcome us.[78] As a result, we would squander our energy or passions on things that are incompatible with our well-being and consequently disperse and finally deplete our passion to act in our own best interests.

Whereas temperance teaches us to manage the dis-passions for the sake of our own thriving, our culture today would seemingly have us believe that we may do as we please with our bodies and lives, without detriment to our physical or emotional wellbeing, let alone our capacity to realize our full potential. In fact, it is often suggested that self-actualization might actually be hindered by a failure to follow personal whims and urges. By thus obscuring the fact that physical and personal limitations call for the discipline to operate in keeping with those limitations, society may deceive us into believing we can obtain the effect of a fulfilled life without its cause, which is temperance.

While our culture might have us self-destruct through the self-centered pursuit of a desire for instant gratification, consequently temperance again instills in us the selfless willingness to deflect this desire, and thus to promote our own self-preservation and thriving.[79] Put differently, temperance gives us the freedom that comes from exercising appropriate restraint. It enables us to follow the rules for our own thriving and so find fulfillment in life.

Admittedly, these rules, dictated by temperance, vary from person to person, as they depend upon individual physical and personal limitations. By leading us to operate in accordance with these limitations, however, temperance creates the conditions in which the operations of prudence and justice may be successfully carried out, even though it cannot perform those operations itself. Where prudent and just plans come to fruition, therefore, this must be credited to temperance, which gives us the daily discipline to live our embodied lives in accordance with who we really are—no more, no less—and to take pleasure in doing this above all else.

Moral Virtue as Rationality

According to the argument I have been developing, the four moral virtues are the means through which we satisfy the conditions for the possibility of promoting the highest which is at once the common good. As I have been insisting throughout the chapter, our ability thus to sustain rationality is contingent upon our willingness to recognize the limited way and extent to which we are able to do so.

Though prudence, justice, fortitude, and temperance allow us personally to fulfill a commitment to the highest good, which is the final arbiter of human rationality, there are a number of other conditions for rationality, so construed. The question whether these conditions are fulfilled must be answered on the basis of whether individuals have habituated themselves in moral virtue and enlisted the intellectual virtues in the service of moral virtue.

While some degree of rationality is certainly attainable apart from a consistent habit of moral virtue, and in cases where intellectual virtue is not cultivated for the sake of moral virtue, such that moral virtue is not conversely substantiated intellectually, rationality defensibly remains to some extent deficient in such cases, precisely because the commitment to the highest good that establishes rationality is inconsistent with and unrelated to the intellectual virtues, which represent our prime resources for exercising moral virtue.

In light of these considerations, my goal in this final section is to demonstrate that rationality in its optimal form must be exercised as a matter of habit and must entail both intellectual and moral virtue. I will make this case as I address four concerns: how to achieve habituation in moral virtue; whether there can be moral virtue in the absence of a habit of virtue, that is, in cases of 'accidental virtue'; whether there can be intellectual without moral virtue; and whether there can be moral without intellectual virtue.

Habituation in Moral Virtue

As mentioned above, a robust commitment to the highest good requires habituation in moral virtue, that is, an ongoing effort first to acquire and then to maintain a virtuous disposition. Since rationality ultimately consists in moral virtue, it must be directly proportional to the degree to which that disposition has been acquired. Though it is possible and even necessary to make an initial resolution to develop such a disposition, virtuous habits cannot be formed in a moment.[80] Rather, it takes practice in order for the will to become accustomed to, and indeed passionate about, following through on the moral directives of the intellect; in short, habits take time to form.

In order to obtain the practice required to perfect a habit of virtue, it is necessary pro-actively to seek out and enter into situations that call for the exercise of a new habit.[81] Conversely, it is imperative to avoid situations in which it would be practically impossible to refrain from indulging in a corresponding vice. This is particularly true early on in the process of habituation, when the temptation to carry on committing old vices is especially strong. In the two aforementioned respects, then, enough effort must be initially and continuously exerted not only to foster a given virtue but also to curb the countervailing vice.[82] As this suggests, it is impossible to work half-heartedly or inconsistently and cultivate any given virtue. A full commitment to forming a habit of virtue is required if such a habit is to be formed at all.[83]

To sustain such a commitment, it is necessary to maintain a clear sense of the kind of quality we are trying to cultivate and the efforts it will take to cultivate it, ordering our lives accordingly. As Aquinas suggests, there is no way around the hard work involved in following through on the decision to replace vicious with virtuous habits.[84] Aristotle echoes this point in his own way when he affirms that, 'the things we have to learn before we can do, we learn by doing.'[85] Though specific acts of justice, for example, may not immediately form in us the just disposition we seek to develop, they dispose us to an increase in the habit of acting justly.[86] Provided we persevere in performing such just acts, we will eventually begin to see the cumulative effect of our work in the formation of a more consistent and automatic habit of acting justly.

On the grounds that the acquisition of virtue is a matter of habit formation, Aquinas following Aristotle names different levels of virtue that correspond to different phases in the process of habituation. The first level is called 'continence.'[87] Although the continent act virtuously, albeit with varying degrees of regularity and success, this takes considerable effort on their part. For while they know their base appetites are base, they do not yet possess a will and passions that are perfectly aligned with the determination of reason to overcome those appetites, which is why they are still fickle and fallible when it comes to doing so.

In ancient and medieval times, many intellectual schools developed various 'tools' or 'exercises' tailored towards helping individuals practice exercising virtue—thus demonstrating continence—until it came naturally to do so.[88] The so-called 'practical syllogism' in Aristotelian thought is one example of this sort of exercise.[89] In such a 'syllogism,' the first line 'consists of a statement of the end to be pursued plus a definition, account, or theory of the nature of that end.'[90]

After the first line indicates the end or good being pursued, the second summarizes the particular situation that calls for striving towards that good, instigating deliberation regarding the most effective means to the end in question. The last line brings the universal or overarching goal to bear on the particular situation in a conclusion about how to think or act under the circumstances. In the most general terms, the premises of a practical syllogism might be spelled out along these lines: 1. the ultimate good is to 'bear things well'; 2. X is a situation that needs to be borne well; 3. Y is what can be done to bear the situation well.

Though such a syllogism is certainly useful as a general guide for bearing things well, it obviously needs to be specified further by particular persons seeking to confront particular vices and cultivate specific virtues in specific circumstances.[91] For example, individuals struggling to check hubris might apply the principles of the practical syllogism by acknowledging that they are 1. responsible to bear their lives well; 2. do not have an aptitude to meet a need or make a valuable contribution in a certain area; 3. such that it is fitting for them to forego involvement in this area in favor of working in another for which they are better suited.

When we strive to specify the practical syllogism in ways appropriate to ourselves and subsequently utilize it on an ongoing basis, the tension we tend to feel between what we know is in our best interests and our desires contrary to these interests will gradually begin to dissipate. For the more the will incites action on the basis of what the intellect knows to be right, the easier it is to appreciate what a life-enhancing thing it is to bear things well. As a result of this realization, our motives or passions will cease to be mixed or to conflict with the intentions of reason, and will increasingly support as opposed to protest the proper purposes of reason and will in the moral context. If we continue along these lines, we may ultimately reach the point where we only will one thing, namely, to be virtuous, such that all our passions support the pursuit of the good life in which we bear all things well.

At this point, virtue is achieved in the true sense of the term, namely, temperance.[92] In a state of temperance, the base appetites or aversions that formerly troubled us no longer pose a hindrance to our thriving, because we no longer take pleasure in doing anything that contradicts our own best interests, as I showed in the section on temperance above. Under these conditions, reason enjoys the full support of the will and the passions, which it lacked in the state of continence. Owing to the union of reason, will, and passions at this point, it is no longer necessary to go through calculations each time we wish to act virtuously. We no longer have to *try* to be good because acting virtuously has now become second nature, and has thus attenuated any power other persons or circumstances might previously have held in terms of dissuading us from virtuous living.

At this stage, the highest possible level of happiness is achieved, namely, the perfect happiness discussed in the section above on fortitude. This again is the happiness we find in continuously deriving pleasure from the only matter that is entirely subject to our control, namely, our ability to act in our best interests by bearing everything well.[93] Though we achieve what is objectively the highest degree of happiness when we are temperate, precisely because we engage fully in the activity of bearing things well, which is convertible with self-actualization, it is arguable that other degrees of happiness are attainable at earlier stages in the process of habituation, when a completely consistent habit of virtue has yet to be developed.

Assuming we do as much as we can at a given point in time to cultivate this habit and thus to engage in self-actualization, the correlative level of happiness we enjoy represents the highest level of happiness that is personally obtainable at that stage. That is not to deny the possibility of cultivating the habit further and thus of experiencing a concomitant increase in happiness. The potential we realize and the happiness we achieve at any given moment is precisely what allows for the further realization of potential and a corresponding increase in happiness, which consists in the activity of bearing things well. As with knowledge, so with virtue, the question whether we have achieved our personal best does not, or not only, call for an objective answer concerning the degree to which we have approximated the ultimate human end of bearing things well at all times. It can also be answered on subjective grounds, or with reference to the extent to which we make the most of every opportunity we have to cultivate virtue—and happiness—while still on the way towards this end.

Moral Virtue without Habituation

The preceding account of habituation in virtue segues naturally into the next question I wish to address, namely, whether there can be virtue without efforts to cultivate virtue, that is, habituation. There are a number of possible ways in which individuals may act virtuously without intending to do so. For instance, they may perform virtuous acts in ignorance, that is, without realizing they act virtuously when they do so. Alternatively, persons may act virtuously for reasons that have nothing do with virtue, namely because virtue happens to be the by-product of other pre-existing and even quite self-serving plans. In other cases, virtuous acts may be performed involuntarily, under force; or semi-voluntarily, when there is a vested interest in doing so—such as that of gaining good repute in the eyes of others. It is even possible to act rightly as a result of being in an altered mental or emotional state.[94]

Though these cases all involve some exemplification of virtue, they do not strictly speaking count as genuine instances of virtue because the subject in all instances lacks a virtuous disposition. In other words, the 'means' to virtue are not in place, despite evidence of the 'ends.' According to Aristotle, these means are only secured in cases where the following three criteria are met.[95] The first criterion posits the necessity of knowing that virtuous acts are virtuous when performing those acts. To guarantee such knowledge, the second criterion stipulates that virtuous acts must be performed precisely because they are virtuous and for no other primary motivation. Where a virtuous act is committed for any reason other than that of fully realizing personal potential to promote the highest good, that act is potentially self-serving and not strictly speaking virtuous.

The last criterion holds that genuine virtue must proceed from a consistent habit of virtue. Put differently, human acts only count as virtuous when they flow from a fundamental impulse to engage in the virtuous activity of bearing things well. Apart from such a conscious and consistent habit of virtue, Aristotle concludes, there is no way to ensure that acts, which appear virtuous, are non-accidental or intentional and can therefore be repeated on a consistent basis, regardless of circumstances. Since circumstances are contingent and subject to considerable variation, only such a habit can predispose moral agents to discern how to act virtuously on short notice or under new or unfamiliar conditions.

This last contention must be bolstered against the deontological and utilitarian moral philosophies, which have sought to delineate external criteria for virtue that guarantee the virtuousness of any given act on the basis of whether it fulfills a preconceived sense of duty or accomplishes the greatest good for the greatest number, respectively. Although these two moral philosophies have held considerable sway during the modern period, both seem to overlook the simple reality that human beings alone are capable of formulating criteria, rules, or principles for moral living in the first place, to say nothing of deciding what rules relevantly apply in the case of particular moral dilemmas.[96]

While such external criteria for virtue—including various binding duties, regulations, or the principle of utility or expediency—are admittedly important for moral judgment in many contexts and for many reasons, they clearly cannot take the place of the moral agent with whom the primary responsibility for moral adjudication inescapably lies, even if external criteria are invoked for this purpose. Conversely, the mere ability to satisfy such criteria or abide by duties, principles or laws does not substitute for a capacity to exercise sound judgment regarding the rules themselves and their appropriate and inappropriate applications.

Though the idea of outlining hard-and-fast criteria for virtue might seem appealing, since a list of these would relieve human beings of the burden of considering what it means to bear things well in every single instance, it emerges for this very reason as a tactic for evading or deferring the whole responsibility associated with being human, indeed, as a rejection of the human condition and its finitude. For these reasons, an ethic of virtue, and specifically one that entails the three criteria for virtue mentioned above, ought to be regarded as foundational to the whole moral task, even if other moral philosophies are invoked to supplement it.

On Aquinas' showing, the satisfaction of these criteria entails the unity of the four virtues I have been discussing.[97] In fact, the absence of any one of the four virtues is likely to generate a vicious act. For example, fortitude without justice results in anger and other forms of aggression and oppression. Temperance without prudence entails mere prudishness or even self-abasement, while fortitude without prudence reduces to recklessness. Though these four virtues are distinct, therefore, they do not ultimately work in isolation but necessarily collaborate to accomplish any given moral act. As I have shown, prudence plans the work that justice executes with the help of the fortitude to overcome difficulties that arise in the process and the temperance or discipline to follow through on prudent and just causes.

Thus, it is as impossible to exhibit prudence without the other virtues, which follow through on prudent purposes, as it is to exemplify the other moral virtues without prudence, which guides all our moral efforts. In harmony, then, and only in that way, the four cardinal virtues foster the unified or holistic style of life in which everything we do promotes rather than thwarts self-actualization.

Together, they create in us the dependable character or habit of virtue through which we are able to make a personal contribution to the highest good and therefore confirm our rationality.

Intellectual without Moral Virtue

Now that the conditions or criteria for authentic virtue have been delineated, I wish to pursue the related questions whether there can be intellectual without moral virtue and moral without intellectual virtue. The answer to the first question is obviously affirmative.[98] There is no reason why a lack of moral virtue should hinder the exhibition of intellectual virtues like prudence, justice, fortitude, and temperance, which hold us accountable to testify to the truth, inasmuch as we can do so through the implementation of our aptitudes in the areas of wisdom, science, or art.

In fact, many who are considerably deficient in moral virtue—who have little or no idea about what is best for them in life or what it would mean to bear things well—enjoy tremendous success when it comes to the use of the intellectually virtuous (prudent, just, courageous, temperate) use of their intellectual virtues (wisdom, science, or art). Nevertheless, I will discuss in what follows some important reasons for casting the quest to cultivate the intellectual virtues in the larger context of a quest to be morally virtuous, or to orientate our lives towards the highest good. Indeed, there are reasons why a moral orientation might in many cases turn out to be the condition for the possibility of exercising intellectual virtue in the optimal way.

The first and arguably most fundamental reason pertains to the fact that moral virtue—particularly prudence—is essential to an accurate assessment of our intellectual virtues in the areas of wisdom, science, or art. Without prudence, we are at risk of over- or under-estimating our capacities in these areas, thus obscuring any sense of what our abilities really are and consequently neglecting to invest our energies where we could make the most effective use of them. In losing a sense of vocation along these lines, we may take up tasks on the basis of what is lucrative or easy to do, or what is likely to please our superiors or enhance our reputation, as opposed to working in the areas where our abilities really lie.

As a result, our own flourishing may be undermined in the very pursuits through which we expect to enhance it. A moral framework provides protection from this end by giving us a proper perspective on our abilities and where we should correspondingly spend our time and energies. In this regard, moral virtue might incline us to use skills and pursue lines of thought and work which we might have neglected if we were striving for an end other than self-actualization. It might even raise our awareness of intellectual virtues we would not have recognized in ourselves any other way.

Another reason why moral virtue is indispensable for the fullness of intellectual virtue concerns the fact that theories and ideas can become objects of undue fixation, like all things. In developing an account of any phenomenon, for instance, it is possible to become so enchanted with an explanation of it as to lose sight of the actual object of our analysis, thus defeating the whole purpose of pursuing knowledge, which is to testify to the way things really are. In this connection, truth that contests our account is often denied or glossed over, even while information is modified or fabricated that supports our own perspectives. By these means, the intellectual virtues of prudence, justice, fortitude, or temperance are clearly undermined rather than enacted through the pursuit of wisdom, science, or art.

As a result, either nonsense or outright falsehoods will invariably be propounded. By means of the former, energy is expended accumulating knowledge and furthering projects that are irrelevant to and a distraction from the actual truth—projects that are simply pointless. Through the latter, human thought and life is built on a foundation that is genuinely incorrect—and potentially destructive. Though the ideas espoused in both cases may be internally consistent, and in that sense valid, the fact that they fail to bear entirely on reality—or contradict it—suggests that their coherency derives from a sort of perverse as opposed to authentic intellectual virtue.

In order to avoid corrupting the truth in these ways, I contended in Chapter 5 that a frame of mind is needed that has the power to check our natural tendency to favor personal intellectual agendas to an inappropriate degree. The four cardinal moral virtues—or a commitment to the highest good—offer the very accountability that is needed in this respect, because they implicitly render us responsible to exhibit an authentic version of those virtues in the intellectual context as well as in the moral context. In cases where it would be tempting or easy to betray the truth for the sake of personal gain, the moral virtues give us a rationale or motivation for manifesting the intellectual virtues; they give 'form' to the 'substance' of intellectual virtue, without which we might fail truly to exhibit intellectual virtue at all.

So far, I have only considered scenarios in which moral virtue would make a difference with regard to an individual's actual competence to exhibit intellectual virtue. But I have already admitted that there are many cases where a lack of moral virtue makes no difference to the exercise of intellectual virtue; where intellectual virtue comes naturally to individuals. In spite of such cases, there are other ways in which moral virtue might prove indirectly necessary for sustaining intellectual virtue.

For example, a moral outlook might help a person perceive their intellectual life and work in the larger context of other activities that are relevant to self-actualization, such as personal relationships or time for rest and refreshment. As important as meaningful work may be when it comes to fostering a sense of fulfillment in life, a fulfilling life cannot normally be reduced to meaningful work. Most people need to feel that their work is part of a larger effort to realize their potential for flourishing, which generally involves various aspects of a personal as well as a professional or vocational life.

Without a balanced lifestyle, feelings of dissatisfaction in life can easily emerge; questions may start to arise as to whether certain lines of work have been taken up for the right reasons and whether they merit further investment of time. As a result of such doubts, appropriate and timely choices to pursue certain lines of intellectual work may be regretted or revoked. By contrast, a moral outlook allows for prioritizing the various areas of life, personal and professional, and thus for maintaining a perspective on work that contributes to a general sense of thriving on account of which intellectually virtuous efforts may be sustained over the long term.

Furthermore, moral virtue makes it possible to face challenges or even outright failures and losses in the professional context. While such experiences would likely devastate those who stake all hopes for happiness on professional success, setbacks can be incorporated into the grander scheme of life in the case of those who do not live to work but work in order to live, or bear things well. A moral outlook further removes some work-related pressures, such as that of collegial competition, which might skew a person's perspective on the work they should undertake or why they should undertake it. In this way, moral virtue allows moral agents to remain true to the demands of their work—and themselves—thus keeping them from becoming disillusioned with their work to the point of giving up on it.

For all these reasons and no doubt others, it is in our best interests to conceive of our intellectual work as part of a larger moral process of self-actualization. As I have suggested, such an outlook heightens our chances of exhibiting the intellectual virtues of prudence, justice, fortitude, and temperance in the fields of wisdom, science, or art. Though it is certainly possible to operate at the purely intellectual level of rationality without a moral outlook, any success in this regard is bound to be accidental, insofar as it is unintentional or unsupported by its proper moral rationale. Since accidental success is generally short-lived, according to my argument at the end of Chapter 4—and is highly likely to be interrupted by any of the factors I mentioned above—it stands to reason that a lifelong commitment to intellectual virtue is most effectively fostered by a commitment of equal longevity to moral virtue.

Moral without Intellectual Virtue

The converse of the preceding question concerns the possibility of exhibiting moral virtue without any of the intellectual virtues of wisdom, knowledge, or art.[99] As noted previously, all human beings possess intellectual virtue in some measure, even if this consists only in the potential to possess intellectual virtue, as in the case of those with mental disabilities or physical disabilities that hinder the life of the mind. Thus, the question in this context is not whether individuals actually possess intellectual virtues; rather it concerns the extent to which it is possible to meet the conditions for moral virtue while neglecting to make the most of personal intellectual virtues.

Under such circumstances, the ultimate criterion for rationality can obviously be met, inasmuch as the four moral virtues are exhibited, which foster an internal ordering towards the highest good.[100] Since the primary purpose of prudence is to identify and govern the use of our intellectual virtues, however, it seems doubtful that we can really bear our lives to the best of our abilities if we bypass those virtues; in other words, it is unlikely that the 'form' of moral virtue can be upheld where the 'substance' afforded by the intellectual virtues is lacking.

That is not to deny that it is possible to be moral in a meaningful sense without recourse to personal aptitudes or intellectual virtues. It is simply to acknowledge that the virtuous activities undertaken in these conditions neglect to optimize intellectual aptitudes, and, as a result, fail to maximize individual contributions to the highest good. This moral deficiency is potentially problematic, both intellectually and morally, because of the separation of the moral from the intellectual it presupposes. As I have already shown, the lack of a moral framework can lead to bearing intellectual resources badly.

In the moral context, moreover, a failure to recognize that the ordinary or intellectual life is the site for moral living can cause morality to be construed in an arbitrary, artificial, or exaggerated manner, as a code to be adhered to over and above ordinary efforts to bear things well in daily life. The moralistic or even legalistic ethical codes produced as a result may then render moral acts immoral and vice versa. When moral judgments are formed in accordance with these codes, the common good may ironically be undermined in attempts to uphold it that are far too restricted in scope and therefore fail to appreciate the diverse ways in which different human beings may bear things well, and flourish.

Because these codes lack intellectual substance, moreover, there can be no grounds for upholding them apart from the sheer will or desire to do so. Since many persons lack the passions necessary to behave morally, however, and most intellectually astute individuals need reasons for acting that have real points of reference, a voluntarist concept of the moral life is not likely to engender much in the way of moral living, at least amongst the intellectually virtuous. As I have been trying to suggest, the moral life as well as the intellectual life, is jeopardized when the two spheres—moral and intellectual—are segregated. For this separation enables us to evade the full measure of our responsibility to be rational in both spheres, depriving both the intellectual and ultimately the moral life of the integrity they enjoy when they stand in a mutually complementary relationship.

Though I have readily acknowledged that it is not out of the realm of possibility to accomplish good intellectually or morally where intellectual and moral virtue do not co-exist, their separation is clearly less than conducive to rationality, because the intellectual virtues need a moral framework in order to maintain the standards of rationality proper to human knowledge, and the moral virtues require the substance provided by intellectual skills in order to seem well founded. In spite of the possibility of an intellectually virtuous life that is lacking in moral virtue, and a morality without intellectual substance, consequently, rationality in its most robust form entails both. To sum up: the paradigm of human rationality consists in intellectual and moral, or, better, intellectual *for* moral virtue.

Endnotes

1   *ST* 2.2.47.6–7; *EN* III.3, 1112b.

2   On these virtues, outlined from Aquinas' point of view, see Josef Pieper's *The Four Cardinal Virtues* (Notre Dame: University of Notre Dame Press, 1966). See also works by Herbert McCabe OP, such as *The Good Life: Ethics and the Pursuit of Happiness* (London: Continuum, 2005); Peter Geach, *The Virtues* (Cambridge: Cambridge University Press, 1977).

3   *EE* III.7, 1234a3: 'the man who represents himself as he is, is sincere.'

4   As mentioned at the end of Chapter 4, intellectual operation at any of the three stages involves the eight 'integral parts' of prudence. The first three of these—'reason,' the 'use of reason,' and 'memory'—necessarily enter into any act of deliberation, where the others may or may not do so (*ST* 2.2.49.1–2, 5). These integral parts also enter into deliberations about how to exercise prudence in the moral sphere.

5   *ST* 2.2.49.6: on foresight.

6   Martha Nussbaum, *Upheavals of Thought: The Intelligence of the Emotions* (Cambridge: Cambridge University Press, 2001): on shame and disgust in children.

7   *EN* II.3, 1104b. Aristotle here suggests that if youth do not develop a sense for the true sources of their pleasure and pain, they will invariably delight in inferior or even bad things and take pleasure in inappropriate things. In short, they will have skewed ideas about what is best for themselves and will therefore act inappropriately in response to stimuli.

8   See Justin L. Barrett, *Cognitive Science, Religion and Theology: From Human Minds to Divine Minds* (West Conshohocken: Templeton Press, 2011), 25ff. Barrett discusses the nature/nurture distinction and argues that both must be appealed to in any adequate account of the factors involved in human development.

9   *EN* II.2, 1104a4–8: 'matters concerned with conduct and questions of what is good for us have no fixity, any more than matters of health. The general account being of this nature, the account of particular cases is yet more lacking in exactness, for they do not fall under any art or set of precepts, but the agents themselves must in each case consider what is appropriate to the occasion.'

10   Thus, in *EE* I.2, 1214b6–10, Aristotle 'enjoins every one that has the power to live according to his own choice to set up for himself some object for the good life to aim at, with reference to which he will then do all his acts, since not to have one's life organized in view of some end is a mark of much folly.' See also *EN* I.1–2, 1094a, on all human activities being directed towards the good.

11   *ST* 2.2.49.3–4: on docility and shrewdness.

12   *ST* 2.2.49.8: on caution.

13   *ST* 2.2.109–10.

14   *ST* 2.1.13.

15   *ST* 2.1.16.

16   *ST* 2.1.15; see also David Burrell, *Aquinas: God and Action* (London: University of Scranton Press, 2008), 141ff.

17   *ST* 2.2.47.9, 49.4; cf. *EN* IV.9, 1142b32–5: 'if, then, it is characteristic of men of practical wisdom to have deliberated well, excellence in deliberation will be correctness with regard to what conduces to the end of which practical wisdom is the true apprehension.'

18   See Martha Nussbaum, *Upheavals of Thought*, chapter 4.

19   *ST* 2.2.49.7: on circumspection.

20   Jean Porter, *Moral Action and Christian Ethics* (Cambridge: Cambridge University Press, 1995), 194. Jean Porter describes the inter-relationship between justice and prudence in this instance in terms of integrity, along these lines: 'the person who attains integrity does not so much move from self-love to altruism as to a new construal of her own good which is now seen in relation to a larger good.'

21 *EN* V: Aristotle on justice and injustice. Though justice motivates its champions to do what is good and refuse to leave the good undone on the one hand, and to thwart evil on the other, the present discussion will not explore what it means to thwart evil or administer correction and punishment, as this involves complex considerations that exceed the scope of the current project (*ST* 2.2.3; 2.2.79.1). For the sake of space and focus, this chapter will also refrain from addressing questions about justice towards non-human animals and the planet, which have been treated at length by other theologians.

22 *ST* 2.2.61.2; cf. *EN* VIII, 1158b.

23 *ST* 2.2.58.11; cf. *EN* VIII.7.

24 *ST* 2.2.80.1. On this, see Martha Nussbaum, *Creating Capabilities: The Human Development Approach* (Cambridge, MA: Harvard University Press, 2011).

25 *ST* 2.2.61.1, 62.

26 Joseph Pieper, *The Four Cardinal Virtues*, 71; see also *EN* 5.

27 See Jean Porter, *Ministers of the Law: A Natural Law Theory of Legal Authority* (Grand Rapids: Eerdman's, 2010).

28 C.S. Lewis, *The Four Loves* (London: Harcourt, 1988), 50: love 'desires the good of the object as such, from whatever source that good comes.'

29 Soren Kierkegaard, *Works of Love* (New York: Harper Collins, 2009), 254: 'for one who has individuality, another person's individuality is no refutation but rather a confirmation or one proof more; it cannot disturb him to be shown as he believes that everyone has individuality. But for small-mindedness every individuality is a refutation.'

30 C.S. Lewis, *The Four Loves*, 8: 'we may give our human loves the unconditional allegiance which we owe only to God. Then they become gods; then they become demons; then they will destroy us and also destroy themselves. For natural loves that are allowed to become gods do not remain loves. They are still called so but can become in fact complicated forms of hatred.' See also page 50: the 'ravenous need to be needed will gratify itself either by keeping its object needy or by inventing for them imaginary needs. It will do this all the more ruthlessly because it thinks in one sense truly that it is [justice] and therefore regards itself as "unselfish".'

31 *EN* IX.11, 1171b32: 'as a man is to himself, so is he to his friend.'

32 C.S. Lewis, *The Four Loves*, 50: 'but the proper aim of giving is to put the recipient in a state where he no longer needs our gift ... Thus a heavy task is laid upon [justice]: it must work towards its own abdication. We must aim at making ourselves superfluous.'

33 Herbert McCabe, *God Matters* (London: T & T Clark, 2005), 179: 'space is not something that is simply there; on the contrary, we are hedged and hemmed around with things. It is only a person who can give us space ... To love is to give to another not possessions or any such good thing. It is to give yourself, which means providing a space in which the other can be himself or herself ... Love in this way is surprisingly like indifference, though it is at the other end of the spectrum.'

[34]   Soren Kierkegaard, *Works of Love*, 255–6.

[35]   *EN* 35 VIII.3ff.

[36]   Josef Pieper, *Death and Immortality* (St Augustine's Press, 1999), 103: we 'possess only what we let go of and lose what we try to hold.'

[37]   Paul Griffiths, *Intellectual Appetite: A Theological Grammar* (Washington, DC: The Catholic University of America Press, 2009), 136–8: greater intimacy is gained by treating others in keeping with their needs and nature as opposed to our own.

[38]   *EN* VIII.3, 1156a.

[39]   *ST* 2.2.79.3.

[40]   *ST* 2.2.101.1: cf. 104, 106. Aquinas argues that we owe respect to some people, especially parents, regardless of how they treat us, simply on account of the role they have in our lives.

[41]   Simone Weil, *Waiting for God* (New York: HarperCollins, 2009): 'a certain reciprocity is essential in friendship. If all good will is entirely lacking on one of the two sides the other should suppress his own affection, out of respect for the free consent, which he should not desire to force. If on one of the two sides there is not any respect for the autonomy of the other, this other must cut the bond uniting them out of respect for himself.'

[42]   *EN* IX.3.

[43]   *EN* VIII.6, 1158b.

[44]   For more on this score, see Lydia Schumacher, 'Forgetting and Forgiving: An Augustinian Perspective,' in *Forgetting and Forgiving: At the Margins of Soteriology*, eds Johannes Zachhuber and Hartmut von Sass (Tubingen: Mohr Siebeck, 2015). See also Martha Nussbaum, *Anger and Forgiveness: Resentment, Generosity, Justice* (Oxford: Oxford University Press, forthcoming).

[45]   Nevertheless, it is possible to have goodwill towards many people, as Aristotle writes in *EN* IX.5.

[46]   *EN* IV.1, 1120b3–5; cf. *ST* 2.2.117.

[47]   *EN* IX.8. Stephen J. Pope, *The Evolution of Altruism and the Ordering of Love* (Washington, DC: Georgetown University Press, 1995).

[48]   *ST* 2.2.26.

[49]   *ST* 2.2.26.7; cf. 2.2.31.

[50]   *ST* 2.2.63.1.

[51]   Rene Girard, *The Scapegoat* (Baltimore: Johns Hopkins University Press, 1989).

[52]   *ST* 2.2.58.5.

[53]   *ST* 2.2.27.1. On disability, see the work of John Swinton, Stanley Hauerwas, and Jean Vanier.

[54]   C.S. Lewis, *The Four Loves*, 132: 'in such a case to receive is harder and perhaps more blessed than to give.'

55   *ST* 2.1.60.2.

56   *ST* 2.1.62.

57   *ST* 2.2.123.1; cf. *EN* III.8.

58   *ST* 2.2.123.3, 125–7.

59   *ST* 2.2.123, 128.

60   *EN* III.8.

61   *ST* 2.2.125.1; cf. *EN* III.7.

62   *ST* 2.2.135.1: contra meanness; *ST* 2.2.134.3–4: magnificence is part of fortitude.

63   *ST* 2.2.137.1.

64   *ST* 2.1.3. Although I draw this distinction from Aquinas' work, I do not follow him in restricting perfect happiness to the vision of God in the afterlife. I argue instead that the sort of 'detachment' from worldly goods we experience when we attain perfect happiness in the afterlife is one we can experience on some level in the present life, even in the midst of sufferings and losses. Though both Aristotle and Aquinas acknowledge that the ideal circumstances associated with imperfect happiness are not always attainable in this life and that an alternative understanding of happiness needs to be developed and invoked in less-than-ideal circumstances, neither seems fully to elaborate this understanding in the way I try to do here in discussing perfect happiness (*EE* I.3), and in the way that Stoic philosophers have evidently attempted to do in their own manner. See Martha Nussbaum, *Upheavals of Thought*; Richard Sorabji, *Emotion and Peace of Mind: From Stoic Agitation to Christian Temptation* (Oxford: Oxford University Press, 2000).

65   *EN* I.8, 1099a32–3, 'it is impossible, or not easy, to do noble acts without the proper equipment.'

66   *ST* 2.1.4.7; cf. 2.1.5.3.

67   *ST* 2.1.4; cf. *EN* I.10.

68   See the Stoic Epictetus' *The Discourses of Epictetus* (Everyman, 1995), I.6; cf. II.1, II.16. On Aquinas' use of Stoic thought, see chapter 4 on 'The Morality of the Passions,' in Robert Miner, *Thomas Aquinas on the Passions* (Cambridge: Cambridge University Press, 2011).

69   *ST* 2.2.123.9.

70   Epictetus, *The Discourses of Epictetus*, III.10: on bearing sickness and other trials well.

71   *ST* 2.1.2, 4.

72   *EN* 1.7–8.

73   Pierre Hadot, *Philosophy as a Way of Life* (Oxford: Blackwell, 1995), 273. According to Hadot, many ancient schools of thought treated philosophy as a way of life which ultimately provides preparation for death.

74   *ST* 2.2.124.

75   *ST* 2.2.141.2; cf. *EN* III.10.

[76]   *ST* 2.2.141.6.

[77]   *ST* 2.1.59.5.

[78]   *ST* 2.1.59.1; *ST* 2.1.59.4; see chapter 4 on 'The Morality of the Passions,' in Robert Miner, *Thomas Aquinas on the Passions*.

[79]   See Pieper's chapter on 'Temperance' in *The Four Cardinal Virtues*.

[80]   *ST* 2.1.51.3.

[81]   *EN* III.5, 1114a6–10: 'for it is activities exercised on particular objects that make the corresponding character ... Not to know that it is from the exercise of activities on particular objects that states of character are produced is the mark of a thoroughly senseless person.'

[82]   *ST* 2.1.52.3.

[83]   *ST* 2.1.53.1–3.

[84]   *ST* 2.1.55.2.

[85]   *EN* II.1, 1103a32.

[86]   *ST* 2.1.53.

[87]   *ST* 2.2.155.1.

[88]   See Pierre Hadot, *Philosophy as a Way of Life* and Richard Sorabji, *Emotions and Peace of Mind*.

[89]   *De Veritate* 17.2; see also Anthony Kenny, *Aristotle's Theory of the Will* (London: Duckworth, 1979), 111.

[90]   Anthony Kenny, *Aristotle's Theory of the Will*, 132. See also Alasdair MacIntyre, *Whose Justice? Which Rationality?* (London: Duckworth, 1988), 129; *EN* VI.11, 1143b, VI.12, 1144a.

[91]   On this, see both Hadot's *Philosophy as a Way of Life* and Sorabji's *Emotions and Peace of Mind*.

[92]   *ST* 2.2.155.4.

[93]   According to Aquinas (*ST* 2.1.3.4–5), happiness is an activity, namely, a life in accord with virtue. As Aristotle also writes in, *EN* I.13, 1102a5–6, 'happiness is an activity of the soul in accordance with complete excellence.' Cf. *EN* X.7, 1177a2–3: 'the happy life is thought to be one of excellence [virtue]; now an excellent life requires exertion, and does not consist in amusement.'

[94]   On the circumstances affecting the voluntariness or involuntariness of actions, see *EN* III.1, 1110a-b and *ST* 2.1.6.

[95]   *EN* II.2, 1105a28–1105b1: 'the acts that are in accordance with the excellences [virtues] themselves have a certain character ... the agent must also be in a certain condition when he does them. In the first place, he must have knowledge [of what he is doing]; secondly, he must choose the acts, and choose them for their own sakes [rather than any other motive]; and thirdly, his action must proceed from a firm and unchangeable character.'

[96]   See the landmark article by Elizabeth Anscombe, 'Modern Moral Philosophy,' originally published in *Philosophy* 33:124 (January 1958).

[97]   *ST* 2.1.65.1; *EN* VI.13, 1144b30–1145a11.

[98]   *ST* 2.1.58.5; cf. *EN* VII.10 1152a8–10, 'a man has practical wisdom not by knowing but only by acting ... [thus] there is nothing to prevent a clever man from being incontinent.'

[99]   *ST* 2.1.58.4.

[100]   *ST* 2.1.58.4–5.

Chapter 8
Towards a Theological Philosophy

In this brief conclusion, I will summarize the steps of the argument that has been advanced over the course of this book's chapters, showing how it lays the foundation for a theological philosophy. The first step in my argument involved a discussion of ontology, more specifically, the defense of an ontology of participation according to which all beings become themselves or actualize their potential to instantiate a certain essence by participating in a particular mode of existence, or characteristic style of life. On the grounds that human beings are defined by the capacity to reason, I further contended that the realization of human potential is made possible by the acquisition of knowledge. The logical corollary of this contention is that human knowledge, like all things, is subject to development through expectant, fulfilled, and informed faith.

Since knowledge is subject to change, a further question arose as to how it can be considered objective or consistently true to reality. At base, this question concerns the way and extent to which human beings can be considered rational. In answering this question, I argued that reason cooperates at every phase in the process of development in understanding with the will, which motivates reason to adapt ideas in accordance with changes in circumstance, as opposed to denying, modifying, or fabricating truth in order to uphold pre-conceived notions. The will or intellectual appetite remains attuned to the particulars of reality for which reason is responsible to account in virtue of the passions, which represent judgments concerning the value objects of knowledge possess with respect to different intellectual purposes.

Though the passions put the will and intellect in touch with reality in the most specific of terms, I pointed out that they can also sever our connection with reality if we lose sight of the fact that their purpose is to enable us to testify to the truth, and instead reduce truth to some specific theory or idea about which we are particularly passionate. Under these conditions, the passions are better described as 'dis-passions.' The four intellectual virtues of prudence, justice, fortitude, and temperance counteract these dis-passions by rectifying the intellect, will, and passions, when it comes to the performance of their joint task of maintaining contact with reality. By these means, the virtues predispose us not only to testify to the truth inasmuch as it is accessible to us through experience but also to adjust our ideas about truth whenever new experiences render this necessary. In these respects, the intellectual virtues act as the arbiters of rationality, which is a matter not only of the intellect but also of the will and the passions, rightly ordered.

As mentioned above, knowledge of what is true, as facilitated by the four intellectual virtues, is merely a means to the greater end of self-actualization, which is an ethical or moral matter. On this basis, I affirmed that rationality in the paradigmatic sense is enacted when cognitive efforts are situated within and informed by the larger moral effort to engage in self-actualization through the cultivation of the four cardinal moral virtues of prudence, justice, fortitude, and temperance, which provide the proper context for the four intellectual virtues.

Before delving into the discussion of these four moral virtues, I explained why the dis-passions may pose a hindrance to self-actualization still more readily than they thwart the pursuit of truth. On account of the long-term and open-ended nature of self-actualization, it is particularly easy for the passions aroused by immediate and particular goods to distract us from self-actualization, which consists in 'bearing well' whatever we have to bear in terms of aptitudes and circumstances, at any given point in time.

Though our sense of thriving and indeed happiness consists in doing just this, the passions may lead us mistakenly to assume that goods, other than that of bearing things well, are the ultimate source of our happiness. For this reason, I insisted, it is necessary to be informed by prudence about the fact that self-actualization is our proper end, and that the means to this end is to bear things well or strive for the highest good through the optimization of personal abilities. On establishing this end, prudence positions us actually to achieve the end in question through the cultivation of the four cardinal moral virtues, whereby we realize our individual type and level of potential to contribute to the welfare of society as a whole, that is, the common good, in our unique and finite ways.

When we strive along these lines to serve the highest good consciously and deliberately, I would add to my preceding arguments, the process through which we realize our personal potential becomes the same process through which we discover the nature and extent of our potential, and consequently, who we are.[1] That is to say, the process through which we explore reality in the awareness that this pursuit is part of a larger effort to make the most of our own interests and abilities is at once the process through which we come to understand the interests and abilities that define us. In sum, our increased understanding of the world proportionally increases self-understanding.

Such self-knowledge is arguably the source of any satisfaction we derive from life, insofar as it enables us to manage and order our lives, limit our activities, and relate to others in ways that allow us to be and consequently know ourselves in increasing measure. By the same token, a lack of self-knowledge renders it virtually impossible to prioritize ordinary activities in a way that is compatible with the realization of personal potential; it is therefore likely to lead to the squandering of any such potential and to a considerable loss of opportunity to flourish in life.

On the account I have been developing, the task of philosophy is to forestall this loss by compelling us to take responsibility for exercising our humanity—through intellectual and moral virtue—in every circumstance. This task is accomplished through the proper delineation of the three main sub-disciplines of philosophy: ontology, the theory of knowledge, and ethics. As I have argued, these sub-disciplines, while distinctive, cannot be divorced from one another, because they collectively describe and prescribe a functional and fulfilling—rational—human life.[2] While ontology underlines the developing nature of all things, and the theory of knowledge extrapolates the implications of this ontology for human knowledge, which is the means by which human beings develop, ethics indicates the larger framework for this development.

So construed, the sub-disciplines of philosophy—and the discipline overall—is accurately described as a 'pro-theology philosophy,' that is, a philosophy that by its very nature gestures towards the rationality of the claims of faith, for two main reasons. One reason has to do with the fact that the theory of knowledge that this philosophy entails presupposes and explains the vital role that faith plays in human reasoning. Although this faith is not specifically religious, the very fact that faith of any kind is indispensable to ordinary rationality suggests that religious and even Christian faith may have a rational substance that is often overlooked in prevailing conceptions of both reason and faith.

Though the account of knowledge I articulated may afford an initial and potentially profitable basis for defending the rationality of Christian faith, there is an even more effective way of doing so, which involves showing how certain articles of faith account for the very possibility of engaging in self-actualization for the sake of others, or maintaining the individual commitment to the common good, that I have described as the final arbiter of human rationality. To demonstrate this will however be the task of a subsequent work of theological philosophy.

Endnotes

¹   *ST* 1.87. As Mark Jordan writes in *Ordering Wisdom: The Hierarchy of Philosophical Discourses in Aquinas* (Notre Dame: The University of Notre Dame Press, 1986), 124: 'there is no intuitive self-knowledge in the intellectual soul. It knows itself in the same way it knows other things. Moreover it knows itself through reflection on knowing its objects.' See also a section on the self-knowledge of the soul in Bernard Lonergan, *Verbum: Word and Idea in Aquinas* (Notre Dame: University of Notre Dame Press, 1967), 75–88.

²   Alasdair MacIntyre, *The Tasks of Philosophy* (Cambridge: Cambridge University Press, 2006), 131. For many, philosophy 'is first of all philosophy conceived as primarily and sometimes exclusively the exercise of a set of analytic and argumentative skills. Subject matter becomes incidental and secondary. Entering into philosophy is a matter of training in the requisite skills and questions about the ends of life that are taken to be of interest to philosophers just insofar as they provide subject matter for the exercise of those skills. Secondly, philosophy may thereby become a diversion from asking questions about the ends of life with any seriousness. I use the word diversion as Pascal used it. On Pascal's view we try to conceal from ourselves how desperate our human condition is and how urgently we need answers to our questions about the ends of life by engaging in a variety of types of activity well designed to divert our attention.' In *EN* II.2, 1105b13–17, Aristotle also speaks of philosophers who are prone to 'take refuge in theory and think they are being philosophers and will become good in this way, behaving somewhat like patients who listen attentively to their doctors, but do none of the things they are ordered to do. As the latter will not be made well in body by such a course of treatment, the former will not be made well in soul by such a course of philosophy.' As the philosopher suggests here, the whole point of philosophical theory is to facilitate practice, that is, functional and flourishing human lives.

Bibliography

Primary Literature

Aquinas, Thomas. *Summa Theologica*, 4 vols. Trans. English Dominican Fathers. New York: Benziger Bros., 1948. Latin text online at corpusthomisticum.org.
—— *Quaestiones disputatae de veritate* (*Saint Thomas On Truth*), 3 vols. Trans. R.W. Mulligan, J.V. McGlynn, and R.W. Schmidt. Indianapolis: Hackett Publishing, 1952–54. Latin text online at corpusthomisticum.org.
—— *De ente et essentia* (*On Being and Essence*). Trans. A.A. Maurer. Toronto: Pontifical Institute of Medieval Studies, 1968. Latin text online at corpusthomisticum.org.
—— *Compendium theologiae ad fratrem Raynaldum* (*Compendium of Theology*). Trans. Richard J. Regan. Oxford: Oxford University Press, 2009. Latin text online at corpusthomisticum.org.
Aristotle. *Categories*; *De interpretatione*; *Prior Analytics*; *Posterior Analytics*; *Topics*; *Sophistical Refutations*; *Physics*; *On the Soul*, in *The Complete Works of Aristotle*, vol. 1. Ed. Jonathan Barnes. Princeton: Princeton University Press, 1984.
—— *Metaphysics*; *Rhetoric*; *Nicomachean Ethics*; *Eudemian Ethics*; *On Virtues and Vices*; *Politics*; *Rhetoric*; *Poetics*, in *The Complete Works of Aristotle*, vol. 2. Ed. Jonathan Barnes. Princeton: Princeton University Press, 1984.
—— *Posterior Analytics*. Ed. and trans. Jonathan Barnes. Oxford: Clarendon Press, 1994.
Epictetus. *The Discourses*; *The Handbook*; *Fragments*. Ed. Christopher Gill. London: Everyman Paperbacks, 1995.

Secondary Literature

Alexander, Peter. *An Introduction to Logic: The Criticism of Arguments*. London: Allen & Unwin, 1969.
Alston, William. *Perceiving God: The Epistemology of Religious Experience*. Ithaca: Cornell University Press, 1993.

Anscombe, G.E.M. 'Modern Moral Philosophy.' In *Human Life, Action and Ethics*. Exeter: Imprint Academic, 2006, 169–94. See also *Philosophy* 33:124 (January 1958).

—— *Intention*. Cambridge, MA: Harvard University Press, 2000.

Baker, Deane Peter. *Tayloring Reformed Epistemology*. London: SCM Press, 2007.

Barnes, Jonathan. 'Aristotle's Theory of Demonstration.' In *Articles on Aristotle, vol. 1: Science*. Eds Jonathan Barnes, Malcolm Schofield, and Richard Sorabji. London: Duckworth, 1975, 65–87.

—— *Aristotle*. Oxford: Oxford University Press, 1982.

Barrett, Justin L. *Cognitive Science, Religion and Theology: From Human Minds to Divine Minds*. West Conshohocken: Templeton Press, 2011.

Bauerschmidt, Ferdinand Christian. *Thomas Aquinas: Faith, Reason and Following Christ*. Oxford: Oxford University Press, 2013.

Beilby, James. 'Plantinga's Model of Warranted Christian Belief.' In *Alvin Plantinga*. Ed. Deane Peter Baker. Cambridge: Cambridge University Press, 2007.

Berti, Enrico (ed.). *Aristotle on Science: The Posterior Analytics: Proceedings of the Eighth Symposium Aristotelicum Held in Padua From September 7–15, 1978*. Padua: Antenore, 1981.

Boland, Vivian, O.P. *Ideas in God According to St Thomas Aquinas: Sources and Synthesis*. Leiden: Brill, 1996.

—— *Eight Deadly Sins*. London: Catholic Truth Society, 2007.

Booth, Edward. *Aristotelian Aporetic Ontology in Islamic and Christian Thinkers*. Cambridge: Cambridge University Press, 2008.

Braine, David. *The Human Person: Animal and Spirit*. Notre Dame: University of Notre Dame Press, 1994.

Burrell, David. *Analogy and Philosophical Language*. New Haven: Yale University Press, 1973.

—— *Aquinas: God and Action*. London: University of Scranton Press, 2008.

—— 'Mulla Sadra on Substantial Motion: A Clarification and a Comparison with Thomas Aquinas.' *Journal of Shi'a Islamic Studies* 2:4 (2009), 369–86.

Byrne, Patrick Hugh. *Analysis and Science in Aristotle*. State University of New York Press, 1997.

Charles, David. *Aristotle on Meaning and Essence*. Oxford: Oxford University Press, 2000.

Coakley, Sarah (ed.). *Faith, Rationality and the Passions*. Oxford: Wiley-Blackwell, 2012.

Cohen, Carl and Copi, Irving M. *Introduction to Logic*, 14th edn. Upper Saddle River: Prentice Hall, 2011.

Craig, William L. *The Cosmological Argument from Plato to Leibniz*. Eugene: Wipf and Stock, 2001.

Crisp, Oliver D. and Rea, Michael C. (eds). *Analytic Theology: New Essays in the Philosophy of Theology*. Oxford: Oxford University Press, 2009.

Crivelli, Paolo. 'Aristotle's Logic.' *The Oxford Handbook of Aristotle*. Ed. Christopher Shields. Oxford: Oxford University Press, 2012, 113–49.

Dixon, Thomas. *From Passions to Emotions: The Creation of a Secular Psychological Category*. Cambridge: Cambridge University Press, 2003.

Faust, Jennifer. 'Can Religious Arguments Persuade?' *International Journal for Philosophy of Religion* 63:1 (2008), 71–86.

Fergusson, David. *Faith and Its Critics: A Conversation*. Oxford: Oxford University Press, 2009.

Foot, Philippa. *Virtues and Vices and Other Essays in Moral Philosophy*. Oxford: Clarendon Press, 2002.

Fortenbaugh, W.W. *Aristotle on Emotion*. London: Duckworth, 1975.

Frankfurt, Harry G. 'On Bullshit.' In *The Importance of What We Care About: Philosophical Essays*. Cambridge: Cambridge University Press, 1988.

—— *On Truth*. New York: Alfred A. Knopf, 2006.

Geach, Peter. *Mental Acts: Their Concepts and Objects*. London: Routledge, 1957.

—— *Reason and Argument*. Oxford: Blackwell, 1976.

—— *The Virtues*. Cambridge: Cambridge University Press, 1979.

Gilson, Etienne. *The Christian Philosophy of St Thomas Aquinas*. Notre Dame: University of Notre Dame Press, 1994.

—— *The Arts of the Beautiful*. Dalkey, 2009.

—— *Thomist Realism and the Critique of Knowledge*. San Francisco: Ignatius Press, 2012.

Girard, Rene. *The Scapegoat*. Baltimore: Johns Hopkins University Press, 1989.

Goldstein, Valerie Saiving. 'The Human Situation: A Feminine View.' *The Journal of Religion* 40:2 (April 1960), 100–112.

Griffiths, Paul J. *An Apology for Apologetics*. Eugene: Wipf and Stock, 2001.

—— *Lying: An Augustinian Theology of Duplicity*. Grand Rapids: Brazos, 2004.

—— 'How Reasoning Goes Wrong: A Quasi-Augustinian Account of Error and Its Implications.' In *Reason and the Reasons of Faith*. Ed. Paul J. Griffiths. London: T & T Clark, 2009, 145–59.

—— *Intellectual Appetite: A Theological Grammar*. Washington, DC: The Catholic University of America Press, 2009.

Hadot, Pierre. *Philosophy as a Way of Life: Spiritual Exercises from Socrates to Foucault*. Oxford: Blackwell, 1995.

Hankinson, R.J. *Cause and Explanation in Ancient Greek Thought.* Oxford: Clarendon Press, 2001.

Hauerwas, Stanley. *With the Grain of the Universe.* London: SCM, 2002.

Herdt, Jennifer. *Putting on Virtue: The Legacy of the Splendid Vices.* Chicago: University of Chicago Press, 2008.

Hibbs, Thomas S. 'Aquinas, Virtue, and Recent Epistemology.' *The Review of Metaphysics* 52:3 (March 1999), 573–94.

Isheguro, Hidé. 'Imagination.' In *British Analytical Philosophy.* Eds Bernard Williams and Alan Montefiore. London: Routledge, 1966.

James, William. *Pragmatism and Other Writings.* London: Penguin, 2000.

Jenkins, J.I. *Knowledge and Faith in Thomas Aquinas.* Cambridge: Cambridge University Press, 1997.

Jordan, Mark D. 'Aquinas' Construction of a Moral Account of the Passions.' *Freiburger Zeitschrift fur Philosophie und Theologie* 33 (1986), 71–97.

—— *Ordering Wisdom: The Hierarchy of Philosophical Discourses in Aquinas.* Notre Dame: University of Notre Dame Press, 1986.

—— 'Thomas Aquinas' Disclaimers in the Aristotelian Commentaries.' In *Philosophy and the God of Abraham.* Toronto: Pontifical Institute of Medieval Studies, 1991.

—— *The Alleged Aristotelianism of Thomas Aquinas.* Toronto: Pontifical Institute of Medieval Studies, 1992.

—— 'Aquinas Reading of Aristotle's Ethics.' In *Ad Litteram: Authoritative Texts and Their Medieval Readers.* Eds Mark D. Jordan and Kent Emery. Notre Dame: University of Notre Dame Press, 1992.

—— *Rewritten Theology: Aquinas after His Readers.* Oxford: Wiley-Blackwell, 2005.

Karamanolis, George E. *Plato and Aristotle in Agreement.* Oxford: The Clarendon Press, 2006.

Kenny, Anthony. *Action, Emotion and Will.* London: Routledge, 1963.

—— 'Intellect and Imagination in Aquinas.' In *The Anatomy of the Soul: Historical Essays in the Philosophy of Mind.* Oxford: Blackwell, 1973.

—— *Aristotle's Theory of the Will.* New Haven: Yale, 1980.

Kerr, Fergus. *Immortal Longings: Versions of Transcending Humanity.* Notre Dame: University of Notre Dame Press, 1997.

—— (ed.). *Contemplating Aquinas: On the Varieties of Interpretation.* Notre Dame: University of Notre Dame Press, 2007.

—— *After Aquinas: Versions of Thomism.* Oxford: Blackwell, 2009.

King, Peter. 'Aquinas on the Passions.' In *Aquinas' Moral Theory.* Ithaca: Cornell, 1999, 101–32.

Kneale, W. and Kneale, M. *The Development of Logic*. Oxford: Oxford University Press, 1962.

Lemmon, E.J. *Beginning Logic*. London: Nelson, 1965.

Lewis, C.S. *The Four Loves*. London: Harcourt, 1988.

Lombardo, Nicholas, O.P. *The Logic of Desire: Aquinas and the Passions*. Washington, DC: The Catholic University of America Press, 2010.

Lonergan, Bernard. *Verbum: Word and Idea in Aquinas*. Notre Dame: University of Notre Dame Press, 1967.

Loughlin, Stephen. 'Similarities and Differences between Human and Animal Emotion in Aquinas' Thought.' *The Thomist* 65 (2001), 45–65.

McCabe, Herbert. *Law, Love, and Language*. London: Continuum, 2003.

—— *The Good Life*. London: Continuum, 2005.

—— *Faith Within Reason*. London: Continuum, 2007.

—— *On Aquinas*. London: Burns and Oates, 2008.

MacIntyre, Alasdair. 'The Antecedents of Action.' In *British Analytical Philosophy*. Eds Bernard Williams and Allan Montefiore. New York: Humanities Press, 1966.

—— *Whose Justice? Which Rationality?* London: Duckworth, 1988.

—— 'The Virtues, the Unity of Human Life, and the Concept of a Tradition.' In *Why Narrative? Readings in Narrative Theology*. Eds Stanley Hauerwas and L. Gregory Jones. Grand Rapids: Eerdman's, 1989.

—— *Three Rival Versions of Moral Inquiry: Encyclopedia, Genealogy, and Tradition*. Notre Dame: University of Notre Dame Press, 1990.

—— *Dependent Rational Animals: Why Human Beings Need the Virtues*. London: Duckworth, 1999.

—— 'Epistemological Crises, Dramatic Narrative, and the Philosophy of Science.' In *The Tasks of Philosophy: Selected Essays*, vol. 1. Cambridge: Cambridge University Press, 2006, 3–24.

—— 'First Principles, Final Ends, and Contemporary Philosophical Issues.' In *The Tasks of Philosophy: Selected Essays*, vol. 1. Cambridge: Cambridge University Press, 2006, 143–78.

—— 'Truth as a Good: Reflection on *Fides et Ratio*.' In *The Tasks of Philosophy: Selected Essays*, vol. 1. Cambridge: Cambridge University Press, 2006, 197–215.

—— *After Virtue: A Study in Moral Theory*. Notre Dame: University of Notre Dame Press, 2007.

Mellone, S.H. *Elements of Modern Logic*, 2nd edn. London: University Tutorial Press, 1945.

Miner, Robert. *Aquinas on the Passions*. Cambridge: Cambridge University Press, 2009.

Moser, Paul. *The Elusive God: Reorienting Religious Epistemology*. Cambridge: Cambridge University Press, 2008.

—— *The Evidence for God: Religious Knowledge Re-Examined*. Cambridge: Cambridge University Press, 2010.

Murdoch, Iris. *The Sovereignty of Good*. London: Routledge, 2001.

Nussbaum, Martha. *The Fragility of Goodness: Luck and Ethics in Greek Tragedy and Philosophy*. Cambridge: Cambridge University Press, 2001.

—— *Upheavals of Thought: The Intelligence of Emotions*. Cambridge: Cambridge University Press, 2001.

—— *The Therapy of Desire: Theory and Practice in Hellenistic Ethics*. Princeton: Princeton University Press, 2009.

—— *Creating Capabilities: The Human Development Approach*. Cambridge, MA: Harvard University Press, 2011.

—— *Anger and Forgiveness: Resentment, Generosity, Justice*. Oxford: Oxford University Press, forthcoming.

Oatley, Keith. 'Two Movements in Emotions: Communication and Reflection.' *Emotion Review* 2 (January 2010), 29–35.

O'Callaghan, John P. 'The Problem of Language and Mental Representation in Aristotle and St Thomas.' *The Review of Metaphysics* 50:3 (March 1997), 499–545.

—— 'Concepts, Beings, and Things in Contemporary Philosophy and Thomas Aquinas.' *The Review of Metaphysics* 63:1 (September 1999), 69–98.

—— 'Aquinas, Cognitive Theory, and Analogy: A Propos of Robert Pasnau's Theories of Cognition in the Later Middle Ages.' *American Catholic Philosophical Quarterly* 76:3 (2002), 451–82.

—— *Thomist Realism and the Linguistic Turn*. Notre Dame: University of Notre Dame Press, 2003.

—— 'Thomism and Analytic Philosophy: A Discussion.' *The Thomist* 71 (2007), 269–317.

Oppy, Graham. *Ontological Arguments and Belief in God*. Cambridge: Cambridge University Press, 2007.

Oliver, Simon. *God, Philosophy and Motion*. London: Routledge, 2005.

Owen, G.E.L. (ed.). *Aristotle on Dialectic: The Topics. Proceedings of the Third Symposium Aristotelicum*. Cambridge: Cambridge University Press, 1968.

—— 'Tithenai ta Phainomena.' In *Articles on Aristotle, vol. 1: Science*. Eds Jonathan Barnes, Malcolm Schofield, and Richard Sorabji. London: Duckworth, 1975, 113–26.

—— *Logic Science and Dialectic: Collected Papers in Greek Philosophy*. Ed. Martha Nussbaum. London: Duckworth, 1986.

Owens, Joseph. 'Aquinas on Cognition as Existence.' *Proceedings of the American Catholic Philosophical Association* 48 (1974), 74–85.

Pasnau, Robert. *Theories of Cognition in the Later Middle Ages.* Cambridge: Cambridge University Press, 1999.

—— *Thomas Aquinas on Human Nature: A Philosophical Study of Summa Theologiae 1a75–89.* Cambridge: Cambridge University Press, 2001.

Pieper, Josef. *Happiness and Contemplation.* London: Faber, 1959.

—— *The Four Cardinal Virtues: Prudence, Justice, Fortitude, Temperance.* Notre Dame: University of Notre Dame Press, 1966.

—— *Living the Truth. Reality and the Good.* San Francisco: Ignatius, 1989.

—— *Guide to Thomas Aquinas.* Ignatius, 1991.

—— *Abuse of Language, Abuse of Power.* Ignatius, 1992.

—— *Leisure: The Basis of Culture.* San Francisco: Ignatius, 2009.

Pinsent, Andrew. *The Second-Person Perspective in Aquinas' Ethics: Virtues and Gifts.* London: Routledge, 2012.

Plantinga, Alvin. *The Ontological Argument from St. Anselm to Contemporary Philosophers.* Garden City: Doubleday, 1965.

—— *God, Freedom and Evil.* Grand Rapids: Eerdman's, 1989.

—— *Warranted Christian Belief.* Oxford: Oxford University Press, 2000.

Polanyi, Michael. *Personal Knowledge: Towards a Post-Critical Philosophy.* Chicago: University of Chicago Press, 1974.

—— *The Tacit Dimension.* Chicago: University of Chicago Press, 2009.

Pope, Stephen J. *The Evolution of Altruism and the Ordering of Love.* Washington, DC: Georgetown University Press, 1995.

—— (ed.). *The Ethics of Aquinas.* Washington, DC: Georgetown University Press, 2002.

Porter, Jean. *The Recovery of Virtue: The Relevance of Aquinas for Christian Ethics.* Louisville: John Knox Press, 1990.

—— 'The Subversion of Virtue: Acquired and Infused Virtues in the *Summa Theologiae.' Annual for the Society of Christian Ethics* (1992), 19–41.

—— 'Openness and Constraint: Moral Reflection as Tradition-Guided Inquiry in Alasdair MacIntyre's Recent Works.' *The Journal of Religion* 73:4 (October 1993), 514–36.

—— 'Virtue and Sin: The Connection of the Virtues and the Case of the Flawed Saint.' *The Journal of Religion* 75:4 (October 1995), 521–39.

—— 'Virtue Ethics and Its Significance for Spirituality: A Survey and Assessment of Recent Work.' *The Way Supplement* 88 (1997), 26–35.

—— *Moral Action and Christian Ethics.* Cambridge: Cambridge University Press, 1999.

——— 'What the Wise Person Knows: Natural Law and Virtue in Aquinas's *Summa Theologiae.*' *Studies in Christian Ethics* 12:1 (1999), 57–69.

——— *Natural and Divine Law: Reclaiming the Tradition for Christian Ethics.* Grand Rapids: Eerdman's, 2000.

——— 'The Common Good in Thomas Aquinas.' In *In Search of the Common Good.* Eds Dennis P. McCann and Patrick D. Miller. New York: T. & T. Clark, 2005, 94–120.

——— *Nature as Reason: A Thomistic Theory of the Natural Law.* Grand Rapids: Eerdman's, 2005.

——— *Ministers of the Law: A Natural Law Theory of Legal Authority.* Grand Rapids: Eerdman's, 2010.

——— 'Nature, Normative Grammars, and Moral Judgments.' In *Evolution, Games and God: The Principle of Cooperation.* Eds Sarah Coakley and Martin A. Novak. Cambridge, MA: Harvard University Press, 2013.

Preller, Victor. *Divine Science and the Science of God: A Reformulation of Thomas Aquinas.* Eugene: Wifp and Stock, 1967.

Rogers, Eugene F. *Thomas Aquinas and Karl Barth: Sacred Doctrine and the Natural Knowledge of God.* Notre Dame: University of Notre Dame Press, 1999.

Ross, W.D. *Aristotle's Prior and Posterior Analytics.* Oxford: Oxford University Press, 1949.

Rousselot, Pierre. *The Intellectualism of Saint Thomas.* Trans. James E. O'Mahoney. London: Sheed and Ward, 1935.

Ryle, Gilbert. *The Concept of Mind.* London: Hutchinson's University Library, 1949.

Sayers, Dorothy. 'Christian Morality.' In *Unpopular Opinions.* London: The Camelot Press, 1946, 9–12.

——— *The Lost Tools of Learning.* London: Methuen, 1948.

——— 'The Other Six Deadly Sins.' In *Letters to a Diminished Church: Passionate Arguments for the Relevance of Christian Doctrine.* Dallas: Thomas Nelson, 2004.

Scholz, Heinrich. *Concise History of Logic.* Trans. Kurt F. Leidecker. New York: Philosophical Library, 1961.

Schumacher, Lydia. *Divine Illumination: The History and Future of Augustine's Theory of Knowledge.* Oxford: Wiley-Blackwell, 2011.

——— 'The Lost Legacy of Anselm's Argument: Re-Thinking the Purpose of Proofs for the Existence of God.' *Modern Theology* 27:1 (January 2011).

——— 'Forgetting and Forgiving: An Augustinian Perspective.' In *Forgetting and Forgiving: At the Margins of Soteriology.* Eds Johannes Zachhuber and Hartmut von Sass. Tubingen: Mohr Siebeck, 2015.

Sherwin, Michael S. *By Knowledge and By Love: Charity and Theology in the Moral Theology of St Thomas Aquinas*. Washington, DC: The Catholic University of America Press, 2011.

Sokolowski, Robert. *Presence and Absence: A Philosophical Investigation of Language and Being*. Bloomington: Indiana University Press, 1978.

Sorabji, Richard. *Emotion and Peace of Mind: From Stoic Agitation to Christian Temptation*. Oxford: Oxford University Press, 2000.

—— 'Aristotle's Perceptual Functions Permeated by Platonist Reason.' In *Platonic Ideas and Concept Formation in Greek and Medieval Thought*. Eds Caroline Mace and Gerd Van Riel. Leuven: Leuven University Press, 2004, 83–105.

Taylor, Charles. *Sources of the Self: The Making of the Modern Identity*. Cambridge, MA: Harvard University Press, 1989.

—— *A Secular Age*. Cambridge, MA: Harvard University Press, 2007.

Tillich, Paul. *Systematic Theology*, vol. 1. Chicago: University of Chicago Press.

Turner, Denys. *Faith, Reason, and the Existence of God*. Cambridge: Cambridge University Press, 2004.

Velde, Rudi te. *Participation and Substantiality in Thomas Aquinas*. Leiden: Brill, 1995.

Wolterstorff, Nicholas. *Reason within the Bounds of Religion*. Grand Rapids: Eerdman's, 1988.

Zagzebski, Linda Trinkaus. *Virtues of the Mind: An Inquiry into the Nature of Virtue and the Ethical Foundations of Knowledge*. Cambridge: Cambridge University Press, 1996.

—— *On Epistemology*. Belmont: Wadsworth, 2009.

Index